MODER

COLLECTING

ROBERT A. WILSON

MODERN BOOK COLLECTING

A Basic Guide to All Aspects of
Book Collecting—What to Collect,
Who to Buy From, Auctions,
Bibliographies, Care, Fakes and
Forgeries, Investments, Donations,
Definitions, and More

Introduction by Nicholas A. Basbanes

Skyhorse Publishing

Skyhorse Publishing books may be purchased in bulk at special discounts for sales promotion, corporate gifts, fund-raising, or educational purposes. Special editions can also be created to specifications. For details, contact the Special Sales Department, Skyhorse Publishing, 555 Eighth Avenue, Suite 903, New York, NY 10018 or info@skyhorsepublishing.com.

www.skyhorsepublishing.com

10 9 8 7 6 5 4 3 2 1

Library of Congress Cataloging-in-Publication Data is available on file.
ISBN: 978-1-62914-791-8

Printed in the United States of America

To N O R R I S   M .   E R B ,

who many years ago, on a hot summer's day,

had the courtesy and patience to explain

to a curious thirteen-year-old boy

just what a first edition was,

thereby planting a seed,

one of the fruits of which

is this book

CONTENTS

INTRODUCTION

Thirty years is a pretty long time for a work of contemporary nonfiction to retain its edge as a work of continuing interest and relevance, especially when the subject is book collecting, for which changes in fashion are endemic to the pastime, and about which there is a bountiful bibliography. One of the many beauties of Robert Wilson's *Modern Book Collecting*, first published in 1980 and as fresh and perceptive today as it was back then, is that it makes no pretension to clairvoyance. Rather, it is precisely what it purports itself to be—a learned guide "on *how* to collect books in the modern world"—something it does in a most engaging and agreeable way.

When I got my first copy of this book—I think we can safely say now that time and widespread approbation have together proven it to be a classic—I was just completing my first year as the literary editor of a good-sized newspaper in Massachusetts. It came to me several weeks prior to its official release, direct from the publisher, a review slip laid in. I still have both in my possession—the first edition and the review slip—though truth be known, I was not a collector then. I certainly was a bibliophile, however, with borderline symptoms of bibliomania, and a professional critic to boot—and I had common sense enough to recognize worthwhile things when they came across my desk.

The short of all this is that I took to Wilson's book in a

heartbeat, and I did so at a time when I knew next to nothing about issue points, variant copies, or the value antiquarian booksellers place on dust jackets, let alone the special alchemy involved in identifying first editions. I was simply someone who had a deep-seated passion for literature and reading, and someone whose work brought him in constant contact with notable authors. Toward the end of the decade, when I began work on what in 1995 would become *A Gentle Madness: Bibliophiles, Bibliomanes, and the Eternal Passion for Books*, I drew on Wilson's sage advice as a useful resource for my own investigations, and appreciatively listed it in my bibliography.

Seven years later, when I was invited to write a little guide of my own about the nuts and bolts of book collecting—I knew I was onto a good thing, and called the effort *Among the Gently Mad*—I appended a highly selective bibliography of books I thought especially worthwhile, and had this to say then about *Modern Book Collecting*: "Now more than twenty years old, this is still the best primer for beginners who plan to buy what are generically known as *modern first editions*, a field that probably applies to most book collectors today. Respected as the owner of the legendary Phoenix Book Shop in New York, Robert Wilson brought a keen sense of the market to his examination, and his sections on author bibliographies and ways to determine if books are first editions make the work must-reading in its own right."

I see no reason to change a word of that assessment in 2010—other than to note that with this edition, Wilson's fine book is available once again to a new generation of readers—and a new generation of collectors.

NICHOLAS A. BASBANES

FOREWORD

This book on the collecting of modern firsts is a welcome addition to the large literature that exists on book collecting. Recent years have seen an enormous growth of interest in this field and the appearance, sometimes transitory, of many new dealers. I can think of few people, whether collectors, librarians, or booksellers, better qualified to write on modern book collecting than Robert Wilson.

Bob Wilson is a literate and bookish man: he reads books, he writes books, he publishes books, he collects books, and he sells books. He is unusual in that he has successfully managed a long career in the book trade, as proprietor of the Phoenix Book Shop in New York City, while also achieving success in the related fields of bibliography and bibliophily. His collections of Gertrude Stein, Ezra Pound, W. H. Auden, and Edward Albee are superb and are well known throughout the collecting world—his Stein collection, in particular, is probably the finest in private hands. The bibliography of Gertrude Stein, which he compiled on the basis of his own collection, is an authoritative one; in addition to Stein's, he has also compiled bibliographies of Gregory Corso and Denise Levertov.

These bibliographies, along with those of Michael McClure by Marshall Clements, Ed Dorn by David Streeter, and Charles Olson by George F. Butterick and Albert Glover, are in the series of "Phoenix Bibliographies" published by the Phoenix Book Shop. Small, handsomely printed editions of contemporary poetry are also published by Wilson under the Phoenix Book Shop imprint "Oblong Octavo Series" and include Marianne Moore, Howard Nemerov, W. H. Auden, John Ashbery, W. S. Merwin, Richard Wilbur, Allen Ginsberg, Louis Zukofsky, LeRoi Jones, Gregory Corso, Diane Di Prima, Galway Kinnell, James Merrill, and Elizabeth Bishop. In addition to the series of bibliography and poetry, the Phoenix Book Shop has also issued occasional publications, the latest of which is a memoir of Greenwich Village by Djuna Barnes. The catalogs that Bob Wilson issues from his book shop, with their recurrent and familiar typos and their home-drawn covers, have paraded the book shop's riches over the years with a characteristic flourish and liveliness.

Each of the manuals, guides, and introductions to book collecting that have been published over the years has contributed something special to the accumulated knowledge about the subject. Some have done so better than others, but all have something to offer, and even those that are outdated present us with important historical perspective and a picture of what was fashionable among collectors of their time. What the good ones have in common is the expression of a new and fresh point of view about their material. Bob Wilson's *Modern Book Collecting* is in this tradition. The lessons learned from his own experiences and achievements, as well as the rules and principles of the past, are gathered together in this book on collecting the moderns. It is a personal and contemporary book, as the best of such books always have been, reflecting the knowledge, flair, integrity, and taste of a fine and individual bookman.

J . M . E D E L S T E I N

Washington, D.C.

PREFACE

A great many people, over a great number of decades, have written essays, pamphlets, whole books even, to justify the collecting of books. This seems to me to be an unnecessary exercise. If you are predisposed to collect books, you don't need any ex-post-facto justification for having done so. And on the other hand, if you are not convinced before you start, the chances are that no argument is going to win you over. Therefore, this book will focus on *how* to collect books in the modern world, with particular reference to twentieth-century authors, not *why*. There are, of course, a great number of books already in existence on the subject of book collecting, some of them excellent. But most of them are rather general, and many seem to be addressed solely to the wealthy collector, going into great detail about the pleasures of collecting incunabula, first editions of Dickens in the original parts, and other such rarities, which, however desirable, are usually far beyond the reach of beginning collectors. This work will concern itself solely with the so-called moderns, a group of writers beginning with such figures as Henry James, Walt Whitman, and Stephen Crane close to a century ago.

As might be expected, this book would not have been possible without the help and encouragement of a number of people. To list them all would be impossible, but it is only polite to mention especially Charles Elliott, without whose insistence this book would never have been written. Others who contributed greatly, in various ways, include Jordan Davies, Marshall Clements, Herman Abromson, Kenneth Doubrava, William S. Wilson III, J. M. Edelstein, Timothy d'Arch Smith, George Bixby, Arthur Uphill, and Nicolas Barker.

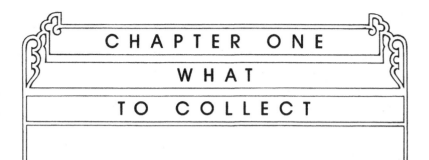

CHAPTER ONE
WHAT
TO COLLECT

A true book collector knows whether he is one or not, just as the old saying has it about being in love. A genuine bibliophile is born rather than made. Thus "what to collect" is a question that answers itself. A collector collects what fascinates him. The fascination, in fact, comes before the collection, because most collectors do not begin to collect deliberately. The first step, inevitably, is buying books that reflect one's interest in a subject or in an author in order to read them. Whether or not they are rare or hard to get is secondary.

My own experience is a case in point. I have a complete collection of Gertrude Stein books; I began to buy them in the first place simply because I wanted to read them. Virtually none were in print. In fact, as recently as 1960, before the intense revival of interest in her work began, only one of her more than sixty titles was available. Anyone who wanted to read Gertrude Stein was forced to seek out copies wherever they could be found—generally in the form of first editions, because only four or five of them had ever existed in any other form. I became deeply involved in the search, and the result is my Stein collection. Nowadays all but two or three of those books are in print again and can be purchased with relative ease. But no matter. In the course of things I had discovered my love of book collecting and the joy that the search can bring.

Once the line between reader and collector has been crossed, there is usually no turning back. There is no cure for the virus. But a distinction should still be made between the collector and the investor. If the acquisition of a rare, long-sought-after book gives you pleasure, a glow, a lift, just because you finally own it, with little or no thought that you may be able to sell it at a profit, then you are undoubtedly a collector and are liable to remain one for the rest of your life. On the other hand, if you buy a book and immediately think, "Aha, I can double the price at X's," then you are primarily a dealer or an investor. It's really as simple and basic as that. (However, as both a collector and a dealer myself, I can testify that the conditions are not mutually exclusive.) In recent years a great many people have begun to collect books as an investment, spurred on, no doubt, by numerous articles in newspapers and magazines written in a breezy, offhand manner and emphasizing the profit motive to the exclusion of almost everything else. Of course, everyone likes to make a profit, and it is normal and human to be pleased when a book you bought a few years ago at publication price or a modest markup starts a price climb in dealers' catalogs or at auction. But the true collector would sooner die than part with his treasures. Many literally skip meals, wear threadbare clothing, are in arrears on the rent—in short, do almost anything to hold on to their books. Once in a while, a collector gives way to the temptation of an enormous profit. In my experience, which stretches over nearly four decades, in every single case the seller regretted the move almost immediately and forever after.

Most book collecting in this century is done in the field of literature, primarily novels, poetry, and plays. There are, of course, other popular fields such as the sciences, biography, criticism, travel, and so on. The literature of chess is particularly popular. The New York Public Library has one entire room devoted to a collection relating solely to tobacco and smoking (although, ironically, the library's rules forbid smoking even in that room). The Black Liberation movement of the sixties and seventies gave tremendous impetus to "black" collections, among white as well as black collectors. Your own taste will dictate what you collect. Some people follow trends and fashions, collecting what is most popular at any given time. But to my mind, these people are not true collectors, but faddists—or, even worse, speculators.

Many factors determine what you can collect, not the least of which is the question of cost. Very few collectors starting today can hope to form a collection of Elizabethan literature, much less of Shakespeare. Cost aside, most of the great pieces of Elizabethan literature have by now gravitated into institutions. For example, all known copies of the first edition of *Romeo and Juliet* are in institutional libraries, so no new Shakespeare collection could ever be complete. Even the great eighteenth-century books, while perhaps slightly more available, are for the most part four-figure items. Important early-nineteenth-century books, particularly those of the Romantic poets such as Byron, Shelley, and Keats, are now fetching prices beyond the reach of the average collector. This has had much to do with the rapid and seemingly endless growth in popularity of modern authors. The term "modern" is bound to be an imprecise one, the meaning of which depends in large measure on one's own age. To some it means only those authors who came into prominence during the twenties and their successors. However, because of the enormous interest in certain late-nineteenth-century American authors, many dealers and collectors start the modern period with Walt Whitman and Emily Dickinson in poetry and Henry James and Stephen Crane in prose. This book uses "modern" in the latter sense.

Another factor, equally as important as price, is availability. If the books are all but unavailable, with only an occasional title surfacing here and there at long intervals, sometimes years apart (as with Shakespearean firsts), there will not be enough activity to keep the collection—and your interest in it—alive. On the other hand, if everything is too easily procurable, if you can expect to gather all the items in a comparatively short time, there will also be little or no excitement. As in almost all other hobbies or sports, the chase is at least half the fun.

The most widespread type of book collecting is undoubtedly the building of author collections, that is, the gathering of all the work of any given author. It can vary from a simple collection of first editions of each book published by the particular author to an intensive, in-depth collection composed of *every* edition of every book, as well as appearances by the author (with prefaces or the like) in books other than his own, original appearances in magazines and periodicals, recordings and photos of the author, books about him, and so on. There is almost no limit to the boundaries of an in-depth collection.

Apart from author collections, collections are often formed on the basis of preestablished guidelines such as those set by "high spot" or category lists. In 1929, for example, Merle Johnson published the first of his lists of important American books, calling it *High Spots in American Literature*; a great many collectors set out to get copies of all of the books listed, a vast undertaking, and for many years catalogs regularly noted when a book was a "Merle Johnson high spot." Prior to that, in 1903, the august and prestigious Grolier Club, whose membership is composed exclusively of book collectors, published a catalog of an exhibit modestly entitled *One Hundred Books Famous in English Literature*. This list was made up of what could reasonably be called the one hundred finest examples of literature in the language, and even today, decades later, there are still collectors who try to assemble the books on this list. It is not uncommon to see a listing of one or more of these titles in dealers' catalogs referred to as "one of the Grolier Hundred."

A few years before his death, Cyril Connolly, an extremely avid collector of first editions as well as an author whose first editions were sought after by fellow collectors, wrote a book entitled *The Modern Movement*, in which he listed and discussed the one hundred books he believed were influential and crucial in the establishment of twentieth-century literature. He did not restrict his list solely to works in English, but also included important French works. This group immediately became known as the Connolly Hundred. At least one institution, the Humanities Research Library at the University of Texas, set out to gather a complete collection of the books named on this list, many of which it already possessed. With the enormous resources at its command, the library soon assembled the entire group and placed it on exhibit, accompanied by a superb illustrated catalog which has in itself become a collector's item, since a great many letters and inscriptions were published in it for the first time.

Still another group of books favored by collectors are those that appear on the list of Pulitzer Prize winners, especially in fiction, drama, and poetry. A collection based on this list is far more difficult to complete than might be imagined. While certain famous books, well loved over many decades— *Gone with the Wind* or *The Bridge of San Luis Rey*—will appear regularly in catalogs, the Pulitzer Prize, in the inscrutable wisdom of the judges, has gone over and over again to authors who subsequently sank into deserved obscurity, along with their works. As a result, these books can be difficult to find, since most dealers, understandably, are loath to stock a book that may remain on the shelf for many years before a Pulitzer Prize collector happens along.

To my way of thinking, it is far more interesting, and considerably more fun, to determine your own area of endeavor, in spite of the satisfaction to be found in achieving a widely recognized standard. Your goal can be challenging despite not being widely recognized or even popular. It can be as simple—but limitless—as making your own list of high spots, especially for the post–World War II period, where very few such guidelines have as yet been published. Indeed, for collectors who are not drawn to the idea of an in-depth collection, this is an excellent field in which to work, since it is flexible enough to admit any item you like and does not force you to acquire anything in which you are not interested merely for the sake of that tantalizing will-o'-the-wisp "completeness." A couple of years ago I prepared my own list of what I thought were the fifty most important and influential books published in the field of American literature after the end of World War II, a date that provided a clear-cut line of demarcation between the literature of the two halves of this century. (This list, along with comments on my reasons for including particular books, will be found as Appendix 4).

Another collecting area that is wide and utterly fascinating is little magazines. There are two guidelines: Frederick J. Hoffman, Charles Allen, and Carolyn F. Ulrich's *The Little Magazine: A History and a Bibliography* (Princeton, 1946), covering the period up through World War II, and the just published *The Little Magazine in America* by Elliott Anderson and Mary Kinzie (Pushcart Press, 1978), covering the postwar period up to the present day. This is also a field that is not overcrowded. I do not mean that such a collection is easy to form—on the contrary. Many dealers will not take the trouble to stock magazines and periodicals with the exception of an occasional outstanding issue or a complete run of a classic, such as *The Little Review, transition, The Dial, Broom*, and *Hound and Horn*, all of them seminal periodicals of the between-the-wars period. "Little" magazines have been an important part of the literary scene for some time, and there was a burst of feverish activity in this area in the 1950s and '60s, coinciding with the "beat" movement. It was caused in part by the classic stimulus behind the existence of such magazines—the inability of the young members of the avant-garde to get their work accepted for publication in the more established literary periodicals of the day. But

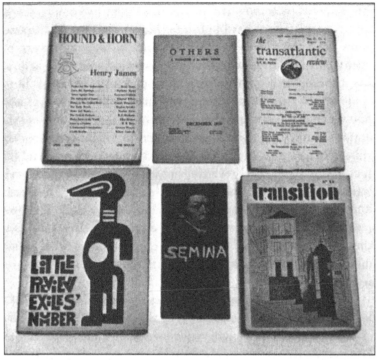

A representative group of little magazines. From the author's collection.

in this period, a new factor entered the picture—the widespread availability of duplicating equipment, particularly the mimeograph, which heretofore had not been generally available to the average citizen. It was now easy to rent or even purchase a relatively inexpensive model, and such a flood of little magazines appeared from these duplicating machines that one writer on the subject, Kirby Congdon, has termed it "the mimeograph revolution." Naturally, very few of these productions were submitted for copyright; many were not for sale, but merely given away to contributors and their friends. Even those that were placed on sale had a relatively limited circulation and almost always a very short life span. Hence they are for the most part extremely scarce and generally very hard to locate. Most institutional libraries were not even aware of their existence until many were already defunct, and few universities were interested in acquiring them even if they were aware of them. While a large majority of these magazines published little work that rose above the mediocre and were often issued mainly to serve the editor's vanity, a surprising number of them contain considerable amounts of worthwhile and important material. In fact, many of the early writings of authors who are now well established—for example, Olson, Duncan, Creeley, Kerouac, and Levertov—first appeared in such magazines. The few people or institutions with the foresight to collect them as they were issued now have collections not only of great monetary value, but also of incalculable historical and research importance.

Private presses have long been a favorite area for collecting, in part because of the great beauty of most examples of their output. Here again, your own taste can set the limits. It is possible to spend much money, time, and effort in trying simply to gather a copy of every book produced by one or more of the famous little presses. Equally interesting and challenging would be a collection of one or two examples from each of the great private presses. There have been many famous private presses in the past, from Horace Walpole's Strawberry Hill and Benjamin Franklin's Passy presses in the eighteenth century to William Morris' magnificent Kelmscott Press of the late nineteenth. More attainable for today's average collector, however, are the products of some of the presses of the twentieth century. These include the Doves Press and the early Nonesuch Press (before it was absorbed commercially), both British, and in the United States, the Mosher Press, operated in Portland, Maine, by Thomas Mosher at the turn of the century.

During the twenties, when most of the young British

and American avant-garde writers flocked to Paris, a number of superb little presses sprang up to meet the need for avant-garde publication in the English language. Many of these books have for collectors the double advantage of being not only finely printed, but also rare and important first editions of some of the twentieth-century literary giants. This, of course, doubles the demand for them, since they are wanted both for press book collections and for author collections. Among these presses of special note, the Black Sun Press is perhaps the most famous of all. Operated by Harry and Caresse Crosby, in the brief span of four years it produced a staggering number of books that are now landmarks of twentieth-century literature. These include Hart Crane's *The Bridge*, as well as significant titles by Joyce, Pound, Lawrence, MacLeish, Boyle, and others, at a time when most of these names were very little known.

Other presses of this period include the Black Manikin Press of Edward Titus, the Contact Press of Robert McAlmon, Harrison of Paris, Nancy Cunard's Hours Press, Plain Edition (run by Alice B. Toklas and Gertrude Stein and publishing, naturally, only books by Stein), the Seizin Press, operated by Robert Graves and Laura Riding from a wide variety of locations, and William Bird's Three Mountains Press. Further details concerning these presses and their products can be had by consulting Hugh Ford's excellent study of them entitled *Published in Paris*. While all this was going on in and about Paris, Leonard and Virginia Woolf were operating their now famous Hogarth Press, with Virginia actually setting the type for many of the early titles.

In the United States there have been several fine presses whose work is actively collected. These include the Grabhorn, Cummington, and Banyan presses, and recently the Windhover Press, the Perishable Press (whose operator, Walter Hamady, even makes all his own paper, the size of the edition of any particular book being determined largely by the amount of paper resulting from the specific paper-making operation), and the Gehenna Press, founded by the artist Leonard Baskin.

Another fascinating and challenging scheme for a collection is first books of prominent authors. Most authors' first books are among their rarest, since very few books by untried, unknown authors are ever issued in large quantities, particularly in the case of poets, where the entire edition may be only a hundred copies or even fewer. The first books of Ezra Pound (*A Lume Spento*, Venice, 1908) and William Carlos Williams (*Poems*, Rutherford, 1909) were privately published in editions of only one hundred copies each. But of these very few have survived (in Pound's case twenty-six copies have been located; in Williams', approximately a dozen). Allen Ginsberg's first book (aside from loose mimeographed sheets of an advance portion of *Howl*), entitled *Siesta at Xbalba*, consisted of only sixty copies, mimeographed on board a Coast Guard cutter anchored off Icy Cape, Alaska. This little pamphlet is thus one of the rarest titles in twentieth-century poetry. While the three examples cited just now are among the most extreme rarities, a first-book collection *can* be assembled, although it is in all likelihood the most difficult of all modern book collecting ventures.

One could go on at great length enumerating other fields, but I shall not. Suffice it to name just a few more: books illustrated by famous artists (many such contain original lithographs or etchings); juveniles, or "children's books," another field presenting extreme difficulties because of the heavy wear and tear most such books are subjected to by their young readers; books in series, such as the books issued by the Limited Editions Club, or signed limited books in a distinct series, as for example the Woburn Books in England in the 1920s or the distinguished Crown Octavo series issued by the House of Books, Ltd., in New York; and also collections of fine bindings. In this latter field the collection

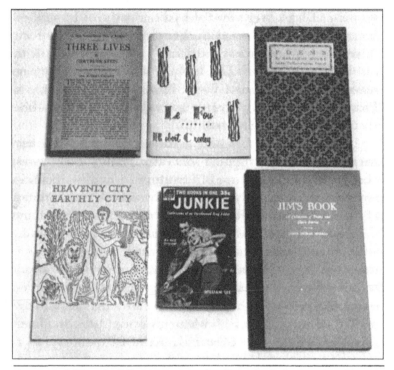

A group of "first books": THREE LIVES *by Gertrude Stein (1909)—this copy has one of only three known surviving dust jackets;* LE FOU *by Robert Creeley (1952);* POEMS *by Marianne Moore (1921);* HEAVENLY CITY, EARTHLY CITY *by Robert Duncan (1947);* JUNKIE, *written by William Burroughs under the pen name William Lee (1953); and* JIM'S BOOK *by James Merrill (1942). From the author's collection.*

can legitimately extend far back into the sumptuous bindings of the sixteenth and seventeenth centuries, as well as more modern fine bindings.

There is one final area of collecting which calls for more extended discussion. I refer to an extremely small group of authors—the innovators or ground breakers, the ones whose work made such an impact that the entire course of English and American literature was altered ever after. A careful scrutiny of book prices over the past century will reveal one incontrovertible fact: that is, theirs are the works that stay in demand, whose prices continually rise, regardless of the fashions in collecting. The books of these writers may not necessarily be the finest flower of an era or an epoch: as Picasso once said, "All creation is ugly the first time—after that any fool can make it beautiful."

In the first half of the twentieth century there have been three such undisputed innovative giants whose works changed the entire course of literature in English. Such innovators are invariably regarded as crackpots or charlatans at first, sometimes for their entire lifetimes. People who buy their books at the time of publication are usually regarded with amused tolerance at best. Yet once the importance of their work is established—and it sometimes takes several decades—there is virtually no interruption to the rise in demand and prices for their books, especially the crucial early ones. The three giants of whom this was true are James Joyce, Ezra Pound, and Gertrude Stein. Of the three, Joyce was the first to be recognized, although as recently as 1960 the price of the signed, deluxe edition of *Ulysses* (of which only one hundred copies were issued, not all of which have survived) still had not reached $1,000. But shortly thereafter, a rapid increase in demand for anything by Joyce began, and this chef d'oeuvre became one of the most sought after of all twentieth-century works. Even now there seems to be no slackening of demand. In fact, one collector I know of who has collected Joyce for many years began a few years ago to buy up all possible copies of *Ulysses* as an investment. His decision seems to have been an extremely astute one. The value of copies of this important book has risen at a far greater—and steadier—pace than that of any stocks, bonds, real estate, gold, or any other form of investment of recent years.

Ezra Pound also came very late to widespread collector

popularity, partly because of his long period of incarceration
in a mental hospital in Washington pending a possible trial
for treason. He had enjoyed a good bit of popularity with
collectors of avant-garde work prior to World War II, but
for a long while after it most of his books could be had at
nominal prices. This period terminated in 1958, when Pound
was released as unfit to stand trial. A policy of forgive and
forget had already begun to manifest itself, although prices
of his books still remained low. Two examples should suffice. The Black Sun Press edition of *Imaginary Letters* was
selling for only $8 a copy in one Park Avenue bookshop
in 1962, with multiple copies available. Now, of course, it
is much sought after both for Pound collections as well
as for Black Sun Press collections. At the time, I bought
all they had at that price, including the signed limited
copies which were thrown in indiscriminately with the regular unsigned copies. The other example is his first book,
discussed previously, *A Lume Spento*, one of the rarest and
most wanted of all twentieth-century books. In 1960 a signed
copy that had three manuscript corrections in the poet's hand,
with a Christmas card bearing the first separate appearance
of one of the poems laid in, appeared for sale in a catalog
issued by the Gotham Book Mart at $185. At the first session
of the Goodwin sale in 1976, an inscribed copy of *A Lume
Spento* fetched $16,000, still the highest price on record for
a modern American book.

Gertrude Stein was the last of this group to be admitted
to sainthood. Scorned and derided by a large part of the
literary and academic world during her lifetime and for the
two decades after her death in 1946, interest in her work
among collectors did not blossom to any significant degree
until the early 1970s. It has most certainly still not peaked.
As with Pound, as late as the end of the 1960s virtually any
title in her large canon of work could be obtained for under
$100. (The single exception was *A Book Concluding with*

As a Wife Has a Cow a Love Story, published in 1926 in an edition of only 110 copies. The high price for this book—whose title is almost as long as the entire brief text—can be explained by the presence in it of four original lithographs, one in color, by Juan Gris. Art dealers cannibalized a large part of the edition by removing the individual plates, framing them, and selling them, quite legitimately, as original Gris lithographs, thereby causing this title to be even rarer than its colophon would indicate.)

In the period after World War II, an entire new generation of writers emerged, and it was only natural that new areas and forms for literature would be explored. Once again, the ground breakers found acceptance difficult. Following the classic pattern, they were scorned by academics and accepted only by disciples and a knowledgeable few until the validity of their revolutionary techniques began to be recognized. The major postwar revolutionaries were Allen Ginsberg, Charles Olson, and William Burroughs. These three men have obviously exerted an enormous influence on the generation of writers succeeding them. The impact of Allen Ginsberg's *Howl* on modern poetry is undeniable. It is the great watershed in American (and probably also British) poetry in the second half of this century. It has undoubtedly had as great and decisive an impact on all subsequent poetry as did Whitman's *Leaves of Grass* in 1855. I do not intend by any means to claim that *Howl* is as great as *Leaves of Grass* (although there are many who feel that such a case could be made). But it is a fact that the entire course of American poetry, even poetry written by "academic poets," was significantly altered when this poem appeared.

An even more controversial figure than Ginsberg is William Burroughs. It is probably too soon to determine how lasting his influence may be, but he is the only prose writer in English since Joyce to introduce a totally revolutionary technique—the so-called cut-up method. Many scholars, critics, and readers maintain that this is not art, or even a technique, but merely an exercise with scissors and paste. This is possibly so, but at least many writers in the two generations since the publication of *The Naked Lunch*— which drew praise from such diverse authors as Norman Mailer and Robert Lowell—have modeled work on his methods. At any rate, for collectors with a flair for inexpensive gambling, Burroughs presents a perfect opportunity. Virtually everything is still available, at modest prices. As of 1979 nothing had reached $100. He is still alive and often available for signing and inscribing books, and he has produced a relatively large body of work, with several items of oddball and interesting formats.

In poetry, one cannot escape consideration of Charles Olson, the most influential American poet since Ezra Pound, whom he parallels on many levels, especially in being acknowledged the paterfamilias of a large literary family. He was the founder of the now famous Black Mountain School of poetry, named for the college where he taught and expounded his theories. Many of those who flowered after World War II acknowledged their indebtedness to Olson, both publicly and by showing his influence in their work. These poets include Robert Duncan, Robert Creeley, Denise Levertov, Joel Oppenheimer, John Wieners, and Paul Blackburn, to mention only the most famous of them. The fiction writer Fielding Dawson was also a member of the group studying with Olson.

Obviously, truly revolutionary ground breakers do not often come along, but when they do, it is important for the collector to recognize them and to acquire their early work without delay.

Beginning collectors, in the first burst of enthusiasm, often tend to dissipate their energies (to say nothing of their funds) in buying without any direction or point of view, on a hit-or-miss basis. It is advisable, when beginning to collect, to lay down some sort of limits or guidelines, no matter how wide or general they may be. I remember, in my beginning days as a book collector while I was still in college, buying anything I could afford by any author I had ever heard of. The result was a hodgepodge of single titles, or at best a dozen common ones, by a great many different authors who had little or no relation to one another. For example, there was a minor play by Coleridge, a political tract by Carlyle, a minor book by John Greenleaf Whittier, a gift annual with an original contribution by Poe, two second-rate novels by Booth Tarkington (those were ex-lending library copies to boot!), a magazine appearance by Shelley, a rebound Byron, along with a few books each by Steinbeck, Hemingway, and Erskine Caldwell, long rows of unimportant titles by Tennyson and Browning, and several books by H. L. Mencken. It was a collection in which I took some pride at that point, since none of my acquaintances had anything like it. Of course, the fact that none of them collected first editions didn't matter to me. But I soon learned the folly of trying to encompass all of British and American literature. Such an ambition requires a millionaire's income. A beginning collector must try to work out a reasonable area of activity, and even though he may wish to collect more than one author, he should think carefully about the systematic acquisition of items. If you are not going to have an in-depth collection of your author or authors, you should set some arbitrary limits. Most author collecting is limited to the primary works, that is, those that would appear in the "A" section of a bibliography. (*See* page 21.) Try not to be diverted by things not germane to your collection. Unless you have virtually unlimited funds (as well as unlimited space) you will find your collection filling up with unrelated items that are not only taking up room but also eating up your book budget, often making either difficult or impossible the purchase of a much needed item that suddenly appears on the market and may not be seen again for a long, long while. A systematic program is essential.

Now, manifestly, one cannot decide to acquire books in "proper" order, waiting to buy the book listed as A-4 in the author's bibliography until one has acquired A-3. You have to be ready to buy anything you need for your collection whenever it is offered. But for this very reason it is important not to stray too far afield. High-spot collectors are less troubled by this problem, as are those assembling a first-book collection, since their aims are already by definition limited.

Incidentally, don't ignore any bibliography on your author that may be available. From even the poorest of them you will gain valuable clues about possible variant editions as well as about unusual, elusive, or ephemeral materials that might otherwise escape your attention.

Many reasons are constantly being put forth to justify the collecting of books, especially first editions. They strike me as quite unnecessary. Scholarly values, investment possibilities—these are all side issues. There is, when you come right down to it, only one basic reason for collecting anything, be it first editions, stamps, coins, Indian arrowheads, baseball cards, or whatever else you like—that is, that it's fun. If you collect for other reasons, all well and good, but you are probably missing out on the best part. All you need is patience, which is necessary for any truly great love affair. Which is exactly what collecting books has always seemed to me—an ongoing affair that never palls, and one that is constantly offering new delights with the arrival of every book, every author.

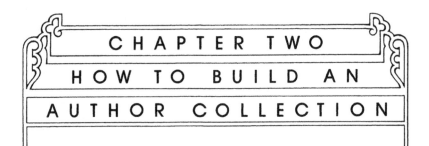

CHAPTER TWO
HOW TO BUILD AN
AUTHOR COLLECTION

Most first-edition collecting is author-oriented. If you collect the work of only one author or a small handful of authors, you can go into far greater depth than if you collect many authors or try to cover a wide area. In my experience, very few collectors are able to limit themselves strictly to a single author, but the author collection is the base type of most important accumulations of books.

As I have said, any collection usually starts before you realize you are actually collecting. You read a book that you especially admire, and then, when its writer publishes a new book, you buy it at once because you are anxious to read it. Chances are that it will be a first edition, particularly if you have purchased it right after publication. This may happen with two or three successive books and, without realizing it, you have the nucleus of a collection—two or three first editions. By then you may be interested enough in your author's work to search for his earlier writings, but when you start looking for them you are disappointed to find that they are o.p.—out of print. Your regular bookseller cannot supply them. So you turn to the used, or secondhand, dealers, and probably find to your surprise that they are also unable to supply any of the titles, particularly if your author is one who has attracted some notice. One of these dealers may suggest that you try a first-edition specialist.

You go to one of these and discover, with mixed emotions, that, indeed, there on his shelves are those elusive early books. Marvelous! But then comes a slight shock when you

learn that you will have to pay a premium for them, anywhere from double the original price on up to lord knows
what, depending upon the popularity of your author and the
scarcity of the book. You gulp, but take the plunge and buy
one. And there you are. You're now a first-edition collector,
and life will never be quite the same again. If the experience
is as heady a one for you as it is for most people, you will
find it so satisfying, so stimulating, that you will most likely
return for another expensive title before you've finished
reading the first one. The race is on.

At this point, a sensible move is to consult a bibliography
of your chosen author, assuming there is one. (See Chapter
10.) It is now standard bibliographic practice to categorize
literary material in terms of its character and the author's
involvement with it, and understanding the way items are
listed in an author bibliography will help you set up your
collecting priorities. You have begun with books in the so-
called A section. Here are listed all works by an author in
their first appearance in whatever format he and his publisher decided to employ—a hardbound book, a paperback, a
small pamphlet, or even a single sheet called a broadside.
Section A of an author bibliography also includes works that
are joint efforts by two authors, but not books to which an
author has merely made a contribution. For example, at the
very beginning of Gertrude Stein's career, while she was
still in medical school at Johns Hopkins University, she co-
operated with a fellow student named Leon Solomons in
writing a scientific article entitled "Normal Motor Automatism." This eventually appeared in book form under the
title *Motor Automatism* and is thus listed in my Stein bibliography in the A section. Another example of joint author-
ship to be found in the A section of a bibliography is *The
Nature of a Crime* by Joseph Conrad and Ford Madox Hueffer
(who later changed his name to Ford Madox Ford).

However, books that contain the work of several authors,

such as the annual "best poems" or "best short stories" collections, appear in the B section. For example, there appeared in Paris in 1925 a volume called *The Contact Collection of Contemporary Writers*. It was published by the Contact Press to give a boost to the careers of such comparatively unknown and struggling young writers as Hemingway, Joyce, Djuna Barnes, William Carlos Williams, and Gertrude Stein. Since each contributed only a few pages and did not work with the others on any of the contents, this is a B section item in bibliographies devoted to any one of these writers.

With anthologies, incidentally, a great deal of care must be taken to ascertain whether the contribution appears in the book for the first time, or if it is merely being reprinted from a previous book appearance. Generally, reprinted items have little value or interest to collectors unless the author has altered the text for the new edition. Certain authors never go back and revise, while others seize every fresh opportunity for making revisions. Among recent poets, Marianne Moore and W. H. Auden were notorious for altering poems every time one was reprinted, thus making the establishment of a definitive text virtually impossible for scholars and providing collectors with either a headache or a field day, depending on your point of view. In fact, Auden once declared "a poem is never finished—only abandoned." In the B section you will encounter a great deal of interesting material that may never find its way into print in any other form, even in collected editions of an author's work. This is particularly true of forewords and prefaces to other writers' books, and variant forms of poems that poets sometimes either forget about when issuing a new volume or prefer to suppress.

The third category in an author bibliography—and in a definitive author collection—is the C section: appearances in magazines, journals, and periodicals. The search for such publications presents the collector with much more of a challenge than the search for books, since many dealers do not take the trouble to carry them. But with a few exceptions, they are not unduly expensive, particularly if you are looking for the work of a current author. Here the aid of a bibliography is virtually indispensable. Yet lacking a bibliography (and many contemporary authors have not been made the subject of a bibliography), there are, fortunately, other sources of information. During the past few decades prior publication information has appeared on the copyright page of a book. In the case of volumes of poetry, it has become common practice to credit the individual magazines where certain poems first appeared. While the specific issues or dates of these magazines are not mentioned, you usually have a definite span of years in which to search, bounded by the date of issuance of the current book and the date of the poet's previous volume. Usually all of the poems in the new volume will have been published between those two dates. You can then check complete runs of the named periodicals to pin down specific issues. Libraries in the larger cities and universities usually have magazine files with either the actual bound copies or microfilms.

Another source of information is the *Periodical Index*. While this does not cover every little magazine, it does index the major periodicals rather thoroughly, and a quick check under your author's name will suffice. This index is issued quarterly, and can be found in the reference department of most major libraries.

For a few authors, there are also newsletters, usually edited by one or more avid fans. These newsletters often act as centers for the dissemination of news concerning appearances in periodicals and magazines. *Menckeniana*, the magazine devoted to lore by and about H. L. Mencken, even prints long lists of references to Mencken appearing in newspapers and magazines. Your first-edition dealer will, in all probability, know about the various author-oriented news-letters and may even carry them in stock.

Many collectors feel that periodical appearances give a truer picture of the era in which a particular work was produced than the actual book itself. Certainly a good argument can be made for this proposition, especially in the case of poets. Individual poems are more likely to appear in magazines than are sections of novels, although it is of course true that novels are sometimes serialized before appearing in book form, and in some cases an entire book will appear in a single issue of a magazine. Two notable examples of this are John Hersey's *Hiroshima*, which filled an entire issue of *The New Yorker*, and Ernest Hemingway's *The Old Man and the Sea*, which appeared complete in a single issue of *Life* magazine. Sometimes the magazine version will be revised considerably by the author before book publication, as was Truman Capote's *In Cold Blood*. The text that appeared in four successive issues of *The New Yorker* differs considerably from that of the Random House edition.

The contents of an issue of an old magazine may show some surprising literary conjunctions. For example, *transition*, one of the classic little magazines, is almost universally thought of as the more or less official house organ of the Paris expatriates, publishing as it did Joyce, Stein, Williams, Hemingway, Boyle, MacLeish, Crane, McAlmon, H.D., Bryher, et al. It may come as a distinct surprise to find in the later issues such writers as James Agee, Muriel Rukeyser, Randall Jarrell, and Dylan Thomas sharing space with Joyce, Beckett, and others who are generally thought of as belonging to entirely different generations and traditions.

Small but illuminating sidelights are the advertisements in the magazines, which usually give the flavor of the period more immediately and more graphically than the mere printed words. One gets also an instant perspective on the literary standing of the author at any particular time by observing the placement of his piece in the magazine. William Faulkner contributed many of his best stories to *The Atlantic Monthly* and to *Harper's Magazine* in the 1930s. In those days the covers of both magazines carried the table of contents, listing titles and authors, in some semblance of what the editors thought was the proper order of importance. Most of the time Faulkner's name did not appear on the cover at all, and when it did it was in the "also ran" category, a catchall in small type at the bottom of the page, usually reading "Also stories by John Doe, Jim Smith, William Faulkner," etc. The important names were such now-forgotten giants as William Beebe, George Davis, and Gerald Johnson.

The next category of an author bibliography, the D section, is customarily devoted to foreign translations of an author's works. Many collectors ignore these on the grounds that they cannot read them, although this seems unwise if you are aiming for a truly complete author collection. It is a field that will provide some surprises, both as to what languages your author appears in, and also as to which of his works have been translated at all. This is another area in which precise information is hard to come by without a bibliography for guidance. There are, however, a couple of aids of great value. Beginning in 1948, the United Nations required its members to report on the issuance of translations of works by citizens of the other member nations. These reports are published annually by Unesco and, happily, are indexed by author. Most large libraries have this volume, catalogued under the title *Index Translationum*. Of course, locating the actual copies of the translations presents another problem, which can be tackled in a variety of ways. First, and easiest, is your specialist first-edition dealer. Many of the more advanced dealers travel a good bit and pick up such titles for their stock simply as a matter of good business. Many major American cities have foreign language book-

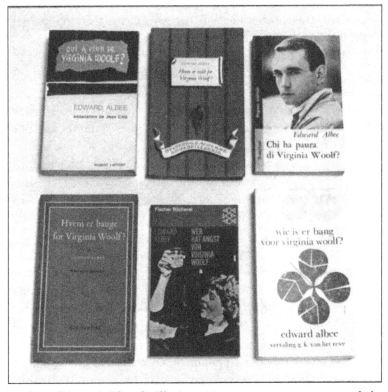

Foreign editions of Edward Albee's who's afraid of virginia woolf? *in French, Norwegian, Italian, Danish, German, and Dutch. From the author's collection.*

shops that carry translations from English. Finally, it is possible to write directly to the publishers in the various countries. The Unesco volume gives their names. It is surprising how many items can be obtained this way. When Truman Capote's *In Cold Blood* became a worldwide sensation, it was translated into at least forty languages. By writing to the publishers of all those that I could learn of, I was able to obtain copies of virtually every one. Only one publisher failed to respond; possibly my letter never reached him.

Some of the larger nations of the world, particularly England and France, also issue an annual volume listing all books published in those countries each year, a book similar to the American Library of Congress *Register of Copyrights*. These volumes will also yield information on foreign editions. The British volume is entitled *The British National Bibliography*.

Another form of foreign publication—which incidentally appears in the A section if the bibliographer is astute enough to note it at all—has sprung up. It causes problems for the authors and their publishers as well as for collectors. These are the notorious Taiwan book piracies. During the last twenty or twenty-five years a number of printers in Taipei have developed a flourishing business of pirating American (and British) books. They are not meant to compete with the American or British editions in their own countries; in fact, it is illegal to import them into the United States on a commercial basis. They are therefore somewhat hard for collectors to come by. Their primary purpose is to satisfy the enormous demand for books in English among students and readers in the Far East at a price that the local buyers can afford.

To produce these, an actual copy of an American book is reproduced by photo offset, printed on cheap thin paper, and usually bound in cloth. There is generally no attempt made to duplicate the original bindings, but the dust jackets are invariably photocopied, although not always in the original colors. Whatever one may think of the ethics—or lack of ethics—surrounding the issuance of these piracies, the books do exist and provide a colorful sideline for any collection. Since the entire operation is outside the law so far as the Western world is concerned, it is difficult to get dependable information on what has been issued, and you must be guided by examples appearing on the market here. Taiwan piracies of collected American authors include books by Baldwin, Bellow, Capote, Cheever, Didion, Doctorow, Gardner, Heller, Jong, Kosinski, Merton, Pynchon, Roth, Rexroth, Salinger, Snyder, Updike, Vidal, Tennessee Williams, and Faulkner, and Burgess, Fleming, Lessing, and Auden among the British—in fact, most authors of importance.

Bibliographic listings now often include musical settings of an author's work. These will usually appear in the E section of a bibliography, the section devoted to miscellaneous items. Most common is the setting of poems to music. The composer Ned Rorem has virtually made a career of writing music for modern poetry. Here again it is difficult to discover just what has been given musical treatment. Help is available from at least two sources. The Performing Arts division of the New York Public Library, located at Lincoln Center, maintains an extensive collection of sheet music, conveniently catalogued both by composer and by author; a check of card catalog entries will reveal most of the modern musical settings of contemporary authors. The Lockwood Poetry Collection at the State University of New York at Buffalo is another repository of such settings. In fact, this library, devoted exclusively to poetry, and especially that of the twentieth century, displays the greatest strength in its chosen field of any library in the United States. Its resources are unrivaled.

In the past three decades many recordings of authors reading their works have been issued. Prior to World War II, when only 78 rpms were available, comparatively little spoken-word recording was done. The boom began with the advent of LPs. Yale University was particularly active in this field at one point, and has issued recordings of well over one hundred modern poets. Now, with the development of tapes and cassettes, even more recordings are being made, and the older ones are being reprocessed and reissued on cassettes. Caedmon and Spoken Arts are the two principal firms engaged in this field. With few exceptions not more

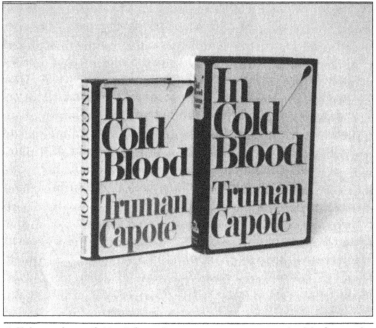

A Taiwan piracy (left) of Capote's IN COLD BLOOD *compared with the regular first edition (right). From the author's collection.*

than one or two recordings of any particular author exist, but even one recording is of inestimable value. It is always interesting to hear an author's own voice, and particularly enlightening to find out how he emphasizes and interprets a given line or passage that may be obscure or in dispute as to meaning. How many Shakespearean problems could be solved simply by being able to hear the Bard read the line himself! Or try to imagine Keats reading the "Ode to a Nightingale" or the "Ode on a Grecian Urn." What wouldn't one give for an hour's tape of Oscar Wilde's conversation, acknowledged by all his contemporaries to outshine his written works? But of course we must be thankful for what has been preserved, even small fragments or short passages. My own two favorite ladies, Gertrude Stein and Alice B. Toklas, were each recorded once. The Stein recording was made at the time of her triumphant return visit to the United States in 1934, and is, happily, still in print on the Caedmon label (TC 1050). Her voice is likely to come as a distinct surprise. It is a rich, colorful contralto, which she uses with great skill and modulation, to such an extent that had she not chosen to communicate in writing, it is easy to imagine her as an actress of distinction, at least on radio. The Alice Toklas record was not made until very late in her life, and may be less of a surprise than an absolute shock. From her diminutive size we might expect a chirping, birdlike voice. Instead, what comes across on the record is something resembling a bass-baritone. But what is also revealed are speech rhythms that closely approximate those of the famous *Autobiography of Alice B. Toklas.* Plainly this work was not wholly Gertrude Stein's invention, but a faithful, almost uncanny reproduction on the printed page of the actual speech pattern and modulations of Alice herself. This record (Verve MG V 15017), alas, was given very little publicity at the time of its release in 1961, and very few copies were sold. In nearly fifteen years of searching, I have never located a copy apart from the one I was lucky enough to buy when it first appeared.

The E section of an author bibliography can be a real grab bag. It contains all the things not classifiable in any other category, including what are called "ephemera." In today's usage, particularly among book collectors, the term has come to mean a variety of oddball objects. Not all will be listed in even the best bibliography. One collector who specializes in ephemera insists that the true definition today is something that was intended to be thrown away after having served a temporary purpose. This definition comes about as close as any, and to tell the truth, I've failed to find any sort of ephemera that would not meet this definition. Yet many of the most fascinating items in a collection will fall into this category, and most of them can pose a huge challenge to the collector. Apart from their intrinsic interest, in some instances they provide valuable information no longer available from any other source. For instance, when Hugh Ford was gathering material for his book *Published in Paris*, a detailed account of the little presses that printed most of the work of the expatriates in and around Paris in the 1920s, a group of publishers' fliers and announcements relating to books by Gertrude Stein served as a unique and valuable source of information for publication dates, prices, sizes of editions, and so forth for several of the presses being studied.

This is a virtually limitless collecting area. It can range from tangential material such as reviews of the author's books (and other newspaper or magazine articles about him) through posters for readings; announcement fliers for forthcoming books; original photos of the author, his home, his family, his pets, and so forth; personal calling cards; even some of his personal possessions. In this latter area some judgment must be exercised. From time to time bits of clothing belonging to an author are offered for sale. Since there has been as yet no recorded instance of any of these relics' performing miracles in the manner of saints' relics, they have, it seems to me, dubious value, especially as there is seldom any way of authenticating their provenance. And in any event fabrics have a tendency to deteriorate at a far more rapid pace than books.

There are some items that help liven up an exhibit where an unbroken run of books, no matter how rare, may furnish dull viewing. Some bibliographies list some of this ephemera, and while such items are often the most difficult things in the entire collection to acquire, they are generally the most fun to search for. Some authors have been school-

teachers for brief periods. Eliot, Pound, and W. H. Auden
served in this line, and issued mimeographed syllabuses for
their courses, as well as exam papers. Many authors have
been physicians; and one collector of my acquaintance prizes
very highly a prescription made out by Dr. William Carlos
Williams. Eliot comes to mind again for a quatrain he wrote
to be printed on the back of a souvenir postcard depicting
Thomas Hardy's home. Many authors have written texts
for art exhibition catalogs: Ezra Pound, Marianne Moore,
Gertrude Stein, and among more recent writers, Donald
Barthelme, the poet John Ashbery, and novelist Donald
Windham. Gertrude Stein, as usual going everyone one step
better, composed a verse to be printed on the wedding announcement of one of her protégés. (Even then, back in the
1930s, long before she was as widely collected as she is today,
the demand for this item was so great that the newlyweds
had to keep reprinting it to satisfy the demand from friends
and admirers. As a result a total of five variants exists. The
groom was enough of a bibliophile to recognize the necessity
of making some distinction among them; yet this bit of
ephemera, in any variant, is among the rarest of all Stein
items.) In the 1930s a major New York department store
sold a rug for a child's room based on illustrations from the
first edition of Stein's immensely successful children's book
The World Is Round. And in 1977 there appeared on the
market a "Stein stein," i.e., a beer stein in the shape of what
was supposed to be Gertrude's face, with a diminutive Alice
perched on the handle. Any absolutely devoted Stein collector would be delighted to have these. (The less devoted
are welcome to be skeptical.)

Ezra Pound, always interested in music, very early in
his career translated groups of songs from the Provençal and
other languages. One group was produced specifically for
Yvette Guilbert, the chanteuse immortalized by Toulouse-
Lautrec. Pound's bibliographer Donald Gallup went so far as

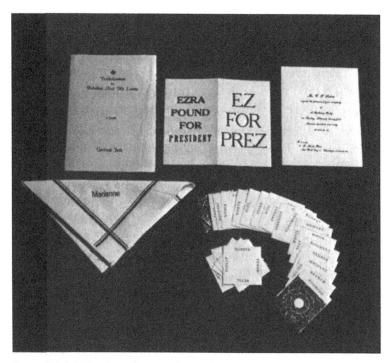

A sampling of literary ephemera: Gertrude Stein's wedding poem for Bobchen Haas; Ezra Pound presidential leaflet; an invitation to W. H. Auden's birthday party; paper napkin from Marianne Moore; and a set of poem-playing cards by Michael McClure. From the author's collection.

to list this item in the B section of his book. Later on, Pound organized concerts in Paris and Rapallo, and many of the programs for these contain texts by the poet. During the war, wall placards were issued in Italy with texts by Pound.

Yeats, with his Celtic interest in things occult, wrote two anonymous pamphlets in 1901, entitled *Is the Order of R.R. & A.C. to Remain a Magical Order?* and *A Postscript to an Essay Entitled "Is the Order of R.R. & A.C. to Remain a Magical Order?"* Miscellanea surely—and among the most difficult of all Yeatsiana to find.

Odd items about an author—as opposed to publications having texts by him—can be even more varied. A pamphlet in my collection promotes Ezra Pound for President, using the slogans "Ez for Prez" and "Let's Have a Round Pound," while he was still incarcerated in St. Elizabeth's Hospital in Washington under indictment for high treason! A greeting card issued by James Thurber contains a drawing by him depicting the moment of shock when an unusually well-endowed male makes his first appearance in a nudist colony.

Poets are especially fond of writing and publishing their own verses as Christmas cards. Most modern poets have issued some of these, usually privately to their own circle of friends. However, Hallmark cards issued one of Auden's commercially, as did the United Nations UNICEF program, which offered pamphlets of eight to ten pages to use as a card, with a verse by Denise Levertov. With Robert Frost, the cards became an annual commercial venture after the first few years. With the proper connections, it was possible to order a supply of the current year's Robert Frost Christmas pamphlet with your own name imprinted thereon. There are thirty-five such Frost Christmas pamphlets, some with as many as twenty different imprints.

I could go on citing specific examples of fascinating ephemera, but I'd prefer to suggest some general areas for consideration when adding ephemera to a modern collection. First of all, with most modern books, especially those from little or private presses, there will be advance fliers or blurb sheets, or perhaps small catalogs listing or announcing these works. These can become an extremely valuable source of information to future researchers or bibliographers. Major publishing houses send out a varying number of review copies in the hopes of gaining favorable reviews or acceptance by a book club, thereby stimulating sales. These copies quite often have a photo of the author laid in, which the

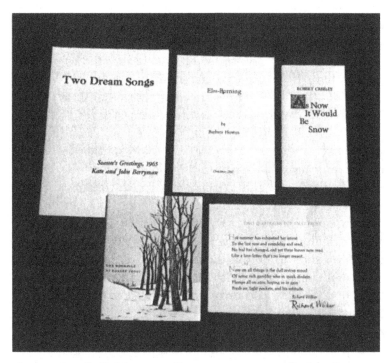

A group of poet's Christmas pamphlets: TWO DREAM SONGS *by John Berryman;* ELM-BURNING *by Barbara Howes;* AS NOW IT WOULD BE SNOW *by Robert Creeley;* THE WOOD-PILE *by Robert Frost; and* TWO QUATRAINS FOR FIRST FROST *by Richard Wilbur. From the author's collection.*

publishers hope will be used to illustrate the review. These photos alone are an area for specialization.

Nowadays, the more popular authors give public readings. This is especially true of poets. There are usually posters or announcements for these readings, some of which may have a photo of the author, or in some cases, a few lines of verse by him or her.

In the case of a novelist whose books are transferred to the screen, a large number of items become desirable. Easiest of all to find are the 8″ x 10″ stills from the picture, along with theater cards (the colored scenes from the film that are usually displayed outside the theater). For a major film there are publicity brochures put out by the studios, including sample ads for use by theaters in local papers. Most desirable of all, but the hardest to come by, is the script for the film version of the book. Sometimes scripts have been written or worked on by the authors themselves, sometimes by studio hacks, and in rare cases by major authors who are under contract to do scriptwriting. When times were hard, F. Scott Fitzgerald and William Faulkner worked as scriptwriters in Hollywood; so did Dorothy Parker, Anita Loos, Tennessee Williams, Terry Sothern, Christopher Isherwood, and Truman Capote, to mention only a few. As I have said, scripts by such people as these are most desirable, and perhaps don't strictly belong in the ephemera category, although they were certainly not designed to be used again after having served their initial purpose. Studios guard these zealously, and very few leak out into the trade, but enough do appear to make this a much sought-after category, with prices usually in three figures.

Sometimes novels are adapted to stage performance, usually before being turned into a film. Programs for such productions form another category of association items. They are particularly rare if the stage version is short-lived, as was the Broadway version of Hemingway's *A Farewell to Arms*. It lasted fewer than ten performances, automatically making a program for it very rare and consequently very high priced.

Recently the passion for illustrated T-shirts has led to several literary imprints; in some cases the authors themselves have had them made up. Poet Anne Waldman recently presented me with one bearing the cover design of her most recent book (which featured a glamorous photo of herself). This may be a sign that things are getting out of hand (the aforementioned Stein stein is another) but you will have to draw your own lines. Luckily, book collecting is not like stamp collecting, where the printed albums, with definite spaces to be filled, leave no leeway for personal judgment.

One very nice thing about ephemera is that most of it will cost very little. In fact, some of your most delightful items may even come free. A number of dealers do not want to be bothered cataloging or handling such relatively insignificant items. Many a charming item has been presented to me as a goodwill gesture by a dealer who knows of my interest in a particular author. If you have established a good relationship with a dealer, he may well do the same; after all, he hates to throw any item away, and he knows that you will like it. And keeping a customer happy is simply a matter of good business, if nothing else.

CHAPTER THREE
STARTING WITH AN
UNKNOWN AUTHOR

For the beginning collector with a modest budget who cannot aspire to the gems of the twenties and thirties—now reaching price levels that only the richest collectors and the most heavily endowed universities can afford—modern book collecting may look like a discouraging field. Few people seem to realize that every author whose work is now highly esteemed and correspondingly high priced was, at one time, relatively unknown and unappreciated—and uncollected. It is here, among the unknowns of today, that the new collector can operate to greatest advantage, financially and in terms of pleasure.

The requirement here is good taste in literary matters. It is essential to read the authors you collect, and not simply assemble copies of their books. Gertrude Stein commented on this in 1933 when *The Autobiography of Alice B. Toklas* brought her worldwide fame after nearly twenty-five years of publishing in relative obscurity, and people started collecting her books avidly. She wanted, she said, "to be read, not collected."

The only way to spot emerging talent is to read. Read, and keep reading. A good deal of such reading of new writers will of necessity have to be done in magazines, for few if any writers have a book published until they have been published in journals for several years. Once in a while something comes along like *Gone with the Wind*, which had neither antecedents nor successors, but this is the exception. Poets particularly are likely to publish in periodicals, because their output is usually not of sufficient bulk or quantity to make a book until several years after they begin. After nine years of publishing poems in magazines, Marianne Moore had only enough to make a pamphlet of twenty-six pages—her first book, *Poems*, published in 1924. Robert Frost's first book, *A Boy's Will*, was published in England in 1913 after Frost had been writing for nearly a decade. So to begin, one must read little magazines with a finely tuned ear. How to develop such an ear can be argued endlessly—and pointlessly. I can only repeat what the opera diva Zinka Milanov told a gushing admirer who asked her how she managed to produce such lovely high C's. Madame Milanov replied succinctly, "Dolling, either you got the voice or you don't got the voice. I got the voice." Yet even if you "don't got the ear," your taste can still be cultivated to some extent. It takes time and patience, but with any degree of sensitivity at all, you will soon be able to discern the good from the bad. Once you have savored quality, mediocrity will never again suffice.

From then on, it is simply a matter of following your chosen author's career. Naturally, some authors—poets particularly—start off brilliantly and then seem to diminish in vigor, strength, and interest. If this happens with one of your choices, you will very likely not have spent an inordinate amount of money—although you may have invested a good amount of reading time. You will almost certainly have found some enjoyment. But all this pales into insignificance when one of your early choices keeps on improving and turns out not only to be an extraordinary poet, but also a writer who is widely recognized and acclaimed. Then you will have an almost proprietary feeling about the author you spotted long ago as a "winner," a feeling confirmed by your own superb collection of his books, with all those early titles, now impossible to find, perhaps even inscribed to you. It may take ten or twenty years, but in the meantime you have been relishing the books, perhaps even getting to know the poet personally, and deserve to feel superior to those collectors who hadn't the courage or taste to decide for themselves which authors were worth collecting.

If you are truly convinced from the beginning that your poet is worthwhile, I'd recommend buying two copies of each of those early works, or even more of some of them if, as is often the case, they are inexpensive pamphlets. In purchasing one you will be forming your own complete collection, one you are unlikely to want to break up later even when market demand rises. Therefore, if you have set aside two or three copies at publication, for a couple of dollars or so, you are in a position to part with them quite happily when they begin to fetch tidy sums. You can use them for bartering for expensive items otherwise unobtainable.

I spoke of the possibility of having the author's early books inscribed to you. Within the existing framework of book collecting, there are several gradations of desirability. At the bottom is an ordinary unsigned copy of a book. One that the author has signed is definitely a notch higher in the scale, while one that bears some writing in addition to the mere signature is even more desirable. At the top of the scale is a presentation copy—that is, one actually given by the author to someone, with an inscription in his hand attesting to this. And within this top category, there are still further refinements. Copies inscribed to other well-known authors are particularly desirable, as are copies inscribed to mothers, wives, or lovers. The ne plus ultra is, of course, the dedication copy, i.e., the copy inscribed to the person to whom the book is dedicated. Obviously there can be only one such, and therefore it achieves top rank in desirability.

Neophyte authors are always particularly anxious for recognition. This is especially true of poets, to whom fame, fortune, and recognition come much more slowly than to novelists or playwrights. They are usually extraordinarily

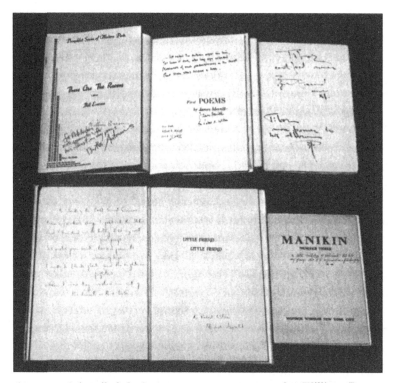

A group of inscribed books: THESE ARE THE RAVENS *by William Everson (Brother Antoninus);* FIRST POEMS *by James Merrill;* A DRAFT OF XXX CANTOS *by Ezra Pound;* LITTLE FRIEND, LITTLE FRIEND *by Randall Jarrell; and* MARRIAGE *by Marianne Moore (published as Manikin #3). From the author's collection.*

grateful when anyone evinces any interest in them at all. A simple letter to a young poet telling him how much you have enjoyed his work, and asking, at the same time, if he would be willing to inscribe your copies of his first two or three books seldom fails to succeed. In many cases the gesture can be the foundation of an interesting and fruitful acquaintance. Quite often poets will have printed some little pamphlet or broadside for their personal use, and they may be willing to give you copies of these if you simply ask about them. More often than not, inscriptions made in the early days of a poet's career, before he is chastened by fame, will be either lengthy or charming, or both. A good example of just what can happen if you develop an interest in a young poet's work early in his career is exemplified in my collection of James Merrill, the American poet who won the Pulitzer Prize in 1975. Merrill had been publishing poetry ever since his undergraduate days at Amherst, and had his first regularly published book issued by Alfred A. Knopf in 1951, a volume entitled simply *First Poems*. In the succeeding years he published several volumes of verse, as well as two novels, one of which bore on its dust jacket high praise from Truman Capote, an author generally not given to lauding a competitor's work. Merrill had over these years a substantial reading public, enough to justify reprintings of many of his earlier books of poetry. While he was collected to some degree, he was never strongly sought after. However, the Pulitzer Prize award, as it sometimes does, changed all that, and now he is widely and eagerly collected. The prices for his early books double and triple every few months, it seems. Collectors now know that *First Poems* was not, in fact, his first book, but his third. The true first, entitled *Jim's Book*, was a substantial hardbound affair, privately published by his father for the family and close friends. It is a book of poems and short stories, all juvenilia, published in 1942 when the author was only sixteen. The work shows talent, but the poet himself considers it immature, prefers to ignore its existence, and is reluctant even to reply to inquiries about it. Since it was a privately published item, intended as a surprise for the author, never for sale, it is of extreme rarity.

Merrill's second book, which appeared some four years later in Athens, was a long poem entitled *The Black Swan*, again privately printed, this time by the poet himself in an edition of only one hundred copies. Since then he has personally published at least one other such long poem in pamphlet form for his personal use, as well as an amusing quatrain on a small card for his mother's use in acknowledging congratulations on his having won the Pulitzer Prize. None of these was ever for sale, and while some of them eventually work their way into dealers' catalogs, it is always an isolated copy that appears on the market, for which there are always many customers. If you become friendly with the poet, there is a chance that such items will be given to you. One of these little pamphlets in my own collection bears a poignant inscription: "For Robert Wilson, my faithful, perhaps only reader, from James Merrill." I bought those extraordinarily rare first two books from another book dealer at a time when Merrill was still not very actively collected. The price was nominal, and the dealer seemed glad to be rid of them—despite the fact that *Jim's Book* was nothing less than the dedication copy! (Late in 1978, the only copy of *Jim's Book* to have appeared in a dealer's catalog thus far was priced at $4,000.)

In my experience, even world-famous and well-established poets can be generous with their time. Two of the very biggest names in twentieth-century poetry, W. H. Auden and Marianne Moore, rarely if ever refused any request they could grant in the way of signing books. They were cooperative even when the signing request involved many volumes, and they invariably invited the importuner into their homes, thereby giving up even more time. A few poets are totally reclusive; Wallace Stevens would not allow even his publisher, Alfred A. Knopf, into the house, but entertained him on the lawn. But such extreme cases are rare. When having books signed by an author, if possible provide the pen yourself. Preferably, if you can find one, use an old-fashioned fountain pen with ordinary ink. A cartridge pen can be used in a pinch. The use of ball-point pens or felt-tip pens is fraught with several dangers. The ink of

felt-tip pens tends to fade quickly, and the pressure needed
to make a ball-point pen work usually makes deep grooves
or impressions on the underlying pages. Especially on soft
book paper, felt-tip ink may spread or bleed through ad-
joining pages. I learned this the hard way when William
Burroughs generously inscribed a group of books for me.
Being in a breezy mood that day, he employed four different colors of felt-tip pens. I was delighted at the time, since
the multiple colors made a brilliant display on the various
title pages. But when I went to show these inscriptions to another collector only a few months later, I discovered that the
colors had bled through as many as eight pages on either
side of the inscription, rather diminishing my joy. Many
authors will have their own pens, but if you have your pen
ready, most of them will accept it. And not a few will
absentmindedly make off with it as well, so it's best not to
offer an expensive model. If you are getting books signed
after a reading or other public appearance, try to remember
that many other people also want books signed, and an author's time and patience have their limits. Generally speaking, two or at the most three books is as many as one should
ask to have signed at a time. Sometimes the author is anxious
to leave promptly and will suggest that you deliver or send
the books to his residence. If you do this, be careful to make
the process as convenient as possible for him. Provide a
return address label, fresh gummed tape for resealing the
parcel, and of course, sufficient postage for the return jour-
ney. After all, authors need their time for writing. Try
not to be another person from Porlock.

Some poets who become aware of your devotion to their
work will send you advance information or announcements
of their forthcoming books. Some even send complimentary
copies, and it is not unknown for a poet to bestow work
sheets or manuscripts upon really earnest enthusiasts.

Paying attention to a rising poet or author for many

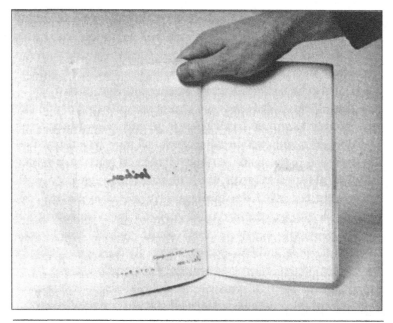

The consequences of using a felt-tip pen for autographing—bleed-through in ink on a copy of William Burroughs' THE EXTERMINATOR. *From the author's collection.*

years may bring about events that you could scarcely have foreseen. Once it becomes known in the book-collecting world that you are particularly interested in a certain author, dealers will often offer you special items in advance of putting them in a catalog. Conversely, dealers will also begin to ask *you* for specific information on bibliographical fine points or variants with which they are personally unfamiliar, especially where no bibliography exists. Thus, by degrees, you may begin to gain a reputation for expertise on your author. You may be *the* expert. This has been known to lead the collector to produce a bibliography of the author in question. It should be noted in passing that bibliographies are generally not moneymakers, particularly if

you count the time expended in gathering the necessary
minutiae. But at some point or other, it is almost inevitable
that you will wish to set down and codify the mass of information that you have gathered in the course of collecting. It may be merely from a sense of self-preservation, to
stop the repeated demands on your time to explain odd details; it may be out of frustration at seeing false information
repeated over and over in catalogs; or it may be simply that
you feel you have to do it. Here again, if you have established a relationship with the author, he may well be willing to help out with the bibliography so far as he can, although in my experience most authors have seldom been
able to hold onto copies of their works (which are usually
given to their friends or, worse, stolen by them), especially
the earlier pieces. Moreover, authors generally have a hazy
knowledge at best of publishing details, since this aspect
of the creation of a book is after all not their prime concern.

In a few cases friendship with the author and his work
may bring still closer involvement. It is not unknown for a
fan to become either a part-time or even a full-time secre-
tary to an author, and in a couple of notable instances, a
lifetime companion, as witness Clara Svendsen's long association with Isak Dinesen. Alice Toklas began her relationship
with Gertrude Stein as a part-time typist of Stein's volumi-
nous longhand works. And recently, a young professor, co-
compiler of a bibliography of one of the century's major
poets, found himself gradually moving into a closer relationship with the poet, eventually editing his later volumes of
prose, and after the writer's death winding up as his literary
executor. Now none of these things is guaranteed to happen
(and you may not even want any of them to happen) but
experience shows that they are entirely possible.

In my own case, a friendship with W. H. Auden grew
out of a simple request to have him sign my copies of his
books, which at that time numbered perhaps a dozen titles.

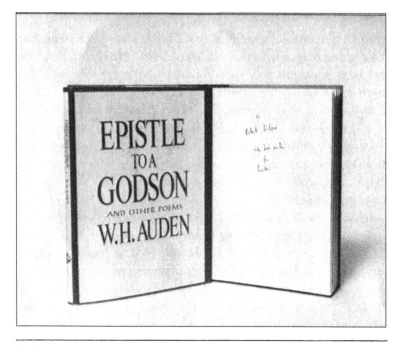

W. H. Auden's last book, with an inscription to the author. From the author's collection.

He was kind enough to invite me to bring them to his apartment on St. Mark's Place, in New York's East Village, at teatime. Tea turned out to mean cocktails—very strong martinis, in fact. Emboldened by his agreeableness, I applied to him again, a year or so later, when I had added further titles to my collection. Again he was lavish with his time. As the years went on, this became a ritual, and I would see him every six months or so. We eventually reached the point where, when I mentioned that I had never been able to find such-and-such a title, he would invariably offer to give it to me if he could find it. Finding it, of course, was the problem; search as he would he could rarely locate the book on his shelves, even though he often looked assiduously. Auden lived in a shambles that had to be witnessed to be believed. His furniture was dilapidated to the point where the springs had burst through the worn fabric of both the sofa and the single easy chair; the padding was oozing out of vital spots in both pieces of furniture, and the end of the sofa was held in place by some tall panels from a packing crate. Piled everywhere were disorderly accumulations of phonograph records, books, magazines, and working drafts of manuscripts. On one unforgettable occasion, he did manage to turn up one of the rarest items in the canon of his work, a tiny pamphlet entitled simply *Poem*, published in 1935 in an edition of only twenty-two copies. He gave it to me.

In 1972, when Auden finally decided to leave America and go back to England, our friendship was firm enough for him to ask me, as a dealer, if I would be interested in purchasing the portion of his library that he did not want to take with him. Of course, I agreed immediately. He then said, "Mind you, I don't have any first editions. I'm not a collector." I agreed nevertheless, realizing that even though his attitude toward books as objects was as far from a book collector's as it is possible to be, there would, of necessity, have to be some first editions—and lord knows what else.

Eventually the time came for him to start the immense task of transplanting himself. When I arrived he had sorted out the books he wanted to keep, piling them in heaps on the floor. Everything else was still on shelves and tables, in every one of the four rooms of his apartment. I looked around and said that it would take me about a week to give him an estimate of what I could pay for the library. He looked a bit surprised. "My good man," he said, "I don't want an estimate. Just get the stuff out of here so that I can start packing. Take it away and send me whatever you think proper." It took the better part of two weeks simply to pack up and move the books. During the course of this work I gained enough courage to ask him why he had chosen me, when any dealer in the world would have jumped at the opportunity. His reply was very matter-of-fact. "Because you're the only one who has taken a personal interest in my work." Needless to say, his library contained, along with what he described as "the world's largest collection of terrible poetry" (wished on him by aspiring poets), some great plums.

Nor was this the only instance of such a happening. I acquired Marianne Moore's library through a similar chain of events. I had made her acquaintance before I met Auden, and long before I had any ideas about becoming a professional book dealer. She was one of the first poets I ever asked to sign books for me. She apparently liked me well enough to allow me to come back from time to time over the years, and once even prepared a memorable, if peculiar, luncheon for me, composed of all the leftovers in her refrigerator. Toward the end of her life, when her family forced her to move back to Manhattan from the disintegrating neighborhood in Brooklyn where she had resided for a quarter of a century, she allowed me to buy several shopping bags full of items she no longer wanted. They ranged from back issues of magazines up through presentation copies of rare books by H. D., William Carlos Williams, and T. S. Eliot. Later, I was entrusted with the job of placing her archive in an institution. As with Auden, this enviable opportunity came about because I had collected her books and ventured to have them signed.

While it is certainly enjoyable and even thrilling when one of your authors rises to immense fame, it is not necessarily disastrous when it fails to happen. A forest is not composed solely of giant trees. It takes all grades and types of writers to make up a literary milieu at any given time. Many authors of less than monumental importance are nonetheless interesting, even if their works are not major landmarks of literature. The giants of course attract the lion's share of the attention with collectors, both private and institutional, but eventually the time comes when scholars and collectors begin to see the charm and importance of some of the lesser lights. One example of this can be seen in the complete exhaustion of possible discoveries in the work of the expatriate authors of the twenties. Hemingway and Fitzgerald have been worked over to the point where there are few finds to be made. But as late as the mid-1960s, the books of Harry Crosby, published by his own Black Sun Press, were literally going begging. I saw stacks of them in a New York bookshop at $4 per copy—with no buyers. And while half a dozen years ago there was some interest in Djuna Barnes, Robert McAlmon, Mary Butts, and others of the period, most of their books could be found easily and were not expensive. Today interest in all these secondary authors is extremely keen, with virtually no copies available of any title. When the occasional copy does surface, the price is high and the demand brisk. So don't be disappointed if your author does not become a giant. As long as there is true literary quality in his work, the collection will always be of interest and value. In fact, because it is focused on a less-collected author, you may find that an institution is much more interested in having it than in acquiring yet another collection of the works of one of the more famous names. It probably already has the latter books—likely in multiple copies.

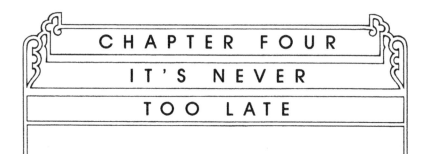

CHAPTER FOUR
IT'S NEVER
TOO LATE

Several times thus far I have emphasized the advisability of beginning early on an author collection. While this always makes sense both financially and in terms of availability of material, a late start is not necessarily impossible. Some of the choicest items turn up after an author has become popular with collectors, sometimes *because* the popularity has driven prices up. People are often willing to sell for a substantial sum things that they wouldn't have wanted to bother selling when prices were low. It is almost a commonplace that an enormous, sudden price rise in an author's work, or of a particular book, almost invariably brings copies out of the proverbial woodwork. A few years ago I discovered in an out-of-the-way shop in upstate New York a dull-looking little pamphlet entitled *12 Occupations* by Jean de Bosschère and dated 1916, with a few pages of woodcuts and some lines of text. A bell rang in the back of my mind. I remembered reading that title and author's name somewhere. So I bought the little pamphlet, and back in New York I was able to confirm the vague memory. The book was a scarce early pamphlet whose text had been translated anonymously by Ezra Pound. I had never seen a copy in a bookseller's catalog, although by this time interest in Pound had already begun to reach fanatic proportions. I priced it at $100, and sold it immediately, with numerous disappointed would-be customers. My suspicions about its real rarity, in both the market as well as in institutional and private collections, were confirmed. To my amazement, five or six additional copies were subsequently offered to me. Several people had owned copies all along, but had not thought them worth selling until the $100 price appeared.

Gertrude Stein's first book, *Three Lives*, one of the most important landmarks in American realism, was privately published in 1909 in an edition of approximately five hundred copies. It has always been a scarce book, and copies have always been extremely difficult to locate. Since the late 1960s, Stein's prices have escalated to a point where a reasonably good copy of this book will fetch several hundred dollars. As a result, more copies are appearing on the market now than when a copy brought less than $100. It thus sometimes becomes easier, albeit more expensive, to find a book once a higher price range has been established.

The collector should realize that it is never too late to start on his chosen collection, despite the fact that everything worth having may seem to have been bought up or to have gone irretrievably into institutional holdings. This is especially true in the manuscript field. An important American museum/library had officially defined its area of collecting interest as ending with the nineteenth century, in spite of having acquired, at the Quinn sale in 1924, the manuscript of what is now generally regarded as the greatest single work in English literature in the twentieth century— James Joyce's *Ulysses*. In the late 1960s, this institution decided that perhaps the twentieth century *had* developed a few authors worthy of its attention. Dylan Thomas and Marianne Moore were named as sufficiently "safe" and important to add to the library's impressive holdings. Miss Moore was still alive, but Dylan Thomas was already dead, and the great period of enthusiasm for him had long since peaked among collectors. The director of the library confided to me his decision to move into the twentieth century, but added, wistfully, that he had been advised against starting on Dylan Thomas because everything worth having was already gone. Without knowing precisely why, perhaps guided by some lucky genie, I encouraged him to go ahead with Thomas, promising to look out for items of interest, all the while thinking to myself that his adviser was probably correct. Within a few weeks the miracle happened. One of the best-known British dealers, on a visit to New York, casually asked me if I might be interested in the handwritten manuscript of Dylan Thomas' *Under Milk Wood*. Trying not to let my enthusiasm show too much, I allowed that I might be, asking for an option for two weeks. The dealer was rather startled, and probably a bit disgruntled, by my response, since I suspect that he had been boasting rather than genuinely offering the manuscript to me. But now he could not back out. I telephoned the library director immediately, and he soon secured the approval of his board of trustees for the purchase. So off to London I flew to bring the treasure home. There was a cloak-and-dagger aspect to the trip, because another American dealer—himself the agent for another (and famously omnivorous) institution—had also got wind of the existence of the manuscript and had likewise flown to London to buy it. I had taken the precaution of sending an advance deposit, however, and had the pleasure of finding that though Mr. F. had been there an hour ahead of me, offering a higher price, the firm of Bertram Rota, Ltd., was honorable in the best traditions of the trade. They politely but firmly told Mr. F. that the manuscript had already been sold. Thus I was able to bring it back in triumph, though not without some difficulties both in taking it on board the plane as hand luggage (it was in a large leather case about three feet square) and again in clearing it through customs on Christmas Eve. The customs officials cared nothing about the manuscript but were intent on charging the duty on the leather case—and since it was Christmas Eve the appraisers were not on duty. This problem was resolved—after a number of firm, not to say excited, words on my part—when the chief inspector declared the whole parcel duty-free.

The day after Christmas I delivered it to my happy librarian, who now faced the problem of building a collection of Thomas' books around this masterpiece. I never actually found out, but I always sincerely hoped that the first person he showed the new acquisition was the adviser who had predicted the impossibility of finding any such thing.

Some few years before his death, William Faulkner deposited all of his manuscripts at the University of Virginia. Virtually everything was there except the manuscript of his first novel, *Soldier's Pay*, which was presumed to have been lost or destroyed. Faulkner himself had no recollection of what had happened to it. Yet a few years ago I discovered it, in the possession of an elderly gentleman who had been Faulkner's roommate in the days after World War I in the French Quarter of New Orleans. Here it was, the entire manuscript with holograph revisions, along with several unpublished short stories, many poems in holograph (some of them unpublished), and even a variant ending for the novel. Everything was still in the original mailing carton addressed to Faulkner by the agent who was returning the material to him. The manuscript itself was in a shirt box. It seems that when Faulkner and the roommate decided to go their separate ways, Faulkner abandoned the material to be thrown away, but the roommate had the prescience to preserve it. The incident shows that once again it was not too late, despite what everyone thought, to acquire an important Faulkner manuscript.

Even more recently, all important literary material by Conrad Aiken was thought to have vanished from the market when his widow sold his entire archive to the Henry Huntington Library and Art Gallery in San Marino, California. But within a year of that transaction, the working draft of his most famous novel, *Blue Voyage*, came to light in the

Working draft of an unpublished poem by William Faulkner. From the author's collection.

estate of one of his lifelong friends. Aiken had inscribed it to the man as a gift, along with several notebooks of poem drafts, and all the manuscripts came up for sale.

Outside the rarefied world of manuscripts, there is no way of knowing when a large collection or cache of books of superb quality will come to light. Many wonderful collections, previously unknown to dealers or other collectors, are continually surfacing. One such nearly incredible collection was sold by the Swann Galleries a few years ago. No one had ever heard tell of the collector or the collection. Put on the market by the lawyers for the estate, it comprised superb runs of Faulkner, Joyce, and Stein, including the long-lost fifth copy of Stein's *The Making of Americans* in the vellum edition, of which only five had been printed. For many years four copies could be located, and the fifth was surmised to have perished during World War II. But suddenly it surfaced along with such other gems as a signed, limited *Ulysses*, a handwritten book by Faulkner, and historically important letters by Stein describing the now famous Salon d'Automne, where Matisse first attracted public attention.

This kind of collection sometimes gravitates into a dealer's hands and forms the basis of an exceptional catalog; sometimes, as mentioned, it comes up at auction; or occasionally it even finds its way into an ordinary secondhand bookshop. More about this aspect will be said in a later chapter. Meanwhile, don't despair.

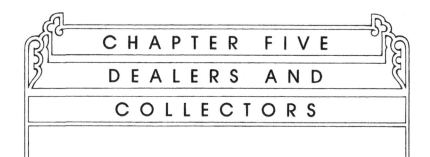

CHAPTER FIVE
DEALERS AND
COLLECTORS

Any collector, as opposed to a general reader who doesn't care whether he has a first or a tenth edition of a book, has to face the fact that most of his books will have to be obtained through specialist dealers. Long gone—if they ever existed—are the days when a superior collection could be built by haunting thrift shops and general secondhand bookshops. The latter are themselves almost an extinct species, victims of the increasingly high rents for the amount of space needed to operate a large general bookstore, the increase in specialization in all fields, extending also into book collecting, and, not least, the prevalence of paperback editions. The resale possibilities of paperbacks is severely limited —many of them literally fall apart after a couple of readings; some don't even last through the first reading. Also, a used-book dealer can hope to make only a slim margin of profit on secondhand paperbacks.

Of course, the occasional instance of serendipity still occurs on outdoor stands and in thrift shops, garage sales, and the like. Every collector has his favorite tale of the gem he obtained in just such a manner. But these finds are isolated instances at best, and happen so rarely that no serious collection can be built by depending on them. Once you are committed to any sort of collecting—first editions, or a subject collection such as chess books, color-plate books, or whatever—you will, of necessity, be obliged to go to specialist dealers to obtain the large majority of your books, especially the rare and more unusual items. Today, whenever a

new, signed, limited edition by a major author is announced
by a publisher, it is almost invariably oversubscribed, and
all available copies taken up by specialist dealers. Very few,
if any, find their way into regular bookstores. If you hope to
get a copy, it will pay to have established a relationship with
a dealer so that you will be guaranteed one of his. This is
especially important when the demand is greater than the
supply, for in that case the publisher is obliged to cut the
number of copies allotted to each dealer.

The first problem, especially for the novice collector, is
to discover which dealer can supply his needs, and where
they are. Fortunately, in the United States and Great Britain
there are several methods, relatively easy, of answering such
questions. First of all, in the United States, there is the directory of the Antiquarian Booksellers' Association of America, commonly known as the ABAA. Founded just after
World War II, this group has over three hundred members
sworn to fair practices and honorable dealings. While a
great many American book dealers are members, there are
several important ones who are not, for a variety of reasons.
One of these is the Association's rule that a prospective member must have been a full-time dealer in business for at least
three years. This, of course, eliminates all fledglings, as well
as part-time dealers. And there are some dealers, long established, with national and even international reputations,
who are not members by reason of personal choice. The Association's membership list is nonetheless a good place to begin
to seek out dealers who can help you. The ABAA maintains
a shop in New York City at 50 Rockefeller Plaza, New York,
N.Y. 10020, where a few representative volumes from several different members are on display. The shop usually has
a supply of the latest catalogs of those members who issue
them. The membership list of the ABAA can be obtained
by going there in person, or by writing to the shop. If you

write, be sure to enclose a self-addressed, stamped envelope for the return of the list.

In Great Britain there is a similar organization known as the Antiquarian Book Dealers' Association, 154 Buckingham Palace Road, London, S.W. 1, England.

The Book Review section of the Sunday *New York Times* always carries a page of advertisements by booksellers, many of whom are specialists. It must be admitted, however, that this group of advertisers is rather small, and tends to remain the same, year in, year out. Furthermore, most of them are members of the ABAA and will already have been located through that membership list. However, in this section there are also advertisements by book searchers, something quite different from regular book dealers. These people will undertake to search for books for a fee. Usually there is no charge if the book is not located. It is generally pointless to ask them to find even run-of-the-mill first editions, and hopeless to request great rarities. However, they are often quite helpful in finding secondary items such as later printings, obscure journals, and the like.

In Great Britain, there is an extremely useful guide to book sellers entitled *A Directory of Dealers in Secondhand & Antiquarian Books in the British Isles*. It is arranged geographically for easy reference to whatever area you may be in at any given time. It further gives a brief description of the kinds of books handled by each dealer, so that you will know at a glance whether or not it is likely to be worth your time to visit a particular shop.

There are several trade journals for the out-of-print, secondhand, antiquarian, or used-book market. Chief among these is the one familiarly known as "The AB" from the initials of its original name, *The Antiquarian Bookmarket*. In recent years the magazine has been called *AB Bookman's Weekly* (Box AB, Clifton, New Jersey 07015). This can be an important source of information for any collector. While its primary function is to serve as a means of getting a dealer's specific and immediate wants known to his fellow dealers (this feature takes up the bulk of every issue), it also issues an annual directory, known as the *AB Bookman's Yearbook*. The *Yearbook* lists many small or part-time dealers who will not be found on the more august membership roll of the ABAA. They are honest, genuine dealers, and potential sources of desirable material. In Great Britain, there is a similar publication known as *The Clique* (75 World's End Road, Handsworth Wood, Birmingham B20 2NS), and another named *The Bookfinder*. Finally, there is a journal catering more directly to collectors than to the book trade, known as the *Antiquarian Book Monthly Review* (30 Cornmarket Street, Oxford OX1 3EY).

The most direct way of getting in touch with dealers is to attend one or more of the various antiquarian book fairs. These are being held with increasing frequency in the United States. The oldest of these is the ABAA's annual fair, held on the east and the west coasts in alternate years, generally in New York and in either Los Angeles or San Francisco. Lately there have been numerous other fairs of major importance. In England there are several regular book fairs in London as well as in the provinces. These fairs usually run for about five days and attract dealers from all over the world. From seventy to one hundred dealers may participate in a given fair and will display their choicest wares at booths. It is here that you can make the personal acquaintance of most of the dealers with whom you have been corresponding. For the neophyte it is an excellent way of ascertaining a dealer's potential value to you, since you can browse in his booth, and from the selection of books he has brought to exhibit you can tell at once whether or not he is ever likely to have the kind of material you seek. Many collectors are reluctant or even embarrassed to enter a shop or even to initiate correspondence without having a specific book in mind to purchase. But at a book fair no one need be shy.

Most dealers save their best pieces for the fairs, and quite often you can obtain a long-sought item that has been kept in reserve for the occasion. So keen is the competition for such material that the admission fee for the opening night of the fair is usually at least double the normal amount, and even so the crowd is so great that it is virtually impossible to get near some of the booths. This apparently deters no one, and most collectors go home with at least one prize in hand. Unfortunately for collectors, there is often a good deal of pre-opening movement of choice items from one dealer to another, with, of course, a price escalation with each move. One such case at a recent California fair involved William Carlos Williams' first book *Poems* (Rutherford, 1909), of which fewer than twenty copies are known to exist. A previously unregistered copy was on display in one dealer's booth. Another dealer spotted it and, realizing that the $3,000 asking price was ridiculously low, bought it and marked it up to $5,000. A third dealer saw it and, still thinking it a bargain, bought it at that price less his 10 percent dealer's discount (dealers customarily give one another 10 percent discount on purchases). When the fair opened, it was resting in the third dealer's booth for sale at $12,000. Of course, such a tremendous price escalation is rare, but it does point up the importance of getting to a fair as early as possible.

Catalogs issued by specialist dealers are probably the most important means of acquiring the better items you need. Most first-edition dealers issue such catalogs, some regularly and frequently, others irregularly and a year or more apart. The physical appearance of these catalogs may vary from a few mimeographed sheets stapled together all the way up to lavishly printed volumes, replete with illustrations and even in some rare cases cloth-bound. The general appearance of a catalog will usually indicate the caliber of material inside and the rough price range to be expected, but this is not always the case. Some of the mimeographed catalogs—my own, I am pleased to say, included—contain material just as rare and desirable as that found in the more finely printed ones. It goes without saying, of course, that the cost of producing and mailing out catalogs has to be taken into account by a dealer when pricing his books, and most collectors realize, if only subconsciously, that the less expensive the makeup of the catalog, the more likely the items in it will be reasonably priced. But whatever the appearance of the catalog may be, it is essential for the collector to get on the mailing list of the dozen or so most important dealers in whatever his field of interest may be, and also to give the dealers in return some sign of interest in their catalogs. Costs force every dealer to scan his mailing list periodically and remove names of persons who have not responded for some time. If you find nothing of interest in a series of catalogs, the chances are that this dealer is not handling the sort of material you want, and he will be justified in removing your name. If, however, you still want to receive his catalogs, you should send a note—a postcard will do—asking to be kept on the list. Most dealers will then be happy to continue to send the catalogs.

Once you have received a catalog in the mail, drop everything and read it immediately. Competition for desirable material is so keen nowadays that often a matter of minutes determines whether or not you get the desired item before someone else does. It is best to look first for the entries under your pet author, or even for a particular book, and then go back and read through the complete catalog. Quite often books you want may be classified under another heading, or even under another author. For example, there exist three plays and one travel book written jointly by

W. H. Auden and Christopher Isherwood, and while you may be interested only in Isherwood, the dealer may catalog these only under Auden. The 1915 *Catholic Anthology*, which contains, among other major items, "The Love Song of J. Alfred Prufrock" and is Eliot's first book appearance, may be listed either in the section devoted to Ezra Pound, who edited the volume and also appears in it, or it may be listed among anthologies. (Once, to my own delight and profit, it appeared very cheaply in the catalog of an innocent dealer under "Religious Books.") If you spot something that you want badly, especially a major item, telephone *immediately*. Any dealer will accept a telephone order, particularly from a customer already known to him. Direct dialing telephone rates are relatively inexpensive, and well worth the extra couple of dollars it may cost to secure an item. It doesn't pay to wait until night rates are in effect. In fact, many wise collectors will telephone immediately on spotting an important item and will then go back and read the rest of the catalog, either making a second phone call for further choices, or perhaps ordering the minor items by mail. Many a collector has failed to get a crucial item merely by delaying an hour or so. Since most dealers who issue catalogs have extensive mailing lists, catalogs are usually sent bulk rate (third class) mail, which means that they are delivered by your local post office after all other mail has been taken care of. In some cases there can be a delay of four or five weeks between the actual mailing of the catalog and your receipt of it—a period of time in which most of the plums will have been plucked. It is thus essential to receive the catalogs by first class mail. Since this is often very costly, a dealer is naturally reluctant to go to such expense. If, however, you are a regular customer and a fairly liberal purchaser, he will usually bear the expense himself of sending your copy first class. If, on the other hand, you are either a new customer, or if you seldom buy, the dealer may ask you to pay for the first-class postage. Usually this will amount to little more than a couple of dollars a year, but will always be worth it in order to have a better chance of obtaining your coveted items.

The dangers of buying a book sight unseen, through the mail, are too obvious to need elaboration. Condition (*see* Chapter 8) is the prime factor in book collecting, as in other hobby fields, and must be ascertained from the dealer's catalog description. It is here that interpretation enters in and disappointment occurs. Shades of meaning and gradations between "fine," "good," "mint," and other terms commonly employed are a matter of judgment, and your standards of what is fine may not be the same as the dealer's opinion. (*See* pages 107–8 for an analysis of commonly used terms.) "Condition cranks," a term applied to collectors whose insistence on perfection borders on mania and who push such standards to illogical extremes, are bound to be disappointed often. But most collectors who adopt a reasonable attitude toward condition will find little to complain of. For one thing, no dealer likes the wasted time, trouble, and expense of returned shipments, to say nothing of the danger to the books in the hands of the postal service. He may have lost a sale to another customer who wanted the particular item. Therefore, if only out of self-interest, most dealers try to be accurate in their cataloging. They have discerning eyes, generally, and it will not take long for you to become acquainted with the general level of each dealer's set of descriptive terms. Very few if any dealers will refuse to take a book back if it is returned within a reasonable length of time. This period is usually specified in the dealer's terms in the front of his catalog, and as a rule is ten days after receipt. If you are going to return a book, notify the dealer at once, either by phone or at least by letter, since the return parcel may take quite a long time to reach him. Particularly with a new catalog, he may have had to turn down one or more other orders for the item. Thus, if he knows it is coming back, he still has time to sell it to another customer.

The most important single aspect of the dealer-customer relationship is the gradual development of friendship and rapport. The buying of books is a unique type of transaction, unlike the purchase of almost any other commodity. Friendly relationships between a dealer and a customer are common. A good dealer will warm almost at once to a customer who indicates a true passion for books. On the other hand he may never find much affection for a customer who is collecting because it is fashionable or—especially in recent years—because books seem to be a good form of investment. Despite the old dictum that a dealer should not be a collector, so as not to compete with his own customers, virtually every dealer does have a personal collection of some sort, and almost without exception, every rare-book dealer started as a collector. It is safe to say that every book dealer is in the business because he enjoys it, a statement that cannot be made of many other professions.

I shall never forget an occasion many years ago when I was browsing in a first-edition dealer's shop while still a novice collector myself. A customer came in and asked for several titles of a particularly scarce and much sought-after author, who happened also to be the favorite author of that dealer, whose collection was rated one of the best in existence. Warming to what he thought was a fellow enthusiast, the dealer not only produced most of the wanted titles, but also brought out several other highly desirable items that he confessed he had been hoarding toward a catalog. The customer said that he would buy them and asked to have them shipped to his address in England. Then he made the cardinal error of boasting, "I can flog them for twice that price in England." The dealer was obviously nettled and immediately froze up, feeling, quite rightly, that he had been taken advantage of by a pretense of personal interest in the author's work. The customer left shortly thereafter, having given his London address, adding that he would send a check as soon as he got back to England. When he was safely out of the shop, the dealer said, as much to himself as to me, "He'll never get those books." If need be, the dealer said, he would advise the man that the shipment had got lost in the mail. "And besides," he added, "he's very slow to pay."

Which brings up another crucial area in your relationship with a dealer. Except for a very occasional item that is in his shop on consignment, every book in a dealer's stock has been bought and paid for by him before placing it on the shelf or in his catalog. He must therefore wait for payments to come in from customers in order to replenish his working capital before he can buy more books. Most dealers are chronically short of immediate cash. The more quickly payments come in, the more stock they can buy and, consequently, the better chance you have of obtaining from them the items you need. Therefore, prompt payment is not only courteous, it is also in your own interest. Most dealers require customers who are purchasing for the first time to pay for the initial shipment in advance, and ask that a charge account be deferred until references can be checked. Usually references from other book dealers are preferred over any credit card or department store account references, which are difficult, if not impossible, to check. Most dealers expect to be paid upon receipt of the merchandise, or at the very least by the end of the month. Naturally, once you have become an established customer, private agreements can be arranged, especially if you are purchasing a particularly expensive item.

When a new customer comes into a shop and asks for "anything" by a particularly prolific author, for example John Updike, Ted Hughes, Gertrude Stein, or any of a large number of major authors, the dealer may hedge a bit, especially if he happens to have a large or varied stock of the particular author. All too often a collector will use just that approach, either in person or by mail, when in actuality he is looking for one specific title or certain rarities. If the dealer's quarters are spacious enough for him to have everything shelved, he will usually point to the place where the author's books are displayed. But most dealers suffer chronically from lack of space, and not everything can be displayed at once. Sometimes there are other considerations, such as the exceptional fragility of an item, or an awkward size, or a rarity of such degree that the book would present too great a temptation to shoplifters. Or, with an unusually prolific author, the sheer bulk of the output may preclude displaying everything in one place. Most dealers will parry such an open-ended request, trying to narrow down the customer's field of interest. It is therefore essential to be specific in stating your wants. It is a false although apparently widely held belief among novices that a dealer instantly increases the price if you ask for a specific title; almost all dealers have prices marked in their books. It is vital for the collector to gain the friendship and goodwill of the dealer, particularly one who specializes in his author or area of interest. Many dealers are eccentrics, most of them charmingly so, but almost all of them like to place especially desirable titles where they think they belong, and if rubbed the wrong way, can very easily deny having the very book you want.

There is another precaution to be observed by someone making his first purchase from a dealer. It is very unwise to try to bargain with a dealer, particularly a specialist who knows his field very well. His prices are usually scaled in accordance with the general levels of the market on most items. Prices are normally set on the basis of the book's cost to the dealer. Most newly issued books are discounted at 40 percent to the dealer (plus, of course, postage or shipping charges, now a considerable figure). Many limited editions from small or private presses carry smaller dealer discounts, usually 30 percent, sometimes only 20 percent, and recently, when several such publishers have seen fit to issue an extremely limited edition of only twenty-six lettered copies, these have been sold to dealers at no discount at all, making it necessary for them to add something on the top in order to make even a modest profit. Many university presses allow dealers only 10 percent discount. When the postage is added to this, the cost to the dealer is often higher than the announced retail price, one reason why university press publications are often difficult to find in bookstores. On out-of-print books, the general practice in the book trade is to double the cost figure. This does not mean that the dealer is doubling his money on each item sold. He has rent, light, postage, printing, salaries—in short, all the expenses that used to be called overhead—to pay before his actual profit can be reckoned. Once in a while an item will come into a dealer's possession on which he can more than double his money, but that is the exception rather than the rule, and only helps to even out items he has bought at a particularly high price—either for the fun or prestige of being able to offer a very rare item, or perhaps as a service to a customer —and ended by selling at a nominal 10 or 15 percent markup.

Most dealers also stockpile a certain number of copies of books by authors in whom they have faith, against future demand or future price rise. These caches, when released some years later, often provide the only available copies of titles suddenly in demand. Here, again, the dealer has invested money and storage space, both of which are chronically in short supply, and hence must charge a premium, if only to compensate for the amount of interest he could have had on the money thus tied up. There is one other form of stockpiling where the dealer can make a higher rate of return, and that is in the case of "remainders," books wholesaled by the publishers at whatever price they will bring. Quite often first editions are remaindered, and many dealers in moderns watch the outlets for these with considerable care, buying quantities of titles by established authors and quietly putting them away until the remainder supply has dried up. Then the dealer will bring them out of storage and place them on the shelf at the original published price, or even at a markup, depending on the demand, how many copies are to be had from other dealers, and how many he himself has. The list of extremely desirable first editions that have been remaindered within the last quarter of a century is truly staggering, making one wonder why everyone was asleep. Just two examples should suffice. In the early 1960s the first four books of Edward Gorey were remaindered at 49c each; they now bring about two hundred times that figure. In 1960 the Yale edition of *The Unpublished Work of Gertrude Stein*, in eight volumes, was remaindered at half the original publication price. Sets now bring at least fifty times that amount and are rarely seen.

It is both unfair and unwise to ask a dealer to lower his price. One dealer, whenever he was asked to change a price, would look at the price penciled in the book, smile, say, "Oh, you're right, that's wrong," and then calmly add another digit. His customers learned very quickly not to haggle. A dealer may offer on his own initiative to lower a price, particularly if it is a book he has had in stock for a long period of time with no apparent interest in it, or he may even wish to give you a break on an item—but the initiative for such a reduction should come from him, not from you, unless your friendship with him is of such a degree that you can politely ask if that's the best he can do. But even such a request as this should be made rarely, only in the most exceptional circumstances, where there is some valid reason to suggest that the price may be too high. It must *never* be used as a standard operating procedure.

Once you have established a firm relationship with a dealer, he will be anxious to help you obtain the items you are looking for. He will take pride in helping build your collection, often spotting items in other dealers' catalogs, buying them for you and passing them on to you for little or no profit, just to have the pleasure of supplying something you need.

While some old-fashioned rare-book dealers felt that a customer should be loyal to only one dealer, this outlook is simply not realistic, and few if any of the dealers now in operation believe that a collector should buy from only one. No one dealer, no matter how active he is, can possibly supply you with every single item you need. Specialist dealers have, of course, many sources from which to draw, but the rare and fugitive items simply cannot be commanded at will. Dealers must also wait for certain items to appear, and be on the spot when they do surface. Some dealers seem to have more luck at this than others, and the talent is inexplicable. If you are determined to have an exceptional collection, you must simply try to establish good relationships with all the major dealers specializing in your area. It is of course not only good taste but wise to exercise some discretion and not talk too much about the foibles, the stock, or the prices of one dealer when in another's shop.

Want lists are both helpful and dangerous. Every collector, of course, has one, be it written on paper or merely carried in his head. But it is unwise to spread your written want lists to the four winds. If you send such a list out simultaneously to every dealer, the net result may well be a sudden false surge of interest in the titles on the list. Many dealers run periodic ads in the trade journals and comb each other's stock, either in person or by telephone. They also alert their book scouts. Several copies of your want list in the midst of all this activity may touch off what looks like a boom in a certain author or in particular titles, and could cause an abnormal escalation of prices. It is best to give the list to one dealer and let him work with it a few weeks or even months before passing it on to one of his competitors. Unless your want list is composed exclusively of "impossibles," a good dealer will normally come up with a few of your items in a reasonable length of time. Of course, if the list is primarily the impossibles, an experienced dealer won't waste much time or energy on it; if he were able to locate such items he'd be happy to buy them anyway. Such difficult books are star items in a catalog and are usually in demand by many people.

Above all, remember that the dealer is the necessary connection between you and most of the books you want. Also remember that he has seen and handled a lot of that material at some time, usually many times over, and will know many fine points that you may be unaware of. Without the dealer, you will never form a significant collection. As one proof of this, consult the acknowledgments page of a bibliography of a modern author published in the last two decades and see how consistently dealers are thanked for their help and advice.

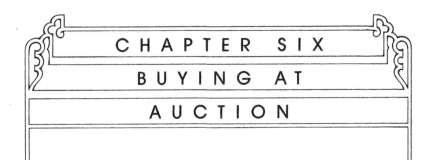

CHAPTER SIX

BUYING AT

AUCTION

Next to buying from a dealer, the most important way of adding to a collection is by purchasing books at auction. It is a method not generally understood as well as it should be. A lack of accurate knowledge about what actually happens at a book auction is partially responsible for the persistence of many popular fallacies, including the one that says prices are bound to be lower at auctions than at first-edition dealers' shops. The auction process seems to begin with to be almost childishly simple: books are offered for sale and people bid on them, the winner receiving the spoils. So it would appear on the surface. However, an experienced bidder knows that there is far more to it.

The easiest way to dispel cherished misconceptions about auctions is to follow the dispersal of a book collection through the auction mill. This process has as many currents and eddies as a millrace, both for the bidder and for the consignor of the collection. The wheels begin to grind long before the books actually come under the hammer and, in fact, before the general public has any notion that the collection will be coming up for sale. The collection may be an inherited one. Strangely, the love for book collecting is seldom inherited with a collection. And even if the heir is a collector, he may well lack interest in a ready-made collection.

Many notable collections, therefore, eventually find their way to auction. The owners get in touch with an auction house. (See Appendix 1 for a list of auction houses handling books in the United States, Canada, and Great Britain.) The gallery will usually request that the books be brought in for examination. If the collection is a very large one, the gallery will assign an expert to appraise the collection *in situ*, for which a fee will be charged. Small galleries generally have only small staffs, with wide but limited knowledge, while the larger galleries such as Sotheby Parke Bernet or Christie's have more expert personnel. At such galleries extensive reference collections of bibliographies are kept along with past auction records, which include their own and other catalogs. The gallery can usually come to a rapid decision as to whether or not a particular collection is suitable for auctioning and whether or not the gallery is interested in disposing of it. The gallery can also advise about the condition of the market at any given moment for a particular type of collection.

The whims affecting book collecting are no different from the whims in collecting art or antiques. What was valued twenty years ago may be passé today or vice versa. F. Scott Fitzgerald went almost totally unregarded a generation ago. Now his works are among the most prized items. A. E. Coppard, on the other hand, was fetching high prices in the thirties, but now is worth almost nothing. Experienced galleries know what is selling well and can advise whether the time is right or whether it may be to everyone's interest to wait for a more opportune moment. It is also in the gallery's interest to tell the would-be consignor when the case is hopeless—when a valuable-seeming accumulation of books is in fact so nearly worthless as to fail to warrant the time and effort to auction them.

If the collection is of interest to the auction house, it is then removed to the gallery premises. A critical phase of the ultimate dispersal takes place here—the separation of the collection into lots. The manner in which this is done will affect the amount of money to be realized by the owners and, frequently, whether dealers and collectors can be induced to bid at all. With highly popular known titles there is little or no problem—each such book is a high spot, and is offered as a single item. Every gallery has its minimum price for a lot to be worth a catalog entry. Of the principal New York book auction galleries, Sotheby Parke Bernet's minimum is $150, Christie's is $100, and the Swann Galleries maintains a minimum of $50. This means books under that price are not accepted for auction singly. The lesser items in a collection are generally "lotted"—that is, lumped together in groups so as not to waste time and effort during the sale. Lotting, however, is a chancy affair. Real treasures may be lotted accidentally together with books of low value, offering an opportunity to the sharp-eyed dealer or collector.

Numerous examples of such finds can be cited. One afternoon, for example, a dealer was the only bidder on a seemingly unpromising group of anthologies offered in one lot near the end of a long, tedious sale. When examining the group a couple of days after the sale, he was startled to discover that one of the books—*Some Imagist Poets* (London, 1915), edited by Amy Lowell—had been signed by each of the contributors. Obviously an industrious collector had gone to a lot of trouble to seek out the various authors for signatures. The one book was consequently worth many times what the dealer paid for the entire lot. It is easy to see that galleries cannot spend time searching through each book for possible hidden values. Every dealer and most collectors can tell tales of finding letters, money, photographs, and other paraphernalia tucked into books by previous owners. Within a space of five years I have personally known of letters by James Joyce, Oscar Wilde, Dylan Thomas, and W. B. Yeats being found slipped in books—and all of them had been overlooked by specialist dealers who had the books on their shelves. This kind of thing happens frequently enough in auction lots to make the time spent in checking them carefully before the sale quite worthwhile.

■ 640 FAULKNER, WILLIAM. Absalom, Absalom!   New York, 1936
8vo. Original cloth, with the dust jacket (worn)
*First edition. Inscribed "For Malcolm Cowley / William
Faulkner / Sherman Conn. / 25 Oct. 1948." Pages 31-58
have been removed, undoubtedly by Cowley. The book is
signed by him and has a few annotations and numerous
pencil markings in his hand*
*Cowley was mainly responsible for the re-establishment
of Faulkner's literary reputation, which led to his Nobel
Prize for Literature in 1950 (see Goodwin Part I, lot 100)*
Petersen A17c

■ 641 FAULKNER, WILLIAM. Intruder in the
Dust   New York, [1948]
8vo. Original cloth, with the dust jacket. Cloth case
*First edition, review copy with the publisher's slip giving
publication details laid in. Signed by the author on the
titlepage and inscribed: "For Malcom Cowley / Bill
Faulkner / Sherman, Conn. 25 Oct. 1948." With a few
pencil markings by Cowley, undoubtedly for his review of
the book in "The New Republic" [October 18, 1948]. A
fine copy·*
Petersen A24b

                [SEE ILLUSTRATION]

■ 642 FAULKNER, WILLIAM. The Reivers
                                    New York, [1962]
8vo. Original cloth, with the acetate dust jacket.
Cloth case
*First edition, one of 500 copies signed by the author. A
very fine copy*
Petersen A37e

■ 643 FAULKNER, WILLIAM. Monnaire de Singe
[Soldiers' Pay], *Grenoble*, [1948], one of 300 copies
on Rives paper, unopened ☆ L'invaincu, [*Paris,
1949*], one of 205 copies on Lafuma Navarre paper,
unopened ☆ Absalom, Absalom! [*Paris, 1953*], one
of 80 numbered copies on Navarre paper, un-
opened ☆ Jefferson, Mississippi, [*Paris, 1956*] ☆ Les
Larrons, [*Paris, 1964*], one of 67 copies on Lafuma
Navarre paper, unopened
Together 5 vols., 8vo. Original wrappers or cloth.
Cloth cases
First editions in French. Fine to very fine copies

Intruder
in the
Dust

by *Wilhm Faslkn*
William Faulkner
for Malcolm Cowley
    Bill Faslkn
    shearm, Conn
    Fel. 1948
    Random House

    New York

                [641]

■ 644 FAULKNER, WILLIAM. The Marionettes
                                [Charlottesville, 1975]
Large 4to. Illustrated by the author. Original unbound quires, publisher's box, as issued. Cloth case
*First edition, one of 100 numbered copies, of an edition of
126. A facsimile of one of the original manuscript copies
made by Faulkner*

Sample page of a catalog from Sotheby Parke Bernet, Inc., New York.

Official conditions of sale printed on the inside front cover of a catalog from the Swann Galleries, Inc., New York.

222 POWYS, LLEWELYN. Skin for Skin * The Verdict of Bridlegoose * Apples Be Ripe * Impassioned Clay. Together, 4 volumes. 8vo, cloth and boards; all but the third in dust jackets.
London, 1926-27-30-31
FIRST EDITIONS; *the first two are large-paper editions, limited to 900 copies each.*
ALSO, *by* JOHN COWPER POWYS—*The Art of Growing Old. (1944); Homer and the Aether. (1959); The Saturnian Quest: a Study of J.C. Powys, by G. Wilson Knight. (1964).*

223 POWYS, T.F. Soliloquies of a Hermit. 12mo, blue boards, cloth back; dust jacket.
London, 1918
FIRST EDITION *of Powys's first book.*

224 POWYS, T.F. A Strong Girl and The Bride * The Rival Pastors. Together, 2 volumes. Thin tall 4to, rebound in patterned boards; top edges gilt, original wrappers bound in.
London, 1926: 1927
LARGE-PAPER FIRST EDITIONS, *each limited to only 100 numbered copies privately printed, and* SIGNED BY ’OWYS.

225 POWYS, T.F. Mr. Weston's Good Wine * Fables * The White Paternoster. Together, 3 volumes. Large 8vo, buckram and boards; top edges gilt.   London, 1927-29-30
LARGE-PAPER FIRST EDITIONS, *limited and numbered, and* SIGNED BY POWYS.
Also, his The Dewpond. Thin 8vo, boards; dust jacket. One of 530, signed. 1928.

226 POWYS, T.F. The Left Leg * Black Bryony * Mark Only * Mr. Tasker's Gods * Mockery Gap * Innocent Birds. Two copies * The House with the Echo. Together, 8 volumes. 12mo, cloth; dust jackets (somewhat frayed). FIRST EDITIONS.   London, 1923-28

227 PROSE QUARTOS. Complete set of 6. Thin 8vo, stiff wrappers, paper labels; boxed
New York 1930
ONE OF 850 SETS. *Tales by S.V. Benet, Bromfield, Aiken, Van Vechten, Sherwood Anderson, and Dreiser.*

228 ROBINSON, EDWIN ARLINGTON. Merlin * The Three Taverns * Lancelot. Together, 3 volumes. 12mo, cloth. FIRST EDITIONS.   New York, 1917-20-30

229 ROBINSON, EDWIN ARLINGTON. Tristram. Tail 8vo, two-toned cloth; top edge gilt, boxed.   New York, 1927
LARGE-PAPER FIRST EDITION, *limited to 350 numbered copies* SIGNED BY ROBINSON.

230 ROBINSON, EDWIN ARLINGTON. Sonnets, 1889-1927 * The Glory of the Nightingales * Matthias at the Door. Together, 3 volumes. Tall 8vo, cloth and boards.
New York, 1928-30-31
LARGE-PAPER FIRST EDITIONS, *each limited and numbered, and* SIGNED BY ROBINSON

231 ROBINSON, EDWIN ARLINGTON. Cavender's House * Nicodemus. Together, 2 volumes. Tall 8vo, cloth and boards; top edges gilt, boxed.   New York, 1929; 1932
LARGE-PAPER FIRST EDITIONS, *limited to 500 and 253 numbered copies* SIGNED BY ROBINSON.

232 ROBINSON, EDWIN ARLINGTON. Modred, a Fragment. Thin 12mo, blue boards, buckram back; boxed.   New York, 1929
FIRST SEPARATE EDITION; *one of 250 numbered copies* SIGNED BY ROBINSON.

— 27 —

Sample page of a catalog from the Swann Galleries.

After the books have been arranged into lots, the gallery prepares the sale catalog. Many factors come into play at this point. Descriptions must be as accurate as possible and, unhappily, as brief as possible due to space and cost restrictions. Only very special items can be given more than three or four lines. All pertinent information must appear within this restricted space, limiting any other comment to a very few words.

The catalogs of many galleries are as a result notoriously inadequate in describing condition. Often no more than the slightest reference is made to condition and frequently none at all, even though a book may be actually disintegrating. Most modern books are of a standard format physically, and auction houses rightly assume that interested collectors and dealers know fairly well what the books look like, so no space is wasted on detailed descriptions. Extraordinary items, such as important presentation inscriptions or significant correspondence, are usually quoted extensively and often reproduced in holograph facsimile, especially in the case of letters, since content normally determines price. Such description is particularly important for bidders who are unable to view the lots in person.

Obviously, then, catalogs are a must, despite the fact that they are usually expensive and may vary considerably in quality, comprehensiveness, and detail. Swann Galleries in New York issues a Spartan no-nonsense catalog, containing only textual descriptions, usually without illustrations, whereas Sotheby Parke Bernet and Christie's issue lavishly illustrated catalogs on glossy paper, often more expensive, but not necessarily more useful. The wisest policy is to subscribe to the catalogs on a seasonal subscription basis; it is less expensive than purchasing the catalogs singly, and they will probably reach you in time for you to research interesting items. This will also give you time to view the books and other materials, of which more will be said later.

It is imperative that you learn how to decipher auction catalogs, mostly for what is left unsaid rather than what actually appears in print. Read *everything*, particularly if you are a novice. Read especially the fine print at the beginning of every catalog entitled "Conditions of Sale." These terms, fairly standard throughout the trade, have a legal basis, and knowledge of them can save you from disputes or unexpected expenses. It is also important to know that each lot is sold as is, regardless of damages that may occur while the books are on display before the sale. Many purchasers have been horrified to receive severely damaged a book that was perfect when they examined it before the sale, and then bid on. It had suffered careless handling during the exhibition. Yet the buyer has no recourse. It is wise to have a precautionary last look immediately before the sale to see if all is still well. In some galleries, such as Swann, this is relatively easy to do because the books remain in full view on the shelves during the sale. Most other galleries, including Christie's and Sotheby Parke Bernet (in both London and New York) halt the viewing the day before the sale. Even at these galleries the head of the book department will usually agree to let you see one specific lot if you arrange to do so in advance, but more than this cannot reasonably be expected.

Most American galleries list lots in their catalogs in alphabetical order by author, although many of the major English firms list the books in the order in which they have been received from the various consignors. The latter procedure makes for a lot of time wasted in searching for your particular authors, and makes it very easy to overlook something of importance to you unless you resign yourself to reading straight through the catalog from beginning to end.

Tradition, laziness, and the unwillingness of the galleries to go to the trouble of alphabetizing seem to explain such lack of organization. With alphabetized catalogs, the natural tendency is to look immediately for your particular favorites, but as soon as you have done this, start back at the beginning and read thoroughly. Unconsidered items that could be treasures may lie hidden in a group lot, or may be mislabeled, or may even be catalogued under a subject heading rather than by author. Remember that you are probably more knowledgeable about your particular author than auction catalogers who have only a limited amount of time for research.

After the catalogs are sent out, the books are generally put on display for several days before the auction. This is an important phase of the auction, but the most dangerous one for the books. Repeatedly, important books have been stolen or have had laid-in items removed or have been carelessly handled and seriously damaged. Much wear and tear is occasioned, with spines ripped and dust jackets snagged and torn. Although the galleries have been slow to act, there has been a recent heartening trend to restrict viewing of valuable books that warrant exceptional care. Sotheby Parke Bernet and Christie's in New York now require appointments to inspect such books. You must examine one book at a time, under the scrutiny of a gallery official. This is a time-consuming procedure, but no other alternative seems practicable.

After the catalogs have been published and before the actual sale, the gallery usually receives many bids by mail and by telephone from out of town. These are noted in a ledger which is referred to during the sale by a gallery assistant who calls them out in competition with bids from the floor of the gallery. Unfortunately it is here that the possibility of irregularity can arise, though auctioneers are usually honest and attempt to obtain lots for absentee clients at the lowest possible figure. When the sale begins, the auctioneer generally opens the bidding at approximately 40 percent of the house's lower estimate. Estimates in recent years have, for the most part, been extremely conservative, and are usually exceeded in the actual bidding. If a book is estimated at $500 to $700, the opening figure would be $200, with the bidding rising by $25 increments. Most galleries have standard increments which the auctioneer automatically announces whenever a bidder indicates his willingness to increase a bid. Rarely if ever is a figure called out by a bidder. At Swann Galleries, bid increases of $1 are accepted on items up to $20. Thereafter bidding goes by $2.50 increments until $50 is reached and then by $5 and $10 increments. At Sotheby Parke Bernet and Christie's, the range is $5 or $10 (depending on the auctioneer and also upon the quality of the sale) until $200 is reached, when the jumps go by $25 up to $500, then by $50 up to $1,000, and by hundreds after that. After $5,000, the increment is usually $250.

One of the many reasons for employing the services of a dealer to do your bidding is to prevent your mail-order bid from being knocked down at precisely your top limit, or just one notch below it. If there is no bid from the floor, an auctioneer can announce your top bid, and the lot may be sold to you at that price; for instance, if you are willing to go to $100, the bidding can be opened at $90 or $100. If you have a dealer on the floor, he can open the bidding considerably below that, and if there is no competition, secure the lot for you well below your limit. A book dealer will undertake to represent you at an auction for a standard fee of 10 percent of the price realized in a successful bid. Many novices feel that they are paying a dealer a lot of money for doing nothing more than waving his arm to obtain the lot. This may be true in the case of a fairly standard item that is not open to much price variation (as for example, a proper first of *Ulysses*, where the only question is one of condition). The fact is, however, that a dealer will often save you frustration, loss of time, and perhaps most important of all, money. Many people fail to remember that the dealer receives a fee only if the bid is successful, regardless of the fact that he may have spent the better part of two or even three days in your service.

If you are a good customer, a dealer will usually go to the trouble of alerting you to items of possible interest. He may obtain photocopies of the pertinent portions of the catalog or even galley proofs of the entire catalog before it is issued. If you decide to try for an item, he will certainly have to go and check the condition and authenticity of the desired lots. He then must attend the auction, including those long stretches during which there are no lots of interest to either of you. (The problem is especially acute in the case of authors at the end of the alphabet. Admirers of Yeats and Zukofsky must have an extra modicum of patience in their makeup.) If successful, the dealer will then have to return to the gallery a third time to obtain the items and, finally, be required to ship them to you. Obviously then, 10 percent may not even recompense him for his efforts, particularly if your lots are relatively inexpensive ones. One veteran New York dealer has been heard to mutter on the way out of a sale, "Didn't even make cabfare on that lot!"

Employing a reliable dealer to bid for you also eliminates the possibility of your mail order bid being opened at your top figure. If a close relationship has developed between you and the dealer, he will know when to use his judgment to exceed, if he thinks advisable, the limit you have stipulated. His experience tells him when an increase or two over your top figure will obtain the book. Also not to be overlooked is the fact that employing a dealer, particularly a specialist, eliminates him as a competitor for a desired lot. One well-known and well-respected dealer solicits bids from customers for important sales with the startlingly frank question, "Well, am I going to bid *for* you or *against* you?"

A dealer also has a broader knowledge of trade trends and values than an individual collector. His profession demands that he attend all important auctions, and he receives and peruses carefully all of his colleagues' catalogs. His finger is on the pulse of the book-collecting field throughout his entire lifetime. (Rare-book dealers practically never retire, and seemingly live forever.) His experience enables him to advise you how much the item will probably cost you, as well as its actual worth—needless to say, not always the same figure.

The dealer will usually know who your likely competitors are and what your probable chances of success in obtaining your lots. Once in a while a new buyer will come into the market, someone eager to form a particular kind of a collection for an institution perhaps, or possibly an institution itself using donated funds to acquire specific items or to build up certain areas. As long as these funds or that particular interest lasts, chances are that there will be an unusually inflated demand for certain books or authors. During these periods only an experienced dealer can advise you when to be bullish and when to be bearish, so to speak. Some items appear so infrequently that if you really covet a particular title, it may be best to go full steam ahead no matter what. On the other hand, an item may appear often enough to make waiting worthwhile until prices level off. There was a classic example of this in 1975 when Faulkner prices began doubling and tripling, in three successive sales, for no obvious reason other than that a couple of avid collectors had suddenly become interested in forming superb Faulkner collections. After they had obtained most of the prime titles, prices rolled back to about where they were before all the excitement started.

A final but no less important reason to enlist the help of a dealer is information. Auction houses will usually answer as many questions as they can. However, it must always be remembered that their time is extremely limited. Most galleries conduct a sale of some kind daily, and book sales with some frequency. An enormous amount of work is required to prepare the catalog and make the myriad arrangements attendant upon a sale. Consequently, even with the kindest intentions, answers must unfortunately be brief. Auction gallery employees cannot be experts. Collectors and specialist dealers almost always have a much deeper knowledge of a particular subject area. Your specialist will know the crucial points of any given title—for example, the different weaves of cloth used in the various bindings of Dylan Thomas' *The Map of Love* that distinguish the four states of the first issue of the first edition of this book. The gallery, even when willing, may not be able to identify them.

Now comes the actual auction. A neophyte attending his first sale usually finds the procedure mystifying and may have a great deal of difficulty identifying who, if anyone, is actually bidding. The auctioneer's rapid-fire style of delivery makes it very difficult to find out where the bidder is located, and a lot may be opened and sold within thirty seconds or, at most, a minute or two. As many as a hundred lots will be run through in an hour, so there is no time for second thoughts or for trying to find out who is bidding against you. Some dealers and experienced bidders do not like it to be known that they are actually bidding and use prearranged signals with the auctioneer. The late Lew Feldman of the House of El Dieff, a New York dealer, one of the most active bidders of recent years, always sat in the last row of the gallery, apparently paying no attention to the proceedings. Even so, lot after lot would be knocked down to him. It took years of careful scrutiny before I penetrated the secret of his signals. It was obvious, simple, and subtle. He placed his glasses across the top of his head, instead of on his nose, as many people do who need them only for reading. Then a small movement of his eyebrows would shift the glasses slightly, just enough for the auctioneer to see and take note of.

The rapid, staccato type of delivery used by auctioneers slows down perceptibly when the bidding reaches higher levels and there are two active bidders. The auctioneer will then be patient, often trying to draw out one more increase, and even, in some cases, allowing the underbidder an increase smaller than the usual unit of escalation to break a tie or to move the price up another notch.

It is not unknown for artificial bidding to take place, although this generally happens more in the art world than in the book world. Some art dealers have been known to try to inflate a particular artist's reputation and price scale in order to increase the value of their own holdings. This is rather more difficult to do in the book world, and few dealers have enough stock of any particular author to make the game worth the candle. It is rumored, however, that the sudden, overnight skyrocketing of the prices of John Betjeman's books after a London auction some years ago was a deliberate ploy by fans who wanted to "put him on the map"— that is, into the realm of high prices. One of them was said to have put up his collection and arranged for a couple of friends to bid each other up. The auction established record prices for Betjeman; but the owner lost nothing but the gallery fees, since the proceeds went to him and he bought back the books from his friends. At least that's the way rumor had it.

The lot legally becomes your property at the fall of the hammer, and it is no longer the gallery's responsibility. You must pay for it within three days unless you have a charge account, which normally gives you the privilege of paying within thirty days. It is prudent to remove your purchases immediately, since in a large establishment books can easily be lost or mixed into the wrong lot. Most of the major galleries have a pickup area separate from the auction room, and you may pay for your lots and remove them even while the sale is still in progress. In smaller galleries, you normally have to wait until the end of the sale or even, in some cases, until the next day.

Important book auctions don't happen very often, partly because of the scarcity of major collections and also because of the growing tendency for such collections to be acquired en bloc by institutions. Two of the most important sales of the first half of the twentieth century were the John Quinn sale, which extended through several sessions in 1923 and 1924, and the Jerome Kern sale, held early in 1929. These two sales dramatically point up the importance of timing in the breakup of a collection by auction. Quinn was a New York lawyer whose taste in both literature and painting was far in advance of the general public's. In addition, his judgment was uncanny. He was wealthy enough to extend financial aid to struggling writers, and in gratitude for his help through crucial times both T. S. Eliot and James Joyce sold him the manuscripts of their major works. Thus, Quinn's collection contained—in addition to superb rarities of most of the writers now the most highly prized of this century—the manuscripts of *The Waste Land* and *Ulysses*, two of the pillars of twentieth-century English poetry and prose. Quinn died suddenly and prematurely, and his heirs, anxious to liquidate his vast holdings, sold off the collection as quickly as possible. Unfortunately for them, the time was ill-chosen. The books and manuscripts went for ridiculously low figures. The manuscript of *Ulysses* was bid on by Dr. A. S. W. Rosenbach for $1,975, far less than the cost of a routine copy of the first edition of the printed book today, and even then a derisory price. Joyce himself was so disturbed by it that he tried to buy it back from Rosenbach, but the doctor knew a bargain when he saw one and shrewdly refused. As a result the manuscript is now one of the choicest items on display at the Rosenbach Foundation in Philadelphia.

Conversely, Jerome Kern's collection came on the market at the very peak of the boom. The sale was held in January 1929, and his collection of high spots of the sixteenth, seventeenth, and eighteenth centuries set record prices, some of which have never been matched since. The Kern sale is still remembered today not only for the prices realized, but also for the quality of the majority of the books in the collection.

The Depression—which began a matter of months after the Kern sale—caused the liquidation of many collections at heartbreaking prices, and in the ensuing debacle of World War II, no major sales occurred. However, in the late fifties interest in first editions started a dramatic upward swing. In October 1958, the Guffey sale took place. It was a sale that illustrates the impact the auction of a major collection can have on the general price structure of a particular author. Don Carlos Guffey had been Hemingway's personal physician through most of the author's life, and had assembled what was probably the world's greatest collection of prime Hemingway material, with every book containing long, important inscriptions. There were letters and manuscripts as well. Until then, while Hemingway had been widely collected, prices were moderate even for the rare two first books, *Three Stories and Ten Poems* and *in our time*, both published by the Contact Press in France. This abundance of important material brought out heavy competition, and at this sale Hemingway prices skyrocketed. He became the number one star in the modern firsts firmament, and has pretty well remained there ever since. Oddly enough, it took Faulkner quite a few more years to move up to the level of Hemingway prices. Today Faulkner and Hemingway are the two most expensive American fiction writers to collect.

Widespread misconceptions regarding auction prices still exist among collectors and even among some new or part-time dealers. Established, knowledgeable dealers in first editions repeatedly make legitimate offers to buy books, only to find the owner saying, "It was sold for five times that at such-and-such a sale last month." It may well be true that a specific copy brought much more than the dealer has offered for the copy in hand, but what is generally unrecognized is that the source of most such quotations, *American Book Prices Current*, does not note unusually fine condition or even the possibility of rare variants that would have accounted for the unexpectedly high price realized. There is usually a reason for an uncommonly high price at auction. It is often caused by two collectors' wanting a relatively scarce item which has not appeared at auction or in a dealer's catalog for a long time; they will hammer away at one another until one is forced to drop out. A similarly fine copy might well appear at a subsequent sale and not bring anywhere near the same price, simply because the loser of the first round has no serious competition this time.

Another possibility is that an important point was not catalogued, but was spotted by the bidders. Quite often a signature or an inscription will appear in an unusual place and be overlooked. Just a few years ago a hawk-eyed librarian spotted Patrick Henry's signature *on the cover* of a copy of *The Statutes of the Commonwealth of Virginia* which he had helped draft, along with Thomas Jefferson—certainly making it a copy of major importance. But this is an unusual place to look for a signature, and the auction gallery cataloger missed it, as did apparently everyone else, because I obtained the lot for the happy librarian for a nominal sum, with no opposition.

The time when a high price was recorded must also be considered. As I have said, the changing fashions in book collecting can cause high prices to be paid for certain titles which, a couple of years later, are so little in demand as to be virtually unsalable. An example of this can be seen in the books of J. D. Salinger, who a decade ago was one of the most sought-after authors. Nowadays, only *Catcher in the*

Rye and *Nine Stories* are salable, and these at prices generally lower than they were in the sixties. The other titles can scarcely be given away.

Grudge fights sometimes occur even in the dignified atmosphere of the poshest galleries, perhaps as often as in the wrestling ring. Rival dealers may run a price up simply to keep the other one from getting a bargain. It is risky, of course, but some enmities transcend mere money. This sort of thing is, alas, indulged in more frequently than one might imagine.

Occasionally a dealer will go beyond the limit given him by a client, since the latter almost invariably says, when being told that his bid was not successful, "Oh, I wish you'd gone another notch." The clever dealer who knows his customer well enough knows whether or not he is risking a refusal. Legally, the customer does not have to pay the difference. Most collectors, however, prefer to do so. That this is not always true is illustrated by the notorious occasion in 1947 when Dr. Rosenbach himself went beyond the limit Yale University had given him to acquire a copy of the rare *The Bay Psalm Book*, the first book printed in colonial America. Yale refused to pay more than the authorized amount and the doctor had to pay the difference out of his own pocket.

From a seller's point of view, the auction process represents the best means of getting the highest possible price for his collection. At least, that is the cherished belief. It is, alas, not always the case; and there can be no guarantee. There are so many variables that affect the bidding at any given sale that you may, after all the charges have been deducted, be left with less than you would have received from a reputable dealer. If you sell to a dealer, you are usually paid immediately, whereas the auction process is a lengthy one, and it may be a year or more before any cash is in your hands. If the collection is a sizable one, the interest alone on the money tied up is an important consideration. The dispersal of the Jonathan Goodwin collection began in March of 1977 and was not completed until more than a year later. When you consider that the collection had been delivered to the gallery nearly a year before the first session of the sale (it takes many months to organize a large collection for auction and to prepare the catalogs) and that a number of weeks passed after the final sale before the owner received settlement, more than two years had actually elapsed between the time the sale was initiated and the time when the payment came in. The Streeter collection of Americana was so vast that it took several years to disperse it. No matter when your collection is accepted by a gallery, you cannot expect it to come up for sale for at least six months, and quite often for nearly a year. Most galleries close in late April for the summer and do not resume sales again until late September. In addition to the pressure on the gallery to accommodate other customers who are also anxious to sell material, it is important not to glut the market with more material of a similar nature than it can comfortably absorb at any given time. To do so would obviously drive prices down, something that neither the gallery nor the owner of a collection desires (however much the acquiring collector may pray for such an event).

Once the sale has actually taken place, you will normally not receive the proceeds for at least sixty to ninety days, since the majority of a gallery's clients have a thirty-day period in which to pay, and payment is not made to you until the gallery has collected from the bidders. Thus, in the normal course of events, it will take *at least* a year from the time you decide to sell, and often longer, before any cash is turned over. Since financial necessity is often the reason for disposing of a collection, this delay must be faced when deciding how to get rid of your books. The auction method may be too slow if your needs are immediate.

Since the gallery's commission is based on the sales price, the auctioneer can be depended upon to extract the last possible bid. Up until the mid 1970s, fees were graduated on a variable percentage of the price realized, with the percentage figure diminishing as the price realized increased. This was true both here and in England. However, in the mid-seventies, the British auction firms began assessing the *buyer* a 10 percent commission, and correspondingly reduced the charge made to the consignor by the same amount. After some reluctance, the major American auction firms also converted to this policy. Since the beginning of 1979, the rates charged a consignor are now flat fees—10 percent from a private individual, 8 percent from a museum or public institution, and 6 percent from a professional dealer (the latter low figure in an obvious bid to attract quality merchandise for auction). It must also be remembered that, aside from this percentage figure, each house has a minimum fee per lot regardless of what it actually brings. This will vary from $20 to $35 per lot, and points up the necessity of grouping minor items so as to avoid disastrous fees for items that may not reach the minimum. In the case of an exceptional item, or even on a very unusual collection, special terms can sometimes be agreed upon.

There are also other charges that must be borne by the owner of the collection. These include insurance while the collection is on the gallery's premises and illustrations in the catalog. The cost of printing and distributing the catalog is paid for by the gallery, but photos of major items are charged to the owner's account, even though the gallery decides which items will be illustrated. However, photos are usually inserted only on those items likely to sell for more than $1,000.

The most confusion and misinformation involves an aspect of the auction business that is often overlooked and often unknown to many of the bidders. This is the question

of reserves—minimum prices set in advance on items to be
sold. In theory, reserves do not exist, since most catalogs state
that the merchandise is "for public sale *without reserve.*" In
actual practice, however, reserves are put on most items of
high value. This is not done to force bidding up to abnormal
levels, but to protect the owner from having to sell a valuable item at a ridiculously low figure because of some fluke.
It is, in effect, a safety net, and generally is placed at about
75 percent of the lower estimate. The assumption—a fair
one, in my opinion—is that it would be ridiculous for an
owner to have to part with a book worth $500 simply because
there was only one bid of $50 or $100. Such circumstances
can develop. For example, a few years back at Sotheby Parke
Bernet a complete collection of the modern poet Charles
Bukowski, which at that time had a retail value of approximately $1,200, was offered as one lot. Only a handful of
dealers are interested in this kind of material. Of the five
present in the gallery that day, one had consigned the lot
and so could not bid on it; another had lost track of his place,
and was one lot behind; the third was leaving town immediately after the sale for an extended period and could not cope
with the problem of removal of such a bulky lot, consisting
of several cartons; and a fourth dealer, to everyone's amusement, had fallen asleep and could be heard gently snoring.
This left only one dealer interested, and to the owner's and
the auctioneer's chagrin, the lot went for $100, since no one
had thought to place a reserve on it. Had the owner done so,
he would have in effect bought it back, paying the gallery only
five percent of the reserve, and could have saved the collection for sale at another more propitious time. Such "buy-
backs" are not announced as such, of course, but are announced as "sold to order," a term that includes all sales
made to bidders not in the room. In recent years, with most
books exceeding the estimates, there is very little buying

back. But the reserve is good insurance, nonetheless, and costs nothing.

Book auctions in the United States are nearly as old as the nation itself. The first book auction was held in the latter part of the seventeenth century, only a couple of generations after the landing of the Pilgrims. They continue with unabated popularity today, despite grumbling and complaining about "outrageous prices" heard after every important sale. Attendance seems to be increasing, partly because an important sale is more than a chance to acquire rarities. In New York and London such sales have become, if not social events, at least tribal rituals where it is important to be seen if only to let your colleagues and competitors know that you are still alive and kicking. The auction sale, John Carter once wrote, "is a mechanical convenience for the bibliophile community" which provides important and valuable secondary services over and above the disposal and acquisition of books. It offers "a continuous barometer of prices; color, romance, and excitement; surprises, upsets, and disappointments; landmarks, records, and historic occasions." It seems likely to remain a permanent feature of book collecting, for what else in the entire field of collecting can offer all that within the space of a couple of hours?

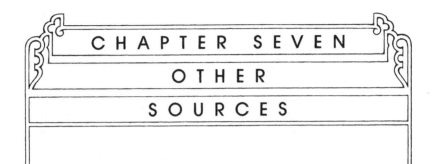

In addition to specialist dealers and the auction galleries, there are of course other means of adding to your collection. They are by no means as fruitful as the two primary methods, and may often be more frustrating than rewarding. But certain items, while desirable and possibly necessary to the completeness of your collection, may be either too insignificant or too low-priced for a dealer to want to take the trouble and expense of acquiring or stocking them. For these things you must turn to other sources.

One such source is always attractive, always fun—and rarely, if ever, productive. That is the general secondhand or used-book store. A great many beginning collectors—and even some of long experience—have the feeling that they have only to walk into such shops to be rewarded with rare volumes that the owner is unaware of, and which have eluded all previous customers and book scouts. The fact is that virtually every dealer in this country and abroad is aware of the potential value of first editions in general. And no matter how ignorant he may appear, or even pretend to be, he usually has some knowledge of particular titles. Such dealers tend to overprice the items they do recognize, mainly out of ignorance of true values, and to overlook condition altogether. Most secondhand dealers keep a copy of *Book Prices Current* (and more recently Van Allen Bradley's biennial compilations of rare-book prices) in order to be able to price, more or less accurately, their out-of-print books. They may also be aware of the auction prices brought by certain first editions. But in their ignorance of the value placed on condition, these dealers are likely to price a dog-eared copy of a rare book at the figure a fine copy would be expected to fetch under more sophisticated circumstances.

Despite these hazards, careful searches in secondhand book shops can still be rewarding. Many books give few hints about what they really are. Quite often a rare or important translation by a much collected author will not display his name in any obvious place on the book. For example, one of the most difficult items to find for any Ezra Pound collection is his 1923 translation of Edouard Estaunié's novel *The Call of the Road*, which nowhere bears Pound's name. Such an obscure novel by an obscure writer may surface in any secondhand bookshop. Likewise, esoteric journals and magazines containing otherwise unpublished articles by major authors can often be found in such places.

Another source, which is sometimes more profitable, is the charity bazaar. I include in this category garage or "tag" sales. Very worthwhile books are sometimes donated to the local charity, and some quite spectacular items have turned up at such affairs. The lucky early bird gets many a prize. These book sales, often conducted for the benefit of various universities, have become annual or semiannual affairs, and attract swarms of customers, some of whom travel hundreds of miles and stand in line for hours to be in the forefront when the doors open. Since the donors are usually college graduates and other presumably literate persons, the quality of the books tends to be a bit higher than that of books generally encountered in the ordinary thrift shop, where the likelihood of making a halfway decent find is remote, But do not despair, even in a thrift shop. A few years ago, in New York City, one of my scouts ran across not just one book, but a treasure trove of superb items. A retired copy editor who had worked all her life at Scribner's died with no known heirs, or at least none who were interested in her library. Her books had been stored in cartons in the basement of her apartment building along with her furniture and other unwanted items. The superintendent of the building eventually took the whole lot to the thrift shop. There they remained all one summer, occasionally thumbed through by apparently ignorant browsers, until my scout finally saw them. There were approximately one hundred books from the thirties, all in superb condition, in their dust jackets. All had long, generous inscriptions from the authors, who ranged from Clarence Darrow to Ernest Hemingway. And in one of the Hemingway volumes was the rough draft manuscript of a chapter of the book!

Now obviously such windfalls seldom happen, but the fact that they sometimes do is sufficient reason to keep these sources in mind. Even as I write this I am arranging for sale by auction of an album of original photos of the San Francisco earthquake and fire, found in a trash can in a New York suburb by a couple of eleven-year-old boys. It can pay to do a little judicious trash-picking.

In the United States still another place to be watched is the type of bookstore specializing in publishers' remainders —that is, books that, for a variety of reasons, the publisher is willing to dispose of at a fraction of their original price. While you will not find older books in such places, it is quite common to find many worthwhile first editions of books issued within the past few years, priced at a dollar or two. Sometimes even signed limited editions appear on these bargain tables. The copies you find will quite often turn out to be later printings, but a careful sifting of the entire stock may well reveal a few first printings mixed in. It pays to check remainder shops regularly and frequently, as their turnover is rapid, and if a particularly desirable title appears on these tables, the entire supply is likely to disappear within a matter of hours.

Church bazaars, roadside stands, garage sales, country

auctions, antique stores, junk stores, and other such unlikely places have all been known to yield the occasional treasure. It doesn't happen often, but the true collector, if only to satisfy his curiosity, will never pass up the most unlikely place. Who knows, he might find an unrecorded copy of Poe's *Tamerlane*, one of which sold at auction in New York in 1974 for $123,000—though I'm fairly certain it did not come from a thrift store.

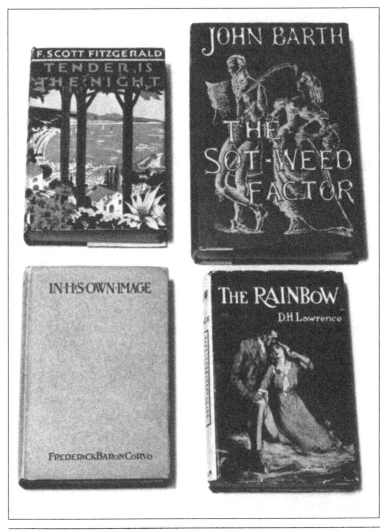

A group of dust jackets: TENDER IS THE NIGHT *by F. Scott Fitzgerald (1934);* THE SOT-WEED FACTOR *by John Barth (1960)—jacket is by Edward Gorey;* IN HIS OWN IMAGE *by Baron Corvo (1901); and* THE RAINBOW *by D. H. Lawrence (1915). From the author's collection.*

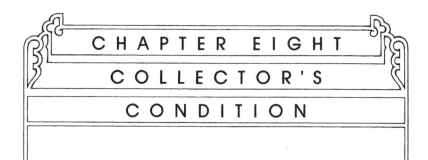

The most important factor in modern book collecting is also probably the most misunderstood and the most often ignored. I speak of condition. As in many other fields of collecting, particularly stamps and coins, condition plays an enormous part in determining prices. The premium placed on condition increases geometrically rather than arithmetically, as has been proven time and time again in the auction house. An example of this phenomenon occurred when the Jonathan Goodwin collection was auctioned in 1977 and 1978, in three landmark sessions. Mr. Goodwin had invariably acquired the best possible copy, and his willingness to pay premium prices for superb examples paid off when the collection was sold. Virtually every book in the collection set record prices precisely because its condition was so unbelievably high. Many beginning collectors (and inexperienced dealers) read of such prices and naïvely assume that they apply to all copies of the books, which they do not.

To a collector, the ideal is a book as fresh and bright and perfect in every respect as it was on the day it was issued. Obviously, it is hard to find copies in such condition, particularly from the period prior to World War II, when collectors were not nearly as concerned with condition as they are today. This is especially true of dust jackets, which were often ignored by even the best collectors of that period. It is for this reason that the books of F. Scott Fitzgerald, for example, often go for ten times as much with jackets as do sound copies without the jackets. One university I know of has a cutoff date of 1930, refusing to buy a book issued after that date without its dust jacket. Some collectors refuse to buy any book without the dust jacket, preferring to wait and pay the premium for a jacketed copy. Obviously, here, as in all phases of collecting, a little common sense has to be employed. There are some books so rare that you would be well advised to purchase whatever copy comes along; you may go the rest of your life and never find another copy in *any* state. (I suspect this may well turn out to be the case with the previously mentioned Pound translation of *The Call of the Road*. The only copy I have ever seen or heard of in twenty-five years is one of three books in my own collection without a jacket.) If a book is that scarce, you will have no trouble in disposing of your unjacketed copy should you be fortunate enough to locate one with a jacket.

The jackets of thick books, such as *Gone with the Wind* or any of the novels of Thomas Wolfe, tend to wear out much faster than the jackets of slimmer volumes, simply in the process of being read. Accordingly, they are likely to be scarce, especially in fine condition. Well-jacketed books thus invariably command premiums over and above the normal price. For most modern books, the price of a copy with a fine jacket will be twice that of a copy without the jacket, and the price for one with a worn or tattered jacket somewhere between the two, the exact difference being determined, of course, by the degree of wear.

Quite a few modern books, particularly little press productions and deluxe, limited editions with fancy bindings, are issued without dust jackets in the usual sense of the term. They may have glassine or clear acetate jackets without printing on them. Glassine, especially, is fragile and over the years tends to become brittle and tear easily. The term "original glassine" is often encountered in dealers' catalogs when such books are being described, with such copies commanding approximately the same premium as books with their original printed dust jackets. But there is widespread disagreement among dealers and collectors over just how much one can depend on such a description, even with the most scrupulous of dealers. Glassine is easily replaced, and, so far as I know, there is no easy way of determining whether glassine is "original" or of fairly recent vintage. Actually, glassine tends to yellow slightly as well as to become brittle, but short of expensive chemical carbon testing, there is no way of proving or disproving its "originality." With clear acetate the problem is almost hopeless. For this reason, many collectors do not attach the same importance to glassine and acetate as they do to printed dust jackets. It is simply a matter of being realistic. And incidentally I have yet to read a catalog description where the glassine was described as anything *but* "original."

One hears a good deal of talk about jackets being "married" to copies of books. This refers to a jacket that was not originally on the specific copy of the book, but was placed on it at a later date. Some people consider this somehow reprehensible, although personally I see no harm in it as long as the correct jacket is placed on the book and the binding of the book itself is not worn or faded. The jackets are usually identical, and at some point in the book's production it had to be "married" to its jacket, so I cannot see why there should be a fuss made. Quite often a dealer will come across a copy of a book with two jackets (it used to be standard practice for a publisher's publicity department to send out review copies with an extra jacket in case the newspaper or magazine wanted to use it as an illustration for the review) and most dealers will save the extra one to place on a copy that they may eventually acquire without a jacket. Most collectors are willing to accept such copies; in fact, virtually every collector I have ever encountered is perfectly willing to perform such a service himself, sometimes continuing to up-grade the condition of jackets throughout his entire collect-ing career.

Of the book itself the area most subject to wear is the binding. This should be, ideally, free from signs of wear or obvious damage. However, what is termed "shelf wear," if not serious, should not be an important factor, for it is virtu-ally inevitable, particularly on most modern novels with three-piece cloth and paper bindings. The bottom edge of such books will become unavoidably darkened from sliding on and off the shelf. Sometimes the paper will split, or break through. At this point the wear must be considered serious. Such worn copies are bound to be less valuable than perfect ones.

Paperbacks are more susceptible to wear than hard-covers. Most commercial paperbacks are bound in a flexible card stock that has been coated with a plastic laminate on the outside. This coating easily crackles if the cover is bent too far, and there is no method of correcting it. Another problem frequently encountered with paperbacks is that of pages loosening and falling out. This happens when a paperback is handled roughly, or too often, since most of the cheaper paperbacks nowadays are "perfect" bound, an am-biguous trade term meaning that loose sheets are glued to-gether and then a cover glued around them (as opposed to groups of folded sheets being sewn together for binding). Obviously, with frequent handling, such a book will begin to disintegrate fairly quickly. With age, moreover, certain glues become brittle and weak. There is a different problem presented by deluxe, little-press limited editions. Their paper is usually of a better quality, but a frequent flaw is the fraying of the overlap edges. Any edge of a book cover that is wider than the actual pages is referred to either as an "overlap" or "wallet" edge. Over the years, since there is no body to support these edges, they become frayed, chipped, and snagged, detracting from the book's value. Even when a protective envelope is used, considerable care has to be taken when removing or replacing the book, since the soft, hand-made papers of these editions are easily caught and snagged. There is little that can be done about snagging once it has occurred. Some collectors place tape on the inside edge of the covers to reinforce them, but this is rather a dangerous procedure; most tapes have chemicals that will eat through the paper, or, at the very least, leave an unsightly stain. If the book is of sufficient value, a trained conservationist can restore the damaged edge by replacing chips where possible and then sealing it with a plastic lamination. This not only preserves it but prevents further deterioration. Depending on the vintage of the book, a moderate amount of such fraying has to be expected, especially on books dating from the first quarter of this century. Perhaps the most famous example of a paperback with a wallet edge is the first edition of Joyce's *Ulysses* published in Paris in 1922. It was an unusually thick book, the paper covers rather insubstantial (in fact the spine was too weak to support the weight of the book). Copies were extremely hard to come by at the time of publication and were usually passed from hand to hand as reading copies, resulting in considerable wear and tear. Quite often the covers were deliberately removed to make the book easier to smuggle past U.S. and British customs agents, who were prepared to seize it as pornography. Thus copies of *Ulysses* with the covers in perfect condition are virtually impossible to find, and correspondingly fetch far higher prices than do copies with some wear and tear or restoration to the spine. With moderately poor condition the norm, most collectors are willing to accept it, so long as the wear is not too disfiguring or too extensive.

This leads to another aspect of condition—rebinding. There are many copies of *Ulysses* that have been rebound, for the reasons cited above. They bring far lower prices than copies with the original blue wrapper covers, even those with some restoration to the spine. Once a book has been rebound, it has lost much of its value as a collector's item. Rebinding of modern books—that is, any books originally issued in publisher's bindings, standard practice since the first half of the nineteenth century—while perhaps aesthetically pleasing, is not only expensive, but also destroys much of the bibliographic interest and a large part of the value of the book. In the case of twentieth-century books, rebinding is seldom done. If a modern book is in such poor condition as to make rebinding imperative, the chances are very much against the game's being worth the candle. There are, of course, a few modern books that are so rare that even a rebound copy can be acceptable. A few years ago I had a rebound copy of Ezra Pound's *A Lume Spento*, his first book and one of the rarest books of twentieth-century poetry. A collector of first books had desired this title for a great many years, and he bought the rebound copy, but not without misgivings. And despite the book's actual rarity (fewer than thirty copies are known to have survived out of the original one hundred printed at Pound's own expense in 1908), within the space of two years he sold it. He is still searching for a copy in the original wrappers. I could mention a few other titles of such rarity as to make rebound condition acceptable, but there aren't many of them, and more common books, such as the novels of John Updike or the later books of Evelyn Waugh, are plentiful enough to make it totally out of the question to consider rebound copies.

Condition is naturally important inside the book, too. There are many things that can detract from value. One of the most common is roughly opened pages. Many books issued with untrimmed pages must be opened before the book can be read. Some careless or lazy persons attempt to do this with a finger, inevitably making uneven edges, and often tearing portions out of a page. It is unwise to use a sharp knife to open pages either, as it may easily slide away from the folded edge and leave a long gash in the page proper. The safest method is to use either a paperknife or, curiously, an ordinary playing card. The card has enough strength to do the job, but none of the dangerous sharpness of a blade. Whether or not the pages of an unopened book should be opened at all is a matter over which there is no agreement among collectors and dealers. If you adhere to the principle that the ideal copy of a book is one in exactly the condition in which it was issued, then the pages should be left unopened. But this of course precludes reading the book at all. The majority of collectors adopt the sensible attitude that a book, even a collector's item, is designed to be read, and while dealers always like to make note of unopened condition when describing a book, I have yet to see any conclusive evidence that an actual premium is placed on an unopened copy in comparison with an opened copy.

Soiled pages are bound to detract from the value of a copy, as will writing or underlining, unless this writing is by the book's author or by some famous person whose comments are themselves of interest. But extreme caution should be taken before erasing anything in a book. Many an unsuspecting person has erased the very thing that would have made a particular copy of a book valuable. One of the most horrifying incidents of this kind occurred some years ago in England, when a collector noticed a clerk in a bookstore erasing penciled notations from a stack of books, then placing each cleaned copy on a bargain table. Finally, the customer's curiosity got the upper hand, and as the clerk was placing the final volume on the table, he asked why such trouble was being taken. "Oh," replied the clerk, "we always erase all previous owner's notations. It makes the books easier to sell." But in this case the books had come from the library of the poet A. E. Housman! It was, of course, too late to salvage anything. All the books had been dutifully purged not only of the markings, but also of their scholarly interest and monetary value.

So it does not pay to be in too much of a hurry to erase traces of previous ownership in modern books. You can never tell who may grow into an important author some few years hence, and what is simply an unsightly signature today may be tomorrow's prized autograph. Let well enough alone. There is usually little if any difference in value between a copy with a signature on the flyleaf and one without, particularly in books dating from before World War II. Elaborate inscriptions or signatures on title pages (always excepting those of noted persons) do detract in general from both appearance and value, although not significantly unless the appearance is truly marred by unsightly effusive scrawling. Soiled spots, fingermarks, and such like can be removed (if you know how), but either let signatures alone or wait until you can find an unsigned copy. Pencil marks are usually easily removed, but ink presents more serious problems. Old-fashioned fountain-pen ink can be removed with standard ink removers, but since these are acid-based, there is the concurrent danger of harming the paper fibers. Ball-point ink is the hardest of all to remove and should be done only by experts. In general, eradication of signatures is best not attempted by amateurs. And even if the signature does not turn out to be a valuable one, a dated sign of ownership may well help establish the date of publication. With little presses, which come and go with very brief life spans, it is often impossible to ascertain even a few years later just when a book was published. Most such little presses do not keep detailed records, and a large majority of the books they issue are never copyrighted; as a result bibliographers are often stymied for even approximate information on publication dates and prices. While it may not be evidence that would stand up in court, a dated signature of ownership is some sort of guide, and may help narrow the possibilities for a bibliographer.

Obvious defects, such as a missing page—especially an illustration or the title page—are virtually fatal. Such copies are termed "cripples" in the trade, for obvious reasons, and I can think of no modern book so rare that a cripple should be bought at all. You will always have an incomplete copy, one that will be difficult if not impossible to resell, and one that is of little interest to anyone. And you yourself will always want a better, perfect copy.

In the chapter on dealers I suggested that some of the terms used to describe condition are at best vague, even though not intentionally so. Simply because certain words can convey a wide variety of meanings and shades of meanings, it may help clarify matters a little to set forth here the terms most often used in book dealers' catalogs describing condition:

MINT, PRISTINE, SUPERB   All three terms are practically synonymous for the perfect copy, bright and fresh as the day it was published.

VERY FINE   Almost the same—flawless. Generally used by the more conservative dealers.

FINE   Slightly below "very fine" but still a copy showing no defects.

VERY GOOD   This term may possibly confuse beginners, who may misunderstand this to mean a fine copy. "Very good" copies are usually rather worn and obviously have been read more than once. Generally speaking, "very good" copies are a bit below acceptable standards for truly serious collectors.

GOOD   Almost at the bottom of the condition scale. The term is often expanded into the phrase "a good working copy," meaning that the book is textually complete, but the binding and other condition factors are below grade. Such copies are of use mainly to students and scholars who want reading copies from which to work.

POOR   The worst possible condition, usually hopelessly bad. It is seldom encountered in a catalog, since most dealers will not stock copies in such condition. There may be the occasional exception where a book is of such rarity that any copy must be considered; and in unusual cases an impecunious collector who cannot ever hope to afford a fine copy will accept a poor copy rather than never own the title at all.

To sum up, the importance of condition is always a matter of personal taste, and though condition determines the price of a book, one must be realistic. It makes no sense to be a "condition crank" or to let condition become an obsession. Remember that even new books are handled several times before they reach a dealer's shelf, and a minuscule flyspeck on the dust jacket is not fatal.

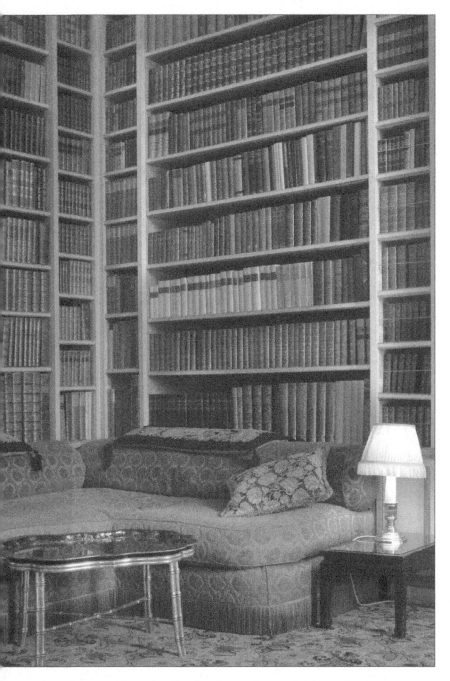
Arranged in a visually pleasing and organized manner,
this is an ideal book collection.

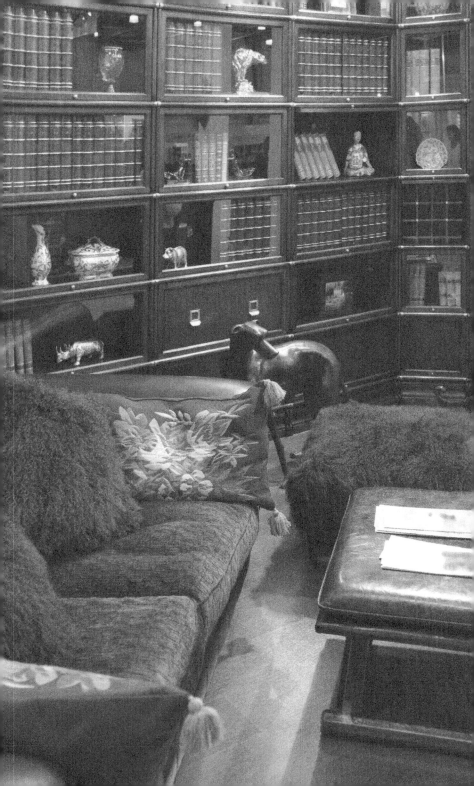

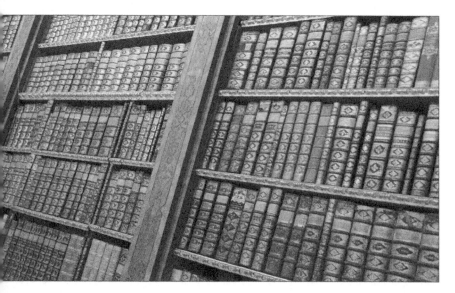

Buying books at an auction can be a great way to jump-start your book collection, especially if you're willing to take a chance on a lotted, or group, collection.

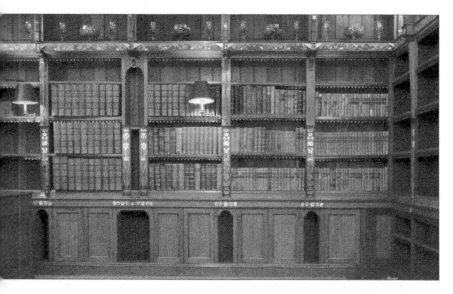

Don't forget to search through used book stores. They can be an excellent resource for the beginner collector.

« A beautiful example of how you can mix two or more collections together, highlighting both. Here, the collector has combined books with antiques.

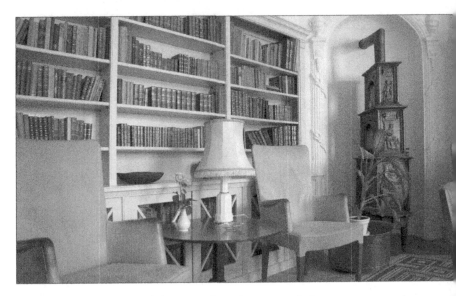

Shelving books too tightly or too loosely can result in torn or warped covers.
Heat from the stove in this room also poses a risk to the collection.

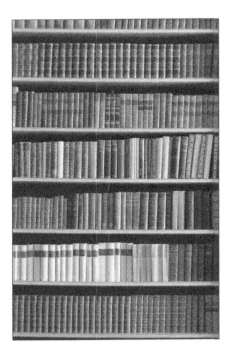

A fine example of a modern book
collection of first and second
editions

The appearance of your books
can be just as important to your
collection as the authors you
collect.

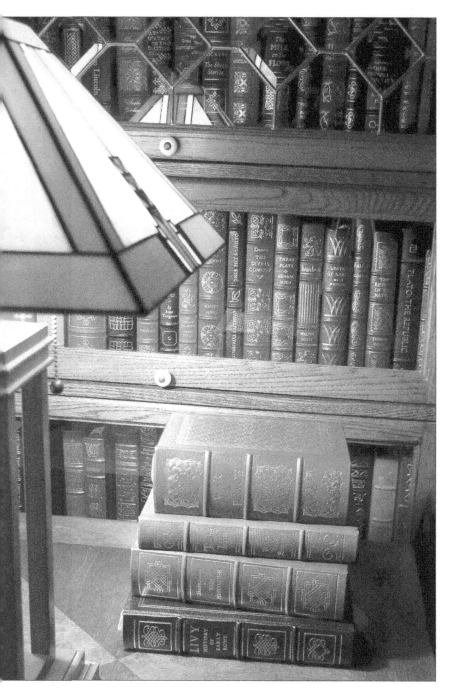

Organize your collection in any manner you choose. This collector has chosen to alternate books based on the color of the spine.

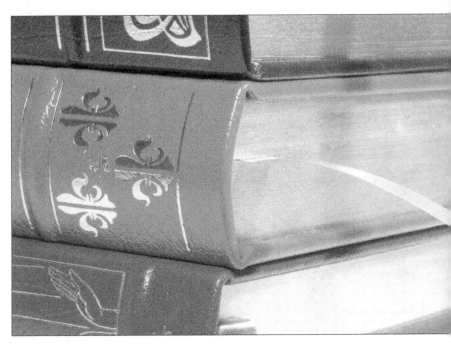

When building your collection, don't feel you can't change your mind about which author you want to focus on. Perhaps you'll find a series by a publisher or an anthology that you would rather own.

Ensure that your collection is protected from insects, children, pets, and direct light.

The pinnacle: a floor-to-ceiling book collection with a ladder. »

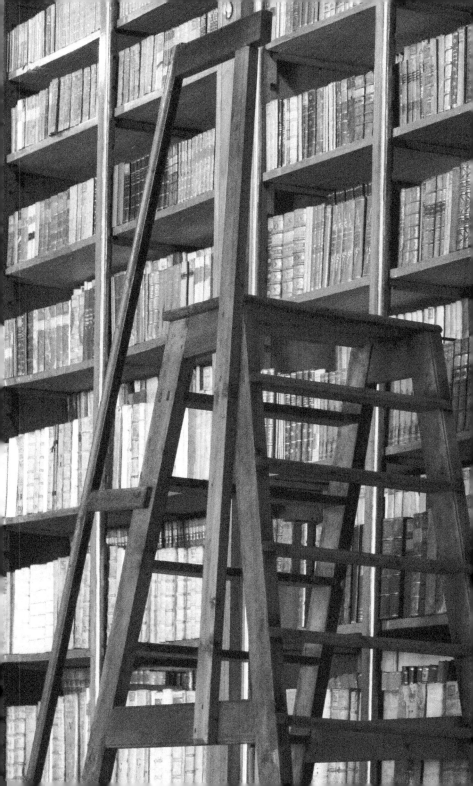

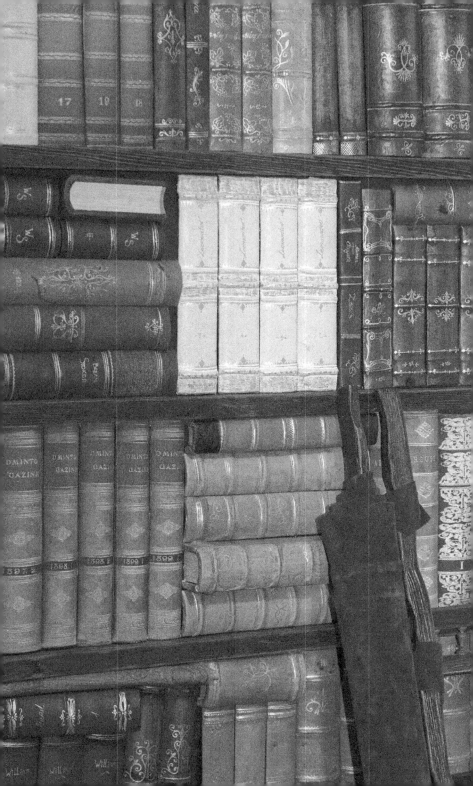

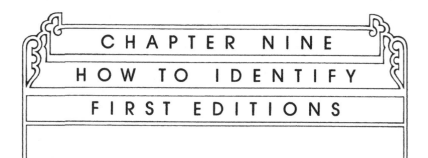

CHAPTER NINE
HOW TO IDENTIFY
FIRST EDITIONS

Knowing how to identify a first edition is plainly a matter of importance in the building of any successful collection. Without such knowledge, even a comparatively advanced collector of considerable sophistication can go wrong, sometimes disastrously so. While no reputable dealer will knowingly sell a book as a first when it isn't, there are many new dealers in the field who have not had sufficient depth of experience to know all the fine points. Even a dealer of many years' experience can come a cropper in an unfamiliar area where he has little or no expertise. And there are, alas, many fledgling dealers who simply haven't taken the time and trouble to learn the standard practices of the major publishing houses.

Which is not to say they are easy to learn. It sometimes seems as though publishers are—or at any rate were in the recent past—deliberately reluctant to make first-edition identification simple. Various handbooks are available—none of them wholly reliable, unfortunately—giving methods of identification, but the circumstances of collecting are such that you may not necessarily have an opportunity to make use of them when you need them. You may be at an auction, or at a neighborhood sale, or even in the shop of a dealer not specializing in firsts. If you leave the item and come back after you have done your checking, the chances are that someone else will have snapped it up in the meantime, especially if it is a truly desirable first edition. So it is wise to learn some key identification tests thoroughly.

On almost all modern books the necessary information will usually be found on the title page or its verso, the copyright page, or both. Knowing what to look for on these two pages will give you the answer in the large majority of cases, though not every time. First of all, check the name of the publisher. Most first editions will bear the imprint of the publishing firm, one recognizable as the original publisher. Especially before the post-World War II paperback revolution, several firms specialized in cheap reprints of popular books that had long since reached a point of no profit for the original publisher. Such books are usually very quickly recognizable by the cheapness of the paper and the binding, and also by the difference between the date of publication (normally on the title page) and the date of the copyright (on the copyright page). In most cases these dates should be identical, although it is possible for a book published near the beginning of a year to have a copyright date at variance with that on the title page. Many inexperienced collectors are also confused by the appearance of a long string of dates on the copyright page. This usually occurs on books of poetry or short stories where the individual pieces were published in periodicals at various earlier dates, and copyrighted then. Novels and plays will generally have a single copyright date.

Among the reprint publishers whose books may present some confusion are Doubleday and Company (formerly Doubleday, Doran & Co.) in Garden City, New York. During the last twenty or thirty years Doubleday has been publishing original works for the most part. But in the period between the two world wars, a large part of the Doubleday output consisted of reprints, and a Garden City imprint in those years should be taken as a clear warning to check further before assuming first edition status. Similarly, Indianapolis as an imprint should be another warning, since Bobbs-Merrill also issued a great many reprints, although once again it has also published first editions—for example, the early work of William Styron and the first books of Vladimir Nabokov published in this country. A book club edition, so marked on the dust jacket or elsewhere, is virtually certain not to be a first edition. An exception, relatively new, is The First Edition Society of the Franklin Library (a subdivision of the Franklin Mint) at Franklin Center, Pennsylvania. (*See* Chapter 14 for further details.)

Some book-club editions present a virtually insoluble problem of identification. Nowadays many books that are taken by book clubs are supplied by the publisher of the trade edition in identical format, with only the dust jacket giving any possible clue, sometimes having the name of the club somewhere on the jacket (although this is not always a positive identification, since in some cases the book's selection as a book-club premium is advertised on the trade edition). One infallible sign, if the dust jacket is still totally intact, is the absence of a price on the flap of the dust jacket. Some book-club editions have a small black dot or a blind-stamped dot at the foot of the rear cover. And on books from the forties, fifties, and even into the sixties, it was common practice to print the book-club editions on much thinner paper, and quite often to use a cheaper binding. Here the beginner must have both copies of both editions in hand to distinguish between them. Once again, the seasoned dealer can guide the collector.

Before describing the ways in which major publishers mark (or fail to mark) their first editions, a word about terminology may be in order. "Edition," "printing," and "issue" are all words used by publishers, bibliographers, and booksellers. However, they are not always used in the same way or even consistently, especially by publishers and booksellers.

To bibliographers (who try to be accurate in all things) an "edition" means all copies of a book printed from a single unchanged setting of type. In the publishing life of a book, the first copy off the press is a "first edition" and so is the five hundred thousandth, even if the latter has a different binding or was printed five years later—*so long as the original typesetting remains unchanged.* A "printing," on the other hand, means only those copies produced during a single press run. "Impression" is synonymous with "printing." Thus an edition may incorporate a whole series of printings. An "issue," finally, is a still smaller category than a printing. Sometimes during a press run the printer may discover an error, stop the press and correct it, then go on to finish the printing. Or a publisher may choose to bind the completed sheets at a different time in different materials. A bibliographer describes the differently bound copies, or those with an error and those without, as two separate issues. The word "state" means much the same thing as "issue." (For fine distinctions, *see* entries under these words in Chapter 16.)

To publishers, "printing" is the key term. Most of them are today fairly careful to indicate the printing a particular copy belongs to (see below). They are much less careful in their use of the word "edition." In publishing usage a "new edition" implies a complete revision or updating or recasting of the book and its contents. But before the book actually goes into a "new edition," many textual changes of greater or lesser importance may be introduced silently at the time of a new printing. The poet Robert Lowell, for example, often took the opportunity offered by a new printing to change words and sometimes whole lines. So did W. H. Auden and Marianne Moore. Errors are usually corrected and minor updating done as a matter of course.

Because of this fairly free and easy attitude toward the words "edition" and "printing" in publishing today, book collectors and dealers have come to regard "first edition" and "first printing" as synonymous. A book listed in a catalog as a first edition will as a matter of course be a first printing. (Some scrupulous—or overhopeful—dealers may list a book as, say, "First edition, fifth printing," which may be technically accurate but unappealing to a collector with no interest in anything but the first printing.)

It will be noted that more and more American publishers are adopting a system of ascending numbers printed on the copyright page, sometimes along with the words "First Edition." These words and the numeral "1" are then removed from the plate at the time of the second printing so that the number series now begins with "2." In this system there is no need for any resetting of type.

$$9 \; 8 \; 7 \; 6 \; 5 \; 4 \; 3 \; 2$$

The following list summarizes the first edition and printing notation practices of most major American and British publishing houses, particularly those who publish— or have published—works of widely collected authors. It is based upon information gathered from several sources, including my own experience, but most of it is the result of a canvass of the publishing houses themselves.

METHODS OF IDENTIFYING
FIRST EDITIONS AND FIRST PRINTINGS
OF BOOKS ISSUED BY IMPORTANT
BRITISH AND AMERICAN
PUBLISHING FIRMS

———————

ABELARD-SCHUMAN, LTD. Later printings are so marked.

ADVENTURES IN POETRY To date no book has gone into a later printing. The colophon bearing publication data is generally the last page of text.

GEORGE ALLEN & UNWIN, LTD. Later printings are so indicated.

ALOES BOOKS Later printings are so indicated.

APPLETON-CENTURY-CROFTS   (formerly D. Appleton and Company) The words "First Edition" appear on the copyright page or the Roman numeral I follows the last line of text on the last page.

ARGUS BOOKS, INC.   (also known as Ben Abramson, Publisher) Lack of any notice of a later printing indicates a first.

ARKHAM HOUSE   All Arkham House books are first editions with the exception of *The Collected Works of H. P. Lovecraft*, where the edition is noted in the colophon.

ARROW BOOKS, LTD.   There must be no indication of a later printing on the copyright page.

ATHENEUM PUBLISHERS   "First Edition" (or "First American Edition" when the book has had a prior European publication) appears on the copyright page. One notable exception is Edward Albee's *Tiny Alice*, where this notice was inadvertently omitted. Since the book did not go into a second printing, all regular trade copies are first editions, but care must be taken not to confuse them with the simultaneous book club edition.

THE ATLANTIC MONTHLY PRESS   The lack of notice of any further printings on the copyright page indicates a first edition. In 1925, the firm merged with Little, Brown, and Company, and since then both names appear on the title page.

THE AUERHAHN PRESS   With the single exception of John Wieners' *Hotel Wentley Poems*, no book ever went into a later printing. The title of the fifth poem is expurgated in the first printing of this book, but is spelled out in full in the later printing.

ROBERT O. BALLOU, INC.   (or Robert O. Ballou, Publisher) The copyright page bears the legend "First published ———" (with year date).

THE BANYAN PRESS   All books are first editions; the press does not reprint.

BARRE PUBLISHING COMPANY   Identical dates appear on the title and copyright pages.

BASIC BOOKS   Identical dates appear on the title and copyright pages.

B. T. BATSFORD, INC.   The copyright page bears the words "First printed 19———." Later printings are usually listed below this line.

BEACON PRESS   Earlier books listed later printings on the copyright page. Since the mid-1970s, the row of ascending numbers has been used, with the lowest number indicating the printing.

BLACK SPARROW PRESS   Later printings are so indicated on the copyright page. A further identification can be made by noting the color of ink on the title page. First editions have title pages in two or more colors, whereas the later printings have title pages in black only.

BLACK SUN PRESS   Most of the books had only one printing. The few that did have second printings are so noted in the colophon.

BOBBS-MERRILL COMPANY, INC.   For many years there was no uniformity of practice regarding identification of first printings, a situation further complicated by the fact that the firm was primarily engaged in issuing low-priced reprints. Some titles bear the words "First Edition," and copies lacking such (as, for example, William Styron's *Lie Down in Darkness*) are either later printings or book club editions. On some other titles, a lack of any indication denotes a first, with later printings being so noted on the copyright page. With this firm it is always wise to consult an author bibliography when possible.

THE BODLEY HEAD, LTD.   First editions are designated by the words "First published 19———" on the copyright page.

ALBERT AND CHARLES BONI   (later, Boni and Liveright) Either the words "First Edition" must appear on the copyright page or the dates on the title and copyright pages must be identical.

R. R. BOWKER CO.   The absence of any notation of a later printing indicates a first edition.

GEORGE BRAZILLER, INC.   The words "First Edition" must appear on the copyright page.

BRENTANO'S   This company's policy through 1927 was to list later printings on the copyright page. Beginning in 1928, the words "First Edition" were placed on the copyright page.

BREWER AND WARREN   (later, Brewer, Warren & Putnam) Identical dates appear on title and copyright pages. Also, a lack of any indication of a later printing denotes a first.

BROADSIDE PRESS   The words "First Edition" must appear on the copyright page.

CALDER & BOYERS, LTD.   (also John Calder [Publisher] Ltd.) Later printings are so noted on the copyright page.

JONATHAN CAPE, LTD.   Later printings are so noted on the copyright page.

JONATHAN CAPE AND HARRISON SMITH (U.S.)   There must be no listing of subsequent printings after the date of publication appearing on the copyright page.

CAPRA PRESS   Later printings are so indicated on copyright page.

CARCANET PRESS   As of 1979 no publication had gone into a later printing.

CAXTON PRINTERS, LTD.   Later printings are so indicated on the copyright page. Lack of any printing information indicates a first.

THE CENTURY CO.   Book must have identical dates on title and copyright pages or the words "First Printing" on the copyright page. Where no date appears on the title page, lack of any indication of a later printing is evidence of a first edition.

CHATTO AND WINDUS   Later printings are noted on the copyright page.

CITADEL PRESS   Either the words "First Printing" appear on the copyright page, or else there is no indication of a later printing.

CITY LIGHTS   This firm has no policy regarding first printings. Sometimes later printings are indicated on the copyright page, and sometimes at the top of the rear cover. Sometimes an increased price is the only indication of a later printing, but obviously in such cases a knowledge of the original price is necessary. With this firm it is absolutely essential to consult author bibliographies.

COACH HOUSE PRESS Normally there is no mention made of first printings, but usually (although not always) later printings are indicated in the colophon.

COLUMBIA UNIVERSITY PRESS Prior to the 1970s, a date on the title page indicated a first printing. On later printings, the date was removed. Currently, the series of ascending numbers is in use.

COPELAND AND DAY Book must have identical dates on title and copyright pages.

CORNELL UNIVERSITY PRESS The copyright page bears the legend "First published ———" (with year date). Later printings are so indicated.

COSMOPOLITAN BOOK COMPANY Book must have identical dates on title and colophon pages.

COVICI FRIEDE (Also Pascal Covici) Either the words "First Edition" appear on the copyright page, or else the dates on the title and copyright pages must be identical.

COVICI-MCGEE, PUBLISHERS The words "First Printing" appear on the copyright page.

COWARD MCCANN, INC. (later, Coward, McCann & Geohegan) There is no mention of first printings, but all later printings are so marked on the copyright page.

CREATIVE AGE PRESS, INC. Either there must be identical dates on title and copyright pages, or, when no date appears on the title, there must be no indication of a later printing on the copyright page.

THOMAS Y. CROWELL COMPANY, INC. This company has had three different ways of marking its first editions. The most common is to have the words "First Printing" on the copyright page. The second is the lack of any indication of a later printing.

The third, and current, is the row of ascending numbers in conjunction with the words "First Edition."

CROWN PUBLISHERS, INC.   Subsequent printings are so indicated on the copyright page.

CUMMINGTON PRESS   The very few second printings by this press are so indicated in the colophon.

DARTMOUTH PUBLICATIONS   Book must have identical dates on title and copyright pages.

THE JOHN DAY COMPANY, INC.   The date in the legend "First Published ———" (with month and year) on the copyright page must agree with the date on the title page; or, lacking this legend, there must be no indication of a later printing. Currently, the words "First Edition" appear on the copyright page.

STEPHEN DAYE PRESS   There must be no indication of a later printing.

DELACORTE PRESS   The words "First Printing" appear on the copyright page, or when the book has had a prior foreign edition, the legend reads "First Delacorte Edition."

THE DERRYDALE PRESS, INC.   The copyright page has a listing of the edition, and usually the number of copies comprising the edition. This occasionally appears in the colophon instead of on the copyright page.

ANDRE DEUTSCH, LTD.   Later printings are so indicated on the copyright page.

THE DIAL PRESS   Either the words "First Edition" must appear on the copyright page, or the dates on the title and copyright page must agree.

DODD, MEAD & COMPANY   Earlier, the dates on the title and copyright pages agreed. Currently, the series of ascending numbers is in use to indicate printings.

THE DOLMEN PRESS, LTD.   Later printings are so indicated, usually (but not always) on the copyright page.

GEORGE H. DORAN & CO.   The copyright page must bear either the words "First Printing" or the "GHD" monogram.

DORRANCE AND CO., INC. Either the words "First Edition" appear on the copyright page or there must be no listing of later printings on the copyright page.

DOUBLEDAY & CO., INC. (Also Doubleday, Doran, & Co.) The words "First Edition" must appear on the copyright page. This is sometimes varied when the book is the first American edition, the legend then reading "First Edition in the United States of America." Finally, if a limited edition preceded the trade edition, the legend reads "First Edition following the publication of a limited edition."

DOUBLEDAY PAGE & COMPANY The words "First Edition" must appear on the copyright page.

DUELL, SLOAN & PEARCE Any one of three indications must appear on the copyright page: "First Edition," "First Printing," or a Roman numeral I.

DUFFIELD & CO. (or Duffield and Green) The words "First Edition" must appear on the copyright page.

DUKE UNIVERSITY PRESS Later printings are generally indicated on the copyright page. Sometimes the presence of more than one copyright date will indicate a later printing if it is not so stated.

DUNSTER HOUSE BOOKSHOP Identical dates appear on title and copyright pages.

PHILIP C. DUSCHNES Identical dates appear on title and copyright pages.

E. P. DUTTON & CO., INC. The earlier practice was to have the words "First Edition" on the copyright page. The current practice is to use the series of ascending numbers in conjunction with the words "First Edition" (or "First American Edition" when the book has had a prior foreign edition).

EAKINS PRESS Usually (but not always) the words "First Edition" appear on the copyright page. However, the question is academic as no books of this press went into later printings.

ECCO PRESS Later printings are so indicated on the copyright page. There is no marking for first editions.

EQUINOX COOPERATIVE PRESS, INC.   Later printings are so indicated on the copyright page.

EYRE METHUEN, LTD.   (formerly Eyre & Spottiswoode, Ltd.) Later printings are so indicated on the copyright page.

FABER & FABER, LTD.   (formerly Faber & Gwyer) Until the mid-1970s this firm consistently used the words "First published in ————" with the year in Roman numerals. Subsequent printings were also listed in Roman numerals. Since that date, the practice has been the same but Arabic numerals are now in use.

FALMOUTH PUBLISHING HOUSE, INC.   Later printings are so indicated on the copyright page.

FARRAR & RINEHART, INC.   (also Farrar Straus & Company, Farrar Straus & Cudahy, and currently, Farrar, Straus & Giroux, Inc.) The earlier practice was to place the firm's monogram "fs" or "frs" in large lower-case italics on the copyright page. Currently, the words "First Edition" (with year date) appear on the copyright page. However, a problem arises with their paperback editions. The practice of this house has been to bind up in paper whatever sheets are on hand from hardcover printings. Thus second or even third printings are often actually the first paperback. Precise information on a given book must be obtained from the publisher or from a reliable bibliography.

FIELDS, OSGOOD & CO.   Identical dates appear on title and copyright pages.

FOLLETT PUBLISHING CO.   First editions are not designated as such. A single date on the copyright page indicates a first, with later editions carrying a dated printing key on the copyright page.

FOUR SEAS COMPANY   No notice of later printings appears on the copyright page.

FOUR SEASONS FOUNDATION   Later printings are so indicated on the copyright page.

SAMUEL FRENCH, INC.   The firm makes no distinction whatever between printings. A bibliography must be consulted, or you must have a sure knowledge of the proper ads to be found on the back cover. These ads change with each printing.

FULCRUM PRESS   Later printings are so indicated on the copyright page.

FUNK & WAGNALLS, INC.   These are three different methods employed by this firm to indicate first editions: the copyright page bears the words "First Published" (with a month and year); or the numeral 1 appears after the copyright date; or, in some rare cases, there is merely no indication of a later printing. Currently the words "First Edition" appear on the copyright page.

GAMBIT   The words "First Printing" appear on the copyright page.

BERNARD GEIS ASSOCIATES   The words "First Printing" appear on the copyright page.

GODINE PRESS   Later printings are so designated on the copyright page.

VICTOR GOLLANCZ, LTD.   There must be no indication of a later printing on the copyright page.

LAURENCE J. GOMME   Identical dates appear on title and copyright pages.

GRANADA PUBLISHING, LTD.   Later printings are so indicated on copyright page.

GREENBERG PUBLISHER, INC.   There must be no indication of a later printing on the copyright page.

GREY FOX PRESS   In some cases, the words "First Edition" appear on the copyright page, but all later printings are so indicated there.

GROSSMAN PUBLISHERS, INC.   This firm was not consistent in its markings. Some books bear the words "First Printing" on the copyright page, others simply lack any indication of further printings. This later style was used on books published in conjunction with the British firm of Jonathan Cape, Ltd.

GROVE PRESS, INC.   The words "First Edition" appear on the copyright page, with later printings also noted there.

HAMISH HAMILTON, LTD.   Later printings are so noted on the copy-
    right page.

HARCOURT, BRACE & COMPANY   (also Harcourt, Brace & World,
    and currently Harcourt Brace Jovanovich, Inc.) At first the
    practice was to place the numeral 1 on the copyright page,
    or to have the legend "Published ————" (with month and
    year), this date being identical with the date on the title page.
    Currently the words "First Edition" (or "First American Edi-
    tion") must appear on the copyright page.

HARPER & ROW, PUBLISHERS   (also Harper & Brothers, and Harper
    & Row, Peterson) First printings of books published by this
    firm between 1960 and 1973 are the most difficult of all to iden-
    tify. Most Harper books published between 1922 and 1960
    should bear the words "First Edition" on the copyright page.
    However this policy was not always adhered to, and from
    1960 until 1973 (except on certain books originating in Great
    Britain) two code letters were used alone on the copyright
    page. (Prior to 1960 the code letters were also used but in con-
    junction with the phrase "First Edition.") These code letters,
    whose use first began in 1912, indicate respectively the month
    and year of the printing of that copy of the book, according
    to the schedule on the next page. With this key you can easily
    determine the month and year of printing of the copy you
    have, but it will still be necessary to ascertain in what month
    and year the book was first published before you know your
    book is a first printing. So you will have to consult an author
    bibliography, if one exists, or to try to obtain publication in-
    formation from the firm itself. Unfortunately, the latter
    method is seldom successful; in some cases the firm no longer
    has records, and in some cases no one has time to reply. Fortu-
    nately, this coding system was discontinued in 1973 in favor
    of the series of ascending numbers in conjunction with two-
    digit year dates.

HARVARD UNIVERSITY PRESS   Later printings are so indicated on
    the copyright page, with the dates on the title and copyright

A — January		G — July	
B — February		H — August	
C — March		I — September	
D — April		J — October	
E — May		K — November	
F — June		L — December	

M — 1912	B — 1927	R — 1942	G — 1957
N — 1913	C — 1928	S — 1943	H — 1958
O — 1914	D — 1929	T — 1944	I — 1959
P — 1915	E — 1930	U — 1945	K — 1960
Q — 1916	F — 1931	V — 1946	L — 1961
R — 1917	G — 1932	W — 1947	M — 1962
S — 1918	H — 1933	X — 1948	N — 1963
T — 1919	I — 1934	Y — 1949	O — 1964
U — 1920	K — 1935	Z — 1950	P — 1965
V — 1921	L — 1936	A — 1951	Q — 1966
W — 1922	M — 1937	B — 1952	R — 1967
X — 1923	N — 1938	C — 1953	S — 1968
Y — 1924	O — 1939	D — 1954	T — 1969
Z — 1925	P — 1940	E — 1955	U — 1970
A — 1926	Q — 1941	F — 1956	V — 1971
	W — 1972		

Key to Harper & Row printing dates.

pages identical. Dates are removed from title pages on later printings.

HASTINGS HOUSE PUBLISHERS, INC. Dates on title and copyright pages are identical, with no indication of later printing on the copyright page.

WILLIAM HEINEMANN, LTD. Later printings are so indicated on the copyright page.

HILL AND WANG Later printings are so indicated on the copyright page.

HODDER & STOUGHTON, LTD. Later printings are so indicated on the copyright page.

HOGARTH PRESS Later printings are so indicated on the copyright page.

HENRY HOLT & CO., INC. (Also Holt, Rinehart and Winston) Earlier books were marked with any one of three different wordings: "First Edition," or "First Published" (with month and year date); or on the copyright page, with the year date corresponding to the date on the title page. Currently, the words "First Edition" appear with the ascending series of numbers.

HORIZON PRESS There must be no indication of later printings.

HOUGHTON MIFFLIN COMPANY Earlier books bore the date on the title page, with no date on later printings. Currently, the series of ascending numbers is in use.

HOWELL SOSKIN PUBLISHERS There must be no indication of later printings on the copyright page.

B. W. HUEBSCH The dates on the title and copyright pages must be identical.

INDIANA UNIVERSITY PRESS There must be no listing of later printings on the copyright page. Recently, the system of ascending numbers has been adopted.

JARGON (Jonathan Williams Publisher) There is no indication of edition on the publications of this firm with the single exception of Irving Layton's *Improved Binoculars,* where a second, expanded edition was issued, and so noted on the front cover. All other books were issued in one printing only.

THE JOHNS HOPKINS UNIVERSITY PRESS Later printings are so noted on the copyright page.

MICHAEL JOSEPH, LTD. Later printings are so noted on the copyright page.

KAYAK Those few books that have gone into second printings are so designated on the copyright page.

MITCHELL KENNERLY Dates on the title and copyright pages are identical.

KENT STATE UNIVERSITY PRESS Until 1973 the words "First Edition" appeared on the copyright page. Since then, the policy has been reversed, with no notice of first printings, but with "Second Printing," etc., on the copyright page to denote later printings.

ALFRED A. KNOPF, INC.   On earlier books, the date on the title page must correspond with the copyright date, as the date on the title page generally indicates the year of the printing, rather than the year of original publication. This is still true, but in recent years the words "First Edition" appear on the copyright page, with subsequent printings also listed there.

JOHN LANE COMPANY   Dates on the title and copyright pages are identical.

SEYMOUR LAWRENCE, INC.   The words "First Printing" appear on the copyright page.

J. B. LIPPINCOTT COMPANY   In earlier books the words "First Edition" must appear on the copyright page, or the dates on the title and copyright pages must be identical. An example of this latter style which confuses many collectors is Thomas Pynchon's *V*, where the first edition is identifiable only in this manner. More recently, the series of ascending numbers has been used in conjunction with the words "First Edition."

LITTLE, BROWN & CO.   The words "First Edition" must appear on the copyright page.

HORACE LIVERIGHT, INC.   (Also Liveright Publishing Co.) There should be no evidence of later printings on the copyright page. In some cases, the words "First Edition" appeared on the copyright page, but the absence of them does *not* indicate a later printing. Since 1970 the series of ascending numbers has been employed along with the words "First Edition."

LONGMANS, GREEN & CO.   The legend "First Published" (with year date) appears on the copyright page. This date must agree with that on the title page.

LOTHROP PUBLISHING CO.   The dates on title and copyright pages must be identical, with no listing of further printings on the copyright page.

LOUISIANA STATE UNIVERSITY PRESS   There must be no listing of additional printings on the copyright page.

JOHN W. LUCE & CO.   There must be no listing of additional printings on the copyright page.

LYLE STUART, INC.   The words "First Edition" appear on the copyright page, with this changed to "Second Printing," etc., on subsequent printings.

THE MACAULAY CO.   There must be no indication of later printings on the copyright page.

ROBERT M. MCBRIDE & CO.   Three different methods of identifying first editions have been employed by this firm: the words "First Edition" on the copyright page; "First Published" (with month and year) on copyright page; or "Published ———" (with month and year) on copyright page. In both the latter styles, the dates on title and copyright pages must be identical.

MCCLELLAND AND STEWART, LTD.   Later printings are usually so indicated on the copyright page. The firm admits that there have been some accidental omissions.

THE MCCLURE CO.   (Also McClure Phillips & Co.) The copyright page must bear either the legend "Published" (with month and year) or "First Impression" (with month and year). In either case the dates on the title and copyright pages must be identical.

A. C. MCCLURG & CO.   The copyright page bears the legend "Published" (with month and year).

MCDOWELL OBOLENSKY CO.   The words "First Printing" must appear on the copyright page.

MACGIBBON & KEE, LTD.   Later printings are so indicated on the copyright page.

MCGRAW-HILL BOOK CO.   The words "First Edition" must appear on the copyright page. More recently, the series of ascending numbers has been in use.

DAVID MCKAY COMPANY, INC.   Prior to the 1970s, there must be no indication of later printings on the copyright page. Since then, the series of ascending numbers has been in use.

MACMILLAN PUBLISHING CO., INC.   Either the words "First Printing" or the legend "First Published" (with month and year date) must appear on the copyright page, in which case the dates on the title and copyright pages must be identical. There have been occasional exceptions to this practice, and it is safer to consult author bibliographies when possible.

METHUEN & CO., LTD.   See EYRE METHUEN, LTD.

MINTON, BALCH & CO.   Dates on the title and copyright pages must be identical.

MODERN AGE BOOKS   The dates on the title and copyright pages must be identical.

WILLIAM MORROW & CO., INC.   Prior to the 1970s the dates on the title and copyright pages must be identical. Occasionally the legend "First Printing" (with month and year) was employed. Since the 1970s the series of ascending numbers has been used in conjunction with the words "First Edition," which are allowed to remain unless there has been a revision of the text.

NASH PUBLISHING CO.   The words "First Printing" must appear on the copyright page.

THE NEW AMERICAN LIBRARY, INC.   The words "First Printing" (with month and year date) must appear on the copyright page. This date must be identical with the date on the title page.

NEW DIRECTIONS PUBLISHING CORP.   Over the years the first-edition indication system of this firm has varied so much that it is jocularly referred to by some dealers as "No Directions." The policy has been particularly inconsistent in respect to its hardbound books. On the paperbacks, the printing has almost always been noted in either the upper left or upper right corner of the rear cover. With the hardbound books, identification of first printings is difficult and often impossible. Generally, any book that does not show evidence of a later printing can be assumed to be a first, but there are numerous exceptions to this rule. Specific information must be sought, or an author bibliography consulted. Frequently, the later printings are noted only on the dust jacket flaps, which may, of course, be clipped, or removed entirely, rendering positive identification difficult at best. In one case, at least, the phrase "First Edition" appearing on the copyright page of Tennessee Williams' *The Rose Tattoo* was allowed to remain on the second printing (which can be identified only by the color of the binding). Recently, later printings have been so indicated on the copyright page.

NEW RIVERS PRESS   The colophon carries all pertinent information regarding the printing and edition.

W. W. NORTON & CO., INC.   The words "First Edition" appear on the copyright page. More recently, the series of ascending numbers is being used in conjunction with the words "First Edition," which are sometimes allowed to remain on later printings—for example, on Adrienne Rich's *Diving into the Wreck.*

IVAN OBOLENSKY   The words "First Edition" must appear on the copyright page.

THE ODYSSEY PRESS, INC.   The words "First Edition" appear on the copyright page, or else a combination of letters and numbers —the letter indicating the state of the text, and the number, the edition. Thus "A-1" indicates a first printing of the original text, whereas "B-1" would be the first printing of a revised text, and "A-2" would be a second printing of the original, unrevised text.

OHIO STATE UNIVERSITY PRESS   Later printings are so noted on the copyright page.

OHIO UNIVERSITY PRESS   Later printings are so noted on the copyright page.

OLIVER & BOYD   Later printings are so noted on the copyright page.

OLYMPIA PRESS   Later printings are so noted on the copyright page.

JAMES R. OSGOOD & CO.   Dates on title and copyright pages must be identical.

PETER OWEN, LTD. Later printings are so noted on the copyright page.

OXFORD UNIVERSITY PRESS All later printings are so noted on the copyright page.

OYEZ Later printings are so noted on the copyright page.

PANTHEON BOOKS, INC. The words "First Edition" or "First Printing" must appear on the copyright page.

PAYSON & CLARKE, LTD. The dates on the title and copyright pages must be identical.

PELLEGRINI & CUDAHY There must be no evidence of later printings on the copyright page.

PENMAEN PRESS This firm issues only first editions, which are *sometimes* so marked.

PERGAMON PRESS, INC. The words "First Edition" must appear on the copyright page.

PERISHABLE PRESS The policy of this firm is to print one edition only, and therefore there is no indication of printing on anything except the first book of the press, *The Disillusioned Solipsist*, which bore the words "First Printing" on the title page. This practice was abandoned immediately thereafter.

PETER PAUPER PRESS Formerly when the books of this press were limited editions notice of such was made in the colophons. Since shifting to the publication of trade books, there has been no definite means of identifying printings. The matter is, however, academic, as virtually everything published by this house consists of reprints of established classics.

THE PHOENIX BOOK SHOP Later printings are so noted on the title page.

THE POET'S PRESS Relatively few books of this press have gone beyond first printings. Those that did are so noted on either the title or the copyright page.

BERN PORTER BOOKS Later printings are so indicated on the copyright page.

CLARKSON POTTER, INC. The words "First Edition" appear on the copyright page, with later printings being so noted.

PRINCETON UNIVERSITY PRESS   Formerly, later printings were so
noted on the copyright page, but this practice has been discontinued and later printings are indicated only when there has
been significant change in the text.

G. P. PUTNAM'S SONS   Later printings are sometimes so noted on
the copyright page. In any case the dates on the title and copyright pages must be identical. Books that are reprinted frequently lack any date whatever on the title page.

RAND, MCNALLY & CO.   The words "First Printing" (with month
and year) appear on the copyright page. The date there must
correspond with the title page date.

RANDOM HOUSE   The words "First Edition" or "First Printing"
must appear on the copyright page. (Two important exceptions to this practice are Faulkner's *Requiem for a Nun* and
Knight's Gambit, in which all indication of first printing status
were inadvertently omitted. These first editions must be distinguished by the colors of their bindings.)

HENRY REGNERY COMPANY   This company follows no set practice.
During the year 1974 it used the series of ascending numbers,
but discontinued it the following year. Bibliographies must be
consulted.

REYNAL & HITCHCOCK, INC.   Most books of this firm bore no indication of printing (there were a few exceptions carrying the
words "First Printing" on the copyright page). Lack of any
indication of a later printing indicates a first.

ROUTLEDGE & KEGAN PAUL, LTD.   Later printings are so noted on
the copyright page.

WILLIAM EDWIN RUDGE   The dates on the title and copyright pages
must be identical.

RUTGERS UNIVERSITY PRESS   Later printings are so noted on the
copyright page.

SAGAMORE PRESS   Later printings are so noted on the copyright
page.

SAGE BOOKS, INC.   Later printings are so noted on the copyright
page.

SAND DOLLAR   To date no book of this press has gone into a later printing. The publisher states that should this happen, he will indicate later printings on the copyright page.

HENRY SCHUMAN, INC.   (now known as Abelard-Schuman, Ltd.) Later printings are so indicated on the copyright page.

CHARLES SCRIBNER'S SONS   This firm has employed three different methods of marking its first editions. Until early in 1929, the dates on the title and copyright pages had to be identical, with no indication of a later printing on the copyright page. Late in 1929, the code letter "A" began to be placed on the copyright page to indicate the first printing. On later printings this was either removed or replaced with subsequent letters of the alphabet. This code letter system was discontinued in 1973 and the series of ascending numbers adopted.

SEARS PUBLISHING CO., INC.   Later printings are so indicated on the copyright page.

MARTIN SECKER & WARBURG, LTD.   Later printings are so indicated on the copyright page.

THOMAS SELTZER   Dates on title and copyright pages are identical.

SHAMBALA PUBLICATIONS, INC.   Later printings are so noted on the copyright page.

SIMON AND SCHUSTER, INC.   The words "First Printing" must appear on the copyright page.

WILLIAM SLOANE ASSOCIATES, INC.   The words "First Printing" must appear on the copyright page.

SMALL MAYNARD & CO.   Dates on the title and copyright pages must be identical.

HARRISON SMITH, INC.   (also known as Harrison Smith & Robert Haas, Inc.) The words "First Printing" must appear on the copyright page.

SOMETHING ELSE PRESS   Later printings are so indicated on the copyright page.

SOUTHERN ILLINOIS UNIVERSITY PRESS   Later printings are so indicated on the copyright page.

STANFORD UNIVERSITY PRESS   Later printings are so noted on the copyright page.

STEIN & DAY, PUBLISHERS   Later printings are so indicated on the copyright page.

FREDERICK A. STOKES & CO.   Dates on the title and copyright pages must be identical.

HERBERT S. STONE & CO.   (also Stone & Kimball) Dates on the title and copyright pages are identical.

STONEWALL PRESS   Dates on the title and copyright pages are identical.

SUMAC PRESS   The words "First Edition" appear on the copyright page in most cases, but not all. However, all later printings are so indicated on the copyright page.

THE SUNWISE TURN   Dates on the title and copyright pages are identical.

THE SWALLOW PRESS   (also Alan Swallow, Publisher) The words "First Printing" (with month and year date) must appear on the copyright page with the year identical with that on the title page. More recently, the wording has been changed to "First Edition, first printing."

SYRACUSE UNIVERSITY PRESS   There must be no indication of a later printing on the copyright page.

TAPLINGER PUBLISHING CO., INC.   The words "First Edition" must appear on the copyright page. If the book had a prior foreign edition, the wording will read either "First American Edition" or "First Published in the United States in ⸺ (year) by Taplinger Publishing Co., Inc."

TICKNOR AND COMPANY   (also Ticknor and Fields) Dates on the title and copyright pages are identical in most cases. There are however some exceptions where the title page date may possibly be a year later than the copyright date. With this firm it is always best to consult either an author bibliography or the Merle Johnson checklist.

TOTEM-CORINTH   There is no specific way of indicating first or later printings by this firm, and extreme care must be taken, as almost all of this firm's important titles have gone into numerous printings, most of which appear similar to the untutored eye. Generally speaking, the later printings will have ads in the back of the books listing titles that were published later than the first printing of the particular book. To identify these, however, requires detailed knowledge of the publishing chronology of all of the firm's books. It is absolutely imperative to consult author bibliographies or reliable checklists.

TRIDENT PRESS   Dates on the title and copyright pages must be identical, or, in some rare cases where the title page date is a year later than the copyright date, there must be no listing of additional printings.

TROBAR   Later printings are so indicated on the copyright page.

FREDERICK UNGAR PUBLISHING CO., INC.   There must be no indication of later printings on the copyright page.

UNICORN PRESS   All information is contained within the colophon, which usually gives the printing dates and the size of the edition.

UNIVERSITY OF ALABAMA PRESS   There must be no indication of later printings on the copyright page.

UNIVERSITY OF ARIZONA PRESS   There must be no indication of later printings on the copyright page.

UNIVERSITY OF CALIFORNIA PRESS   Dates on the title and copyright pages are identical.

UNIVERSITY OF CHICAGO PRESS   Later printings are so indicated on the copyright page.

UNIVERSITY OF COLORADO PRESS   Later printings are so indicated on the copyright page.

UNIVERSITY OF ILLINOIS PRESS   Later printings are so indicated on the copyright page (or very occasionally on the title page).

UNIVERSITY OF KENTUCKY PRESS   Later printings are so indicated on the copyright page.

UNIVERSITY OF MICHIGAN PRESS   Later printings are so indicated on the copyright page.

UNIVERSITY OF MINNESOTA PRESS   Later printings are so indicated on the title page.

UNIVERSITY OF NEBRASKA PRESS   Later printings are so indicated on the copyright page.

UNIVERSITY OF NORTH CAROLINA PRESS   Later printings are so indicated on the copyright page.

UNIVERSITY OF OKLAHOMA PRESS   The words "First Edition" appear on the copyright page.

UNIVERSITY OF PENNSYLVANIA PRESS   Later printings are so indicated on the copyright page.

UNIVERSITY OF PITTSBURGH PRESS   Later printings are so indicated on the title or copyright page.

UNIVERSITY OF SOUTH CAROLINA PRESS   The words "First Edition" appear on the copyright page.

UNIVERSITY OF TENNESSEE PRESS   Later printings are so indicated on the copyright page.

UNIVERSITY OF TEXAS PRESS   Later printings are so indicated on the copyright page.

UNIVERSITY PRESS OF VIRGINIA   Later printings are so indicated on the copyright page.

UNIVERSITY OF WASHINGTON PRESS   Later printings are so indicated on the copyright page.

VANDERBILT UNIVERSITY PRESS   Later printings are so indicated on the copyright page.

VANGUARD PRESS, INC.   Prior to the mid-1970s, later printings were so indicated on the copyright page. Currently, the series of ascending numbers is used.

VIKING PRESS, INC.   (now Viking Penguin, Inc.) Later printings are so indicated on the copyright page, which usually bears the words "Published ———" (with month and year). On juveniles, the words "First Edition" appear on the copyright page along with both a numerical and a year code—1 2 3 4 5 82 81 80 79 78. On the second printing the words "First Edition" are removed, along with the numeral 1, and also the year date if the printing is in a succeeding year.

FRANKLIN WATTS, INC. On earlier books, the words "First Edition" must appear on the copyright page. Since the mid-1970s the series of ascending numerals has been in use.

WEIDENFELD & NICHOLSON, LTD. (also Weidenfeld [Publishers], Ltd.) Later printings are so indicated on the copyright page.

WESLEYAN UNIVERSITY PRESS The words "First Edition" must appear on the copyright page, where later printings are also indicated.

WEYBRIGHT & TALLEY, INC. Later printings are so indicated on the copyright page.

WHITE RABBIT PRESS Almost no books of this press went into later printings. The one known exception is Robert Duncan's *As Testimony*, where the second printing can be distinguished by the presence of illustrations.

WHITLESEY HOUSE Either the words "First Edition" will appear on the copyright page, or there will be no notice of later printings.

THE H. W. WILSON CO. The dates on the title and copyright pages must be identical. Later printings are also usually indicated on the copyright page.

WINGBOW PRESS The words "First Edition" or "First Printing" usually occur on the copyright page, where later printings are so indicated.

WORLD PUBLISHING CO. The words "First Printing" or "First Edition" must appear on the copyright page.

YALE UNIVERSITY PRESS Later printings are so indicated on the copyright page.

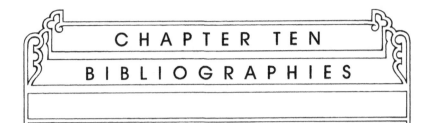

CHAPTER TEN

BIBLIOGRAPHIES

Several times in this book I have recommended that collectors refer to author bibliographies in identifying first editions, as well as for other information. A great many bibliographies now exist for twentieth-century authors, although, sad to say, only a small handful of them are really accurate. Some, because of sketchiness or errors, are not even useful. Particularly noteworthy for their excellence are those compiled for Ashbery, Auden, Cummings, Eliot, Frost, Hemingway, James, Kerouac, Lawrence, Pound, the Sitwells, Stevens, Wilder, William Carlos Williams, and Virginia Woolf. I will immodestly include my own bibliography of Gertrude Stein in this list. There are, unfortunately, many important twentieth-century authors who are widely collected, but who have not as yet received the attention of a serious or competent bibliographer. And there are also a great many so-called bibliographies that need total revision to be of any real use. Bibliography is a field with a great many opportunities for good, solid work to be done. This chapter lists all the bibliographies currently available for modern authors. I begin with a handful of general works that comprise, in the main, short title checklists of a large number of authors in one or more volumes. Of these, the most useful single volume ever produced in the United States for the aid of collectors is Merle Johnson's *American First Editions*, which first appeared in 1929 and was periodically revised and updated in 1932, 1936, and 1942, the latter two under the aegis of Jacob Blanck following Johnson's death in the early thirties. (Curiously there seems never to have been a comparable British volume.) All editions of Johnson have long been out of print, including a small pocket format reprint of the 1942 edition which appeared in 1962. This was quickly sold out and is much sought after. Many dealers will have a copy that you can consult, and (if it hasn't been stolen) most major libraries usually have one on their reference shelf. The book covers the first editions of approximately two hundred American authors, beginning with the post-Revolutionary literary pioneers such as Robert Bird, Hugh Henry Brackenridge, and Philip Freneau, proceeding through all the nineteenth-century giants, and ending by doing yeoman service on the moderns who rose to prominence in the first three decades of this century. While there are, of course, some curious omissions, and even more curious deletions (the 1942 edition dropped Hart Crane, Gertrude Stein, and Ezra Pound "as there is not sufficient interest in these authors to continue listing them"), there are very few errors of fact. *American First Editions* is still one of the most reliable volumes for quick, handy reference.

Blanck did not issue another revision of Johnson for the simple reason that he had become involved in a far more extensive project—the multivolume definitive *Bibliography of American Literature*, commonly referred to by its initials, "the BAL," or sometimes by its editor's name, "Blanck." Mammoth in scope, it proposes to cover in minute detail every known printing of every book or pamphlet by any American author of any degree of literary merit who died prior to 1930. It has never been revealed just how the relative degrees of "literary merit" were ascertained, or just why 1920 was chosen as a cutoff date. In any event, if the project has any fault, it is on the side of generosity, since it includes some extremely minor authors, as well as all those of importance and collector interest. The volumes have appeared irregularly at intervals of a few years. So far six volumes have

been published, covering authors whose names begin with
the letters *A* through *O*. Volume Six, published in 1973,
is the last one to have benefited from the guidance of Jacob
Blanck, who, alas, has since died. The series will be continued nonetheless, under the general direction of the Yale
University Press, but the loss of its master spirit has dealt
it a staggering blow.

Each entry in the BAL is numbered, and it has already become standard practice for knowledgeable dealers to
identify an item in their catalogs, particularly nineteenth-
century titles, by listing its BAL number. This avoids any
possible confusion among collectors or librarians about
which edition is being offered. The series is rather costly for
a private collector to own and, when completed, will take
up nearly as much space as the unabridged *Oxford English
Dictionary*. Nor is it particularly geared for collectors of
twentieth-century material, because of its cutoff date. But
it is invaluable for authors who straddle the last century
and this, and it is without doubt the definitive work for
eighteenth- and nineteenth-century American authors.

Unfortunately, there is nothing, at least as yet, that
takes the place of the BAL for British authors. I. Brussell's
pioneering work *Anglo-American First Editions* is invaluable in the tricky field of twentieth-century authors who
published on both sides of the Atlantic. Beginning with the
first full-fledged American expatriate author, Henry James,
the problem of whether the British or the American edition
of a title takes precedence has been a constant plague and
a problem for collectors. The old maxim of "follow the
flag" (i.e., collect only the books published in the native land
of the author) is rather a Procrustean solution and often
flies in the face of facts. And it is also difficult to apply in the
case of such authors as Henry James, T. S. Eliot, and W. H.
Auden, who changed their citizenship in mid-life. While a
rough rule of thumb will sometimes apply—the books of

Aldous Huxley, W. H. Auden, and Christopher Isherwood usually appeared first in the countries where they were living at the time of publication—this was not always true. From 1940 onward, the American editions of books by that trio are firsts, whereas the British editions are the true firsts for books published prior to that date. Of course, exceptions are numerous, and the only safe method is to check author bibliographies. Fortunately, the revised edition of the bibliography of W. H. Auden, compiled by B. C. Bloomfield and Edward Mendelson, is meticulous in detail and totally accurate, one of the best author bibliographies ever published. On the other hand, there has been no good bibliography of Huxley, and the Isherwood bibliography, while listing both British and American editions, fails to make plain which is the proper first. Luckily, work is being done on a revised and fully detailed study of Isherwood, and it is to be hoped that its publication will fill one of the major gaps in twentieth-century bibliography.

There are three other helpful guides which must be used with extreme caution. The least dubious is the first, Van Allen Bradley's *Handbook of Values*, now in its third edition, with many of the errors that marred the two previous editions removed. It does not attempt to be a bibliography as such, concentrating as it does on current market prices for an extremely large number of books that are popular with collectors, and not only in the literary field. Such an undertaking cannot go into much detail, and book descriptions are necessarily perfunctory. But it does list specific "points" and usually gives prices for both first and second issue varieties. Its main fault, aside from omissions, is the fact that the prices have been compiled from dealers' catalogs and auction records, with no apparent effort to edit out patently ridiculous prices. Many a dealer will put an outrageous price on an item in his catalog, either out of ignorance or out of greed, or perhaps from a combination of both.

Such a figure does not by any means represent a true value, and the book in all probability will not find a buyer at that price, at least not for many years to come. Thus one must read Bradley's quotations with awareness of the fact that the reported prices are simply a cross-section of dealers' asking prices. Under the circumstances there are bound to be occasional bloopers, both high and low. But in the main it is fairly accurate, and will tell you at least what sort of ball park you are in with regards to any given title—that is, whether it is a book likely to cost $50 or $500. Incidentally, to prevent his book from becoming unwieldy and bulky, Bradley does not list any title valued at less than $25. However, the absence of a listing does not mean per se that the title is worth less than $25: it can mean merely that the book is so scarce that no copy has been offered in the past few years, and there is, accordingly, no price on record. For example, Gertrude Stein's *Is Dead* was privately issued in an edition of only twenty-five copies. No copy has appeared at auction or in a dealer's catalog, at least not for the past twenty years, and one would easily bring several hundred dollars, regardless of the fact that Bradley does not list it.

The second book referred to is Gary Lepper's *A Bibliographical Introduction to Seventy-five Modern American Authors*. Despite its title, this work contains virtually no bibliographic data whatever, the contents comprising the briefest of checklists of the authors covered. It is a pioneering work, bringing to light a great many fugitive pamphlets and broadsides whose existence was known to very few dealers or collectors, and does provide the only checklists thus far available for a great many contemporary authors. But unfortunately it is so badly flawed with errors of fact that it is dangerous for a beginner to use. I have counted more than two hundred such errors, including listings of books that were never published and of pages removed from magazines described as "broadsides," to say nothing of incorrect priorities being given in dozens of cases where a book was published in more than one format. Lepper's is a book that can be used with safety only with outside guidance, either from a knowledgeable dealer or from a veteran collector who already knows the intricacies of the books being described.

The third reference guide is somewhat similar—Gale Research's *First Printings of American Authors*. It is more ambitious than Lepper in that it includes nearly five times as many authors, but like Lepper, it gives only the scantiest information, with no mention of dust jackets. Also like Lepper, it is badly flawed with errors of fact. In some cases it reprints Lepper's mistakes, thereby reproducing and reinforcing many glaring and obvious errors. The book is weirdly arranged—not by alphabet but by the order in which the editors received the various lists from the compilers, often necessitating a search through four cumbersome volumes, all too large to fit upright on shelves. *First Printings* is also overloaded with many virtually unknown authors as well as a great many of dubious merit. Once again, as with Lepper, it is not a book a beginning collector can rely on. But it does provide checklists, inaccurate though some of them may be, for many authors about whom no other publication information is available. It has one feature possessed by no other reference work in this field: a generous number of reproductions of title pages for each author covered. This is a great aid in identifying proper editions.

LIST OF TWENTIETH-CENTURY AUTHOR BIBLIOGRAPHIES

Æ [GEORGE RUSSELL]. *Printed Writings by George Russell (Æ): A Bibliography with Some Notes on His Pictures and Portraits* compiled by Alan Denson. Northwestern University Press, Evanston, Ill., 1961. 255 pp.

AGEE, JAMES.   "A Bibliography of the Works of James Agee" by
Genevieve Fabre. *Bulletin of Bibliography* Vol. 24, No. 7
(May–Aug. 1965), pp. 145–48, 163–66.

ALDINGTON, RICHARD.   *A Bibliography of the Works of Richard
Aldington from 1915 to 1948* by Alister Kershaw. Introduction by Richard Aldington. The Quadrant Press, London,
1950.   57 pp.

ALGREN, NELSON.   *Nelson Algren: A Checklist* compiled by Kenneth G. McCollum. Introduction by Studs Terkel. Gale Research Company, Detroit, 1973.   107 pp.

ANDERSON, MAXWELL.   *A Catalog of the Maxwell Anderson Collection at the University of Texas* by Laurence G. Avery.
University of Texas, Austin, 1968.   175 pp.

ANDERSON, SHERWOOD.   *Sherwood Anderson: A Bibliography*
compiled by Eugene P. Sheehy and Kenneth Lohf. The Talisman Press, Los Gatos, Calif., 1960. (Reprinted by H. P.
Kraus, New York, 1968.)   125 pp.

ASHBERY, JOHN.   *John Ashbery: A Comprehensive Bibliography
Including His Art Criticism and with Selected Notes from
Unpublished Materials* by David Kermani. Foreword by
John Ashbery. Garland Publishing, Inc., New York & Lon-
don, 1976.   244 pp.

AUDEN, W. H.   *W. H. Auden: A Bibliography 1924–1969* by B. C.
Bloomfield and Edward Mendelson. Second edition. University Press of Virginia, Charlottesville, 1972.   420 pp.

AUERHAHN PRESS, THE.   *A Bibliography of the Auerhahn Press &
Its Successor Dave Haselwood Books*. Poltroon Press, Berkeley, 1976.   89 pp.

BALDWIN, JAMES.   *James Baldwin: A Checklist 1963–1967* by
Fred L. Standley. *Bulletin of Bibliography* Vol. 25, No. 6
(May–Aug. 1968), pp. 135–37.

BARNES, DJUNA.   *Djuna Barnes: A Bibliography* by Douglas Mes-
serli. David Lewis, New York, 1976.   131 pp.

BARTH, JOHN.   *John Barth: A Descriptive Primary and Annotated Secondary Bibliography Including a Descriptive Cata-*

log of Manuscript Holdings in United States Libraries by Joseph Weixlman. Garland Publishing, Inc., New York & London, 1976. 214 pp.

BARTHELME, DONALD. *Donald Barthelme: A Comprehensive Bibliography and Annotated Secondary Checklist* by Jerome Klinkowitz, Asa Pieratt, and Robert Murray Davis. Archon Books, Hamden, Conn., 1977. 128 pp.

BECKETT, SAMUEL. *Samuel Beckett—His Works and His Critics: An Essay in Bibliography* by Raymond Federman and John Fletcher. University of California Press, Berkeley/Los Angeles/London, 1979. 383 pp.

BEERBOHM, MAX. *A Bibliography of the Works of Max Beerbohm* by A. E. Gallatin and L. M. Oliver. Harvard University Press, Cambridge, 1952. 60 pp.
Sir Max Beerbohm, Man and Writer: A Critical Analysis with a Brief Life and a Bibliography by J. G. Riewald. Martinus Nijhoff, The Hague, 1955. Bibliography, pp. 213–343.

BELLOW, SAUL. *Saul Bellow–His Works and His Critics: An Annotated International Bibliography* by Marianne Nault. Garland Publishing Inc., New York & London, 1977. 191 pp.

BENNETT, ARNOLD. *Arnold Bennett: An Annotated Bibliography 1887–1932* by Anita Miller. Garland Publishing, Inc., New York & London, 1977. 787 pp.

BERRYMANN JOHN. *John Berryman: A Checklist* compiled by Richard J. Kelly. Foreword by William Meredith. Introduction by Michael Berryhill. Scarecrow Press, Inc., Metuchen, N.J., 1972. 105 pp.
John Berryman: A Descriptive Bibliography by Ernest C. Stefanik, Jr. University of Pittsburgh Press, Pittsburgh, 1974. 285 pp.

BISHOP, ELIZABETH. *A Bibliography of Elizabeth Bishop* by Candace MacMahon. University Press of Virginia, Charlottesville, 1980. Forthcoming.

BLACK SPARROW PRESS, THE. *A Checklist of the First One Hundred Publications of the Black Sparrow Press* by Seamus

Cooney. With 30 Passing Remarks by Robert Kelly. Black Sparrow Press, Los Angeles, 1971.   39 pp.

BLACK SUN PRESS, THE.   *A Bibliography of the Black Sun Press* by George Robert Minkoff. Introduction by Caresse Crosby. G. R. Minkoff, Great Neck, N.Y., 1970.   60 pp.

BLUNDEN, EDMUND.   *A Bibliography of Edmund Blunden* by B. J. Kirkpatrick. Clarendon Press, Oxford, 1979.   725 pp.

BOGAN, LOUISE.   *Louise Bogan: A Woman's Words* by William Jay Smith. Library of Congress, Washington, D.C., 1971. 81 pp.

BOTTEGHE OSCURE.   *Botteghe Oscure Index* (with an appendix *Index of Commerce 1949–1960*) compiled by several hands. Introduction by Archibald MacLeish. Wesleyan University Press, Middletown, Conn., 1964.   36 pp.

BRADBURY, RAY.   *The Ray Bradbury Companion* by William F. Nolan. Gale Research, Detroit, 1975.   339 pp.

BROOKE, RUPERT.   *A Bibliography of Rupert Brooke* compiled by Geoffrey Keynes. Third edition, revised. Rupert Hart-Davis, London, 1964.   158 pp.

BUKOWSKI, CHARLES.   *A Bibliography of Charles Bukowski* by Sanford Dorbin. Black Sparrow Press, Los Angeles, 1969. 93 pp.

BUNTING, BASIL.   *Basil Bunting: A Bibliography of Works and Criticism* by Roger Guedalla. Norwood Editions, Norwood, Pa., 1973.   183 pp.

BURROUGHS, WILLIAM S.   *William S. Burroughs: An Annotated Bibliography of His Works and Criticism* by Michael B. Goodman. Garland Publishing, Inc., New York & London, 1975.   96 pp.
William S. Burroughs: A Bibliography, 1953–73 compiled by Joe Maynard and Barry Miles. Bibliographical Society of the University of Virginia, Charlottesville, 1978.   242 pp.

CABELL, JAMES BRANCH.   *James Branch Cabell: A Revised Bibliography* by I. R. Brussel. The Centaur Bookshop, Philadelphia, 1932.   133 pp.

James Branch Cabell: A Bibliography of His Writings, Biography, and Criticism by Frances Joan Brewer. Foreword by James Branch Cabell. University Press of Virginia, Charlottesville, 1957. 206 pp.

CAPOTE, TRUMAN. *Truman Capote: A Checklist* by Kenneth Starosciak. Kenneth Starosciak Publisher, New Brighton, Minn., 1974. 29 pp.

CARY, JOYCE. *The Books of Joyce Cary: A Preliminary Bibliography of English and American Editions* by James B. Meriwether. Offprint from the University of Texas *Studies in Literature and Language* Vol. I, No. 2 (Summer 1959). 12 pp.

CATHER, WILLA. *Willa Cather: A Checklist of Her Published Writings* compiled by JoAnna Lathrop. University of Nebraska Press, Lincoln, 1975. 118 pp.

CHANDLER, RAYMOND. *Raymond Chandler: A Checklist.* Kent State University Press, Kent, Ohio, 1968.
Raymond Chandler: A Descriptive Bibliography by Matthew J. Bruccoli. University of Pittsburgh Press, Pittsburgh, 1979. 120 pp.

CHESTERSON, G. K. *G. K. Chesterton: A Bibliography* by John Sullivan. University of London Press, London, 1958. 208 pp.
Chesterton Continued: A Bibliographical Supplement by John Sullivan. Together with some uncollected prose and verse by G. K. Chesterton. University of London Press, London, 1968. 120 pp.

CIARDI, JOHN. *John Ciardi: A Bibliography* by William White. Note by John Ciardi. Wayne State University Press, Detroit, 1959. 65 pp.

CLARK, WALTER VAN TILBURG. "Walter van Tilburg Clark: A Bibliography" by Richard Etulain. *The South Dakota Review*, Vol. 3, No. 1 (Autumn 1965), pp. 73–77.

CONRAD, JOSEPH. *A Bibliography of the Writings of Joseph Conrad (1895–1921)* by Thomas J. Wise. Printed for private circulation, London, 1921. 126 pp.

Joseph Conrad at Mid-Century: Editions and Studies, 1895–1955 by Kenneth A. Lohf and Eugene P. Sheehy. University of Minnesota Press, Minneapolis, 1957.

COPPARD, A. E.   *The Writings of Alfred Edgar Coppard: A Bibliography* by Jacob Schwartz. Foreword and notes by A. E. Coppard. The Ulysses Bookshop, London, 1931.   73 pp.

CORSO, GREGORY.   *A Bibliography of Works by Gregory Corso 1954–1965* compiled by Robert A. Wilson. The Phoenix Book Shop, New York, 1966.   40 pp.

CORVO, BARON.   *A Bibliography of Frederick Rolfe, Baron Corvo* by Cecil Woolf. Second edition, revised and enlarged. Rupert Hart-Davis, London, 1972.   213 pp.

COZZENS, JAMES GOULD.   *James Gould Cozzens: A Checklist* compiled by James B. Meriwether. Gale Research Company, Detroit, 1972.   88 pp.

CRANE, HART.   *Hart Crane: A Descriptive Bibliography* by Joseph Schwartz and Robert C. Schweik. University of Pittsburgh Press, Pittsburgh, 1972.   168 pp.

CRANE, STEPHEN.   *Stephen Crane: A Bibliography* by Ames W. Williams & Vincent Starrett. John Valentine, Glendale, Calif., 1948.   161 pp.

CREELEY, ROBERT.   *Robert Creeley: An Inventory, 1945–1970* by Mary Novik. Foreword by Robert Creeley. Kent State University Press, Kent, Ohio, 1973.   210 pp.

CROWLEY, ALEISTER.   *Aleister Crowley: The Man the Mage the Poet* by C. R. Cammell. Richards Press, London, 1951.   Bibliography, pp. 207–18.

CULLEN, COUNTÉE.   *A Bio-Bibliography of Countée P. Cullen 1903–1946* by Margaret Perry. Foreword by Don M. Wolfe. Greenwood Publishing Corp., Westport, Conn., 1971.   134 pp.

CUMMINGS, E. E.   *E. E. Cummings: A Bibliography* by George J. Firmage. Wesleyan University Press, Middletown, Conn., 1960.   129 pp.

CUMMINGTON PRESS.   "The Cummington Press" by Mary L. Richmond. *Books at Iowa* No. 7 (Nov. 1967), pp. 9–31.

H. D. [HILDA DOOLITTLE]   "H. D.: A Preliminary Checklist" by Jackson R. Bryer and Pamela Roblyer. Pp. 632–75 in the special H. D. issue of *Contemporary Literature*, Vol. 10, No. 4 (Autumn 1969), University of Wisconsin Press, Madison.

DAHLBERG, EDWARD.   *A Bibliography of Edward Dahlberg* by Harold Billings. Introduction by Edward Dahlberg. Humanities Research Center, University of Texas at Austin, 1971. 22 pp.

DAY-LEWIS, C.   *Day-Lewis—The Poet Laureate: A Bibliography* compiled by Geoffrey Handley-Taylor and Timothy d'Arch Smith. Letter of introduction by W. H. Auden. St. James Press, Chicago & London, 1968.   42 pp.

DICKEY, JAMES.   *James Dickey—The Critic As Poet: An Annotated Bibliography with an Introductory Essay* by Eileen Glancy. Whitston Publishing Co., Inc., Troy, N.Y., 1971. 107 pp.
James Dickey: A Checklist compiled by Franklin Ashley. Introduction by James Dickey. Gale Research Company, Detroit, 1972.   98 pp.

DINESEN, ISAK.   *Isak Dinesen—Karen Blixen: A Bibliography* by Liselotte Henriksen. Gylendal, Cophenhagen, 1977.   224 pp.

DORN, ED.   *A Bibliography of Ed Dorn* compiled by David Streeter. The Phoenix Book Shop, New York, 1973.   64 pp.

DOS PASSOS, JOHN.   *A Bibliography of John Dos Passos* by Jack Potter. Introduction by John Dos Passos. Normandie House, Chicago, 1950.   95 pp.

DOUGLAS, NORMAN.   *A Bibliography of the Writings of Norman Douglas* by Edward D. McDonald. Notes by Norman Douglas. The Centaur Bookshop, Philadelphia, 1927.   165 pp.
A Bibliography of Norman Douglas by Cecil Woolf. Rupert Hart-Davis, London, 1954.   201 pp.

DOYLE, ARTHUR CONAN.   *A Bibliography of First Appearances of the Writings of A. Conan Doyle* by Benny R. Reece. Furman University, Greenville, S.C., 1975.   48 pp.

DREISER, THEODORE. *Dreiserana: A Book About His Books* by Vrest Orton. Chocorua Bibliographies, New York, 1929. 84 pp.
Theodore Dreiser: A Checklist by Hugh C. Atkinson. Kent State University Press, Kent, Ohio, 1971. 104 pp.

DRINKWATER, JOHN. *John Drinkwater: A Comprehensive Bibliography of His Works* by Michael Pearce. Garland Publishing, Inc., New York & London, 1977. 157 pp.

DUBOIS, W. E. B. *W. E. B. Dubois: A Bibliography of His Published Writings* by Paul G. Partington. Paul G. Partington, Whittier, Calif., 1977. 202 pp.

DURRELL, LAWRENCE. *Lawrence Durrell: A Study* by G. S. Fraser. with a Bibliography by Alan G. Thomas. Faber & Faber, London, 1968. Revised edition, 1973. 256 pp.

EBERHART, RICHARD. *Richard Eberhart—The Progress of an American Poet* by Joel Roache. Oxford University Press, New York, 1971. Bibliography, pp. 263–93.

EIGNER, LARRY. *A Bibliography of Works by Larry Eigner 1937–1969* compiled by Andrea Wyatt. Oyez, Berkeley, 1970. 82 pp.

ELIOT, T. S. *T. S. Eliot: A Bibliography—A Revised and Extended Edition* by Donald Gallup. Harcourt, Brace & World, New York, 1969. 414 pp.
Checklist of T. S. Eliot compiled by Bradley Gunter. Charles E. Merrill Publishing Company, Columbus, Ohio, 1970. 43 pp.

ELLISON, RALPH. "A Ralph Waldo Ellison Bibliography" by R. S. Lillard. *The American Book Collector* Vol. 19, No. 3 (Nov. 1968), pp. 18–22. The Nov./Dec. 1969 issue (Vol. 20, No. 3) contains an "Addendum" by Carol Polsgrove, pp. 11–12.

EVERSON, WILLIAM. *William Everson: A Descriptive Bibliography 1934–1976* by Lee Bartlett and Allen Campo. Scarecrow Press, Metuchen, N.J., & London, 1977. 119 pp. (For a large part of his writing career Everson published under his clerical name, Brother Antoninus.)

FAULKNER, WILLIAM. *"Man Working," 1919–1962 William Faulkner* compiled by Linton Massey. Introduction by John Cook Wyllie. Bibliographical Society of the University of Virginia, Charlottesville, 1968. 249 pp.
Each in Its Ordered Place: A Faulkner Collector's Notebook by Carl Petersen. Ardis, Ann Arbor, 1975. 311 pp.

FIRBANK, RONALD. *A Bibliography of Ronald Firbank* by Miriam Benkowitz. Rupert Hart-Davis, London, 1963. 103 pp.

FITZGERALD, F. SCOTT. *F. Scott Fitzgerald: A Descriptive Bibliography* by Matthew J. Bruccoli. University of Pittsburgh Press, Pittsburgh, 1972. 369 pp.

FORD, FORD MADOX. *Ford Madox Ford 1873–1939: A Bibliography of Works and Criticism* by David Dow Harvey. Princeton University Press, Princeton, 1962. 633 pp.

FORD, JESSE HILL. *Jesse Hill Ford: An Annotated Checklist of His Published Works and of His Papers* by Helen White. Memphis State University, Memphis, Tenn., 1974. 55 pp.

FORSTER, E. M. *A Bibliography of E. M. Forster* by B. J. Kirkpatrick. Foreword by E. M. Forster. Second, revised edition. Rupert Hart-Davis, London, 1968. 205 pp.

FROST, ROBERT. *Robert Frost: A Bibliography* by W. B. Shubrick Clymer and Charles Green. Foreword by David Lambuth. Jones Library, Inc., Amherst, Mass., 1937. 158 pp.
Robert Frost—A Descriptive Catalogue of Books and Manuscripts in the Clifton Waller Barrett Library, University of Virginia compiled by Joan St. C. Crane. University Press of Virginia, Charlottesville, 1974. 280 pp.

GALSWORTHY, JOHN. *A Bibliography of the Works of John Galsworthy* by E. V. Marrot. Elkin Matthews & Marrot, London & New York, 1928. 252 pp.

GEHENNA PRESS. *A Bibliography of the Gehenna Press 1942–1975* by Stephen Brook. J. P. Dwyer, Northampton, Mass., 1976. 77 pp.

GINSBERG, ALLEN. *A Bibliography of Works by Allen Ginsberg October 1943 to July 1, 1967* compiled by George Dowden.

Foreword by Allen Ginsberg. City Lights Books, San Francisco, 1971. 343 pp.

GLASGOW, ELLEN. *Ellen Glasgow: A Bibliography* by William W. Kelly. Bibliographical Society of Virginia, University Press of Virginia, Charlottesville, 1964. 330 pp.

GOODMAN, PAUL. *Adam and His Work: A Bibliography of Sources by and About Paul Goodman* by Tom Nicely. Metuchen, London, 1979. 336 pp.

GOREY, EDWARD. "Edward Gorey: An American Gothic" by Thomas M. McDade. *American Book Collector* Vol. 21, No. 7 (May 1971), pp. 12–17.

GRAVES, ROBERT. *A Bibliography of Works by Robert Graves* by Fred H. Higginson. Nicholas Vane, London, 1966. 328 pp.

GREENE, GRAHAM. *The Portable Graham Greene.* Viking, New York, 1973. Bibliographic notes, pp. xix–xxiii.

GUNN, THOM. *Thom Gunn—A Bibliography 1940–1978* by J. W. C. Hagstrom and George Bixby. Bertram Rota, Ltd., London, 1979.

HAGGARD, SIR H. RIDER. *A Bibliography of the Writings of Sir Rider Haggard* by George L. McKay. The Bookman's Journal, London, 1930. 110 pp.
A Bibliography of the Works of Sir Henry Rider Haggard 1856–1929 by J. F. Scott. Elkin-Mathews, Ltd. Takeley, London, 1947. 258 pp.

HAMMETT, DASHIELL. *A List of the Original Appearances of Dashiell Hammett's Magazine Work* assembled by E. H. Mundell. Kent State University Press, Kent, Ohio, 1968. 52 pp.
Dashiell Hammett: A Descriptive Bibliography by Richard Layman. University of Pittsburgh Press, Pittsburgh, 1979. 162 pp.

HARDY, THOMAS. *Thomas Hardy: A Bibliographical Study* by Richard Little Purdy. Oxford University Press (Geoffrey Cumberlege), London & New York, 1954. 387 pp.

HAWKES, JOHN. *Three Contemporary Novelists: An Annotated*

Bibliography of Works by and about John Hawkes, Joseph Heller, and Thomas Pynchon by Robert M. Scotto. Garland Publishing, Inc., New York & London, 1977. 97 pp.

HEARN, LAFCADIO. *Lafcadio Hearn: A Bibliography of His Writings* by P. D. and Ione Perkins. Introduction by Sanki Ichikawa. Houghton-Mifflin, New York & Boston, 1934. 444 pp.

HELLER, JOSEPH. (*See* Hawkes, John.)

HELLMAN, LILLIAN. *The Lillian Hellman Collection at the University of Texas*. Humanities Research Division, Austin, 1966. 167 pp.

HEMINGWAY, ERNEST. *A Bibliography of the Works of Ernest Hemingway* by Louis Henry Cohn. Random House, New York, 1931. 116 pp.

A Hemingway Checklist by Lee Samuels. Charles Scribner's Sons, New York, 1951. 64 pp.

Ernest Hemingway: A Comprehensive Bibliography by Audre Hanneman. Princeton University Press, Princeton, 1967. 568 pp.

Supplement to Ernest Hemingway: A Comprehensive Bibliography by Audre Hanneman. Princeton University Press, Princeton, 1975. 393 pp.

HIMES, CHESTER. "Chester Himes's Published Work: A Tentative Checklist" by Michel Fabre. *Black World* Vol. 21, No. 5 (March 1972), pp. 76–78.

HOFFMAN, DANIEL. *Daniel Hoffman: A Comprehensive Bibliography* by Michael Lowe. Norwood Editions, Norwood, Pa., 1973. 64 pp.

HOGARTH PRESS. *A Checklist of the Hogarth Press with a Short History of the Press by Mary E. Gaither* compiled by J. Howard Woolmer. Woolmer & Brotherson, Ltd., Andes, N.Y., 1976. 177 pp.

HOURS PRESS, THE. "The Hours Press Restrospect Catalogue Commentary" by Nancy Cunard. *The Book Collector* Vol. 13, No. 4 (Winter 1964), pp. 492–96.

HOUSMAN, A. E. *A. E. Housman: An Annotated Hand-List* by

John Carter and John Sparrow. Rupert Hart-Davis, London, 1952. 54 pp.

HUDSON, W. H. *A Bibliography of the Writings of W. H. Hudson* by G. F. Wilson. The Bookman's Journal, London, 1922. 69 pp.

W. H. Hudson: A Bibliography by John R. Payne. Foreword by Alfred A. Knopf. Archon Books, Dawson, Hamden, Conn., 1977. 248 pp.

HUGHES, LANGSTON. *A Bio-Bibliography of Langston Hughes 1902–1967* by Donald C. Dickinson. Preface by Arna Bontemps. Archon Books, Hamden, Conn., 1967. 267 pp.

HUXLEY, ALDOUS. *Bibliographies of the First Editions of A. L. and T. F. Powys* compiled by P. H. Muir and B. van Thal. Dulau & Co., Ltd., London, 1927. 61 pp.

Aldous Huxley: A Bibliography 1916–1959 by Claire John Eschelbach and Joyce Lee Shober. University of California Press, Berkeley & Los Angeles, 1961. 150 pp.

ISHERWOOD, CHRISTOPHER. *Christopher Isherwood. A Bibliography 1923–1967* by Selmer Westby and Clayton M. Brown. California State College at Los Angeles Foundation, Los Angeles, 1968. 51 pp.

JAMES, HENRY. *A Bibliography of Henry James* by Leon Edel and Dan H. Laurence. Second edition, revised. Rupert Hart-Davis, London, 1961. 427 pp.

JARGON PRESS. *The Jargon Idea* by Millicent Bell. Brown University, Providence, R.I., 1963. Offprinted from *Books at Brown* Vol. XIX (May 1963). 12 pp.

The Jargon Society 1951–1975. The Book Organization, Millerton, N.Y., 1976. 12 pp.

A Jargon Society Checklist by J. M. Edelstein. Books and Company, New York, 1979. 11 pp.

JARRELL, RANDALL. *Randall Jarrell: A Bibliography* by Charles M. Adams. University of North Carolina Press, Chapel Hill, 1958. 72 pp.

Supplement to the above, in *Analecta* Magazine, Spring 1961, Vol. I, pp. 49–56.

JEFFERS, ROBINSON. *A Bibliography of the Works of Robinson Jeffers* by S. S. Alberts. 1933. Reprinted in 1966 by Cultural History Research, Inc., Rye, N.Y. 262 pp.

JONES, DAVID. *David Jones: An Annotated Bibliography and Guide to Research* by Samuel Rees. Garland Publishing, Inc., New York & London, 1977. 97 pp.

JONES, JAMES. *James Jones: A Checklist* compiled by John R. Hopkins. Foreword by James Jones. Gale Research Company, Detroit, 1974. 67 pp.

JONES, LEROI. *LeRoi Jones (Imamu Amiri Baraka): A Checklist of Works by and about Him* by Letitia Dace. The Nether Press, London, 1971. 196 pp.

JOYCE, JAMES. *A Bibliography of James Joyce (1880–1941)* by John J. Slocum and Herbert Cahoon. Yale University Press, New Haven, 1953. 195 pp.

KEROUAC, JACK. *Jack Kerouac: A Bibliography 1939–1975* compiled by Ann Charters. Revised edition. The Phoenix Book Shop, New York, 1975. 136 pp.

KIPLING, RUDYARD. *Bibliography of the Works of Rudyard Kipling* by Flora V. Livingston. Edgar H. Wells & Co., New York, 1927. 523 pp.
Rudyard Kipling: A Bibliographical Catalogue by James M. Stewart. Edited by A. W. Yeats. Dalhousie University Press, Halifax, and University Press of Toronto, Toronto, 1959. 673 pp.

LARDNER, RING. *Ring W. Lardner: A Descriptive Bibliography* by Matthew Bruccoli and Richard Layman. University of Pittsburgh Press, Pittsburgh, 1976. 424 pp.

LAWRENCE, D. H. *A Bibliography of D. H. Lawrence* by Warren Roberts. Rupert Hart-Davis, London, 1963. 399 pp.
The Frieda Lawrence Collection of D. H. Lawrence Manuscripts: A Descriptive Bibliography by E. W. Tedlock,

Jr. University of New Mexico Press, Albuquerque, 1948. 333 pp.

LAWRENCE, T. E.   *T. E. Lawrence: A Bibliography* by Jeffrey Meyers. Garland Publishing, Inc., New York & London, 1974.   48 pp.

LESSING, DORIS.   *Doris Lessing: A Checklist of Primary and Secondary Sources* by Selma R. Burkom and Margaret Williams. Whitston Publishing Co., Inc., Troy, N.Y., 1973.   88 pp.

LEVERTOV, DENISE.   *A Bibliography of Denise Levertov* compiled by Robert A. Wilson. The Phoenix Book Shop, New York, 1972.   98 pp.

LEWIS, ALUN.   *Alun Lewis 1915–1944: Biographical Note, Original Works and Contributions to Periodicals, Critical Articles.* Welsh Arts Council, Adran Llenyddiaeth, 1968.   7 pp.

LEWIS, WYNDHAM.   *Wyndham Lewis: A Descriptive Bibliography* by Omar S. Pound and Phillip Grover. Archon Books, Dawson, Hamden, Conn., 1978.   198 pp.
A Bibliography of the Writings of Wyndham Lewis by Bradford Morrow and Bernard Lafourcade. Introduction by Hugh Kenner. Black Sparrow Press, Santa Barbara, 1978.   373 pp.

LITTLE MAGAZINES.   *The Little Magazine: A History and a Bibliography* by Frederick J. Hoffman, Charles Allen, and Carolyn F. Ulrich. Princeton University Press, Princeton, 1946. 440 pp.
The Little Magazine in America: A Modern Documentary History edited by Elliott Anderson and Mary Kinzie. Pushcart, Yonkers, N.Y., 1978.   770 pp.

LONDON, JACK.   *Jack London: A Bibliography* compiled by Hensley C. Woodbridge, John London, and George H. Tweney. Talisman Press, Georgetown, Calif., 1966.   422 pp.

LORCA, FEDERICO GARCÍA.   "Federico García Lorca, 1899–1936: A Bibliography of His Works in English Translation" by Remigio Ugo Pane. *Bulletin of Bibliography and Dramatic Index*, Vol. 20, No. 3 Whole Number 184 (Sept.–Dec. 1950), pp. 71–75.

LOWELL, ROBERT. *The Achievement of Robert Lowell: 1939–1959* by Jerome Mazzaro. University of Detroit Press, Detroit, 1960. 41 pp.

LOWRY, MALCOLM. *A Malcolm Lowry Catalogue*, essays by Perle Epstein and Richard Hauer Costa. J. Howard Woolmer, New York, 1968. 64 pp.

MCALMON, ROBERT. *Robert McAlmon: Expatriate Publisher and Writer* by Robert E. Knoll. University of Nebraska Press, Lincoln, 1959. Contains "The Published Works of Robert McAlmon," pp. 85–89.

MCCARTHY, MARY. *Mary McCarthy: A Bibliography* by Sherli Evens Goldman. Harcourt, Brace & World, New York, 1968. 80 pp.

MCCLURE, MICHAEL. *A Catalogue of Works by Michael McClure 1956–1965* compiled by Marshall Clements. The Phoenix Book Shop, New York, 1965. 36 pp.

MCCULLERS, CARSON. "Carson McCullers, 1940–1956: A Selected Checklist" by Stanley Stewart. *Bulletin of Bibliography and Magazine Notes*, Vol. 22, No. 8 (Jan.–April 1959), pp. 182–85. Supplement in Vol. 24, No. 5 (Sept.–Dec. 1964) by Robert S. Phillips, pp. 113–16.

MACDONALD, ROSS. *Kenneth Millar/Ross MacDonald: A Checklist* compiled by Matthew J. Bruccoli. Introduction by Kenneth Millar. Gale Research Company, Detroit, 1971. 86 pp.

MACLEISH, ARCHIBALD. *A Catalogue of the First Editions of Archibald MacLeish* by Arthur Mizener. Yale University Library, New Haven, 1938. 30 pp.

MACNEICE, LOUIS. *A Bibliography of the Works of Louis MacNeice* by C. M. Armitage and Neil Clark. University of Alberta Press, Edmonton, 1973. 136 pp.

MALAMUD, BERNARD. *Bernard Malamud: An Annotated Checklist* by Rita Nathalie Kosofsky. Kent State University Press, Kent, Ohio, 1969. 63 pp.

MANSFIELD, KATHERINE. *The Critical Bibliography of Katherine Mansfield* by Ruth Elvish Mantz, M.A. Introductory Note by

John Middleton Murry. Originally published in 1930; reprinted by Burt Franklin, New York, 1968.   204 pp.

MASEFIELD, JOHN.   *John Masefield O.M.: A Bibliography* compiled by Geoffrey Handley-Taylor. The Cranbrook Tower Press, London, 1960.   96 pp.

MAUGHAM, W. SOMERSET.   *A Bibliography of the Works of W. Somerset Maugham* by Raymond Toole Stott. The University of Alberta Press, Edmonton, 1973.   320 pp.

MELTZER, DAVID.   *David Meltzer: A Sketch from Memory and Descriptive Checklist* by David Kherdian. Oyez, Berkeley, 1965.   9 pp.

MENCKEN, H. L.   *H. L. M.: The Mencken Bibliography* compiled by Betty Adler with the assistance of Jane Wilhelm. The Johns Hopkins Press, Baltimore, 1961.   367 pp.
H. L. M.: The Mencken Bibliography, A Ten-Year Supplement compiled by Betty Adler. Enoch Pratt Free Library, Baltimore, 1971.   84 pp.

MERRILL, JAMES.   *The Merrill Notebook: A Provisional Checklist* compiled by Mary Johnsen. In preparation.

MERTON, THOMAS.   *Thomas Merton: A Bibliography* compiled by Frank Dell' Isola. Farrar, Straus and Cudahy, New York, 1956.   116 pp.

MILLAY, EDNA ST. VINCENT.   *A Bibliography of the Works of Edna St. Vincent Millay with an Essay in Appreciation by Harold Lewis Cook, Introductions and Three Poems by Edna St. Vincent Millay* compiled by Karl Yost. Originally published in 1937; reprinted by Burt Franklin, New York, 1968, in his Bibliography and Reference Series No. 149.   248 pp.

MILLER, HENRY.   *Henry Miller: A Chronology and Bibliography* collected and published by Bern Porter, n.p., 1945.   36 pp.
Bibliography of Henry Miller edited by Thomas H. Moore. The Henry Miller Literary Society, Minneapolis, 1961.   32 pp. plus one page addendum leaf.
Henry Miller: An Informal Bibliography 1924–1960 by Esta Lou Riley. Fort Hays Studies—New Series Bibliography

Series No. 1, Fort Hays Kansas State College, Fort Hays, June 1961. 52 pp.

A Bibliography of Henry Miller 1945–1961 by Maxine Renken. Allan Swallow, The Swallow Pamphlets No. 12, Denver, 1962. 13 pp.

MOORE, GEORGE. *A Bibliography of George Moore* by Edwin Gilcher. Northern Illinois University Press, DeKalb, 1970. 274 pp.

MOORE, MARIANNE. *The Achievement of Marianne Moore: A Bibliography 1907–1957* compiled by Eugene Sheehy and Kenneth A. Lohf. New York Public Library, New York, 1958. 43 pp.

Marianne Moore: A Descriptive Bibliography by Craig S. Abbott. University of Pittsburgh Press, Pittsburgh, 1977. 265 pp.

MORLEY, CHRISTOPHER. *A Bibliography of Christopher Morley* by Alfred P. Lee. Doubleday, Doran and Company, Garden City, N.Y., 1935. 277 pp.

MUIR, EDWIN. *A Bibliography of the Writings of Edwin Muir* by E. W. Mellown. Alabama University Press, University, Ala., 1964. 139 pp.

MUMFORD, LEWIS. *Lewis Mumford: A Bibliography 1914–1970* by Elmer S. Newman. Introduction by Lewis Mumford. Harcourt Brace Jovanovich, New York, 1971. 167 pp.

MURDOCH, IRIS. "An Iris Murdoch Checklist" by R. L. Widmann. *Critique (Magazine) Studies in Modern Fiction,* Vol. X, No. 1 (1967), pp. 17–29.

NABOKOV, VLADIMIR. *Vladimir Nabokov Bibliographie des Gesamtwerkes* by Dieter E. Zimmer. Rowohlt Verlag, Hamburg, 1963. 50 pp. (In German)

Nabokov: A Bibliography by Andrew Field. McGraw-Hill Book Company, New York, 1973. 249 pp.

NATHAN, ROBERT. *A Checklist of First Editions.* Preface by Robert Nathan. Casanova, Inc., Milwaukee, n.d. 15 pp.

NEW YORKER, THE. *An Index to Literature in The New Yorker*

by Robert Owen Johnson. 3 vols. Scarecrow Press, Metuchen, N.J., 1969–71.

Vol. One covers 1925–1940 (Vols. I–XV)   543 pp.

Vol. Two covers 1940–1955 (Vols. XVI–XXX)   477 pp.

Vol. Three covers 1955–1970 (Vols. XXXI–XLV   523 pp.

NEWTON, A. E.   *A. Edward Newton: A Collection of His Works* edited by Robert D. Fleck. Oak Knoll Books, Newark, Del., 1977.   38 pp.

NIN, ANAIS.   *Anais Nin: A Bibliography* by Benjamin Franklin V. Kent State University Press, Kent, Ohio, 1973.   115 pp.

O'CONNOR, FLANNERY.   "Flannery O'Connor: A Bibliography" by Joan T. Brittain. *Bulletin of Bibliography* Vol. 25 No. 4 (Sept.–Dec. 1967), pp. 98–100. Continued in Vol. 25 No. 5 (Jan.–Apr. 1968), pp. 123–24.

O'FLAHERTY, LIAM.   *Checklist of Twentieth Century Authors: First Series*, pp. 12–13. Casanova Booksellers, Milwaukee, 1931.

O'HARA, JOHN.   *John O'Hara: A Checklist* compiled by Matthew Bruccoli. Random House, New York, 1972.   136 pp.

OLSON, CHARLES.   *A Bibliography of Works by Charles Olson* compiled by George Butterick and Charles Glover. The Phoenix Book Shop, New York, 1967.   90 pp.

OLYMPIA PRESS.   *The Olympia Press Paris: 1953–1965. A Handlist* by P. J. Kearney, London, 1975.   34 pp.

O'NEILL, EUGENE.   *A Bibliography of the Works of Eugene O'Neill together with the Collected Poems of Eugene O'Neill* compiled and edited by Ralph Sanborn and Barrett H. Clark. Random House, New York, 1931; reprinted by Benjamin Blom, New York, 1965.   171 pp.

Eugene O'Neill: A Descriptive Bibliography by Jennifer McCabe Atkinson. University of Pittsburgh Press, Pittsburgh, 1974.   410 pp.

OPPENHEIMER, JOEL.   *Joel Oppenheimer: A Checklist of His Writings* by George F. Butterick. The University of Connecticut Library Bibliography Series No. 4, Storrs, March 1975.   12 pp.

OWEN, WILFRED. *Wilfred Owen (1893–1918): A Bibliography* by William White. Prefacing note by Harold Owen. Kent State University Press, Kent, Ohio, 1967. 41 pp.

PATCHEN, KENNETH. *Kenneth Patchen 1911–1972: An Annotated Descriptive Bibliography* by Richard G. Morgan. Paul P. Appel, Mamaroneck, N.Y., 1979. 174 pp.

PERREAULT, JOHN. "These Repeats Repeat: A Beginning Bibliography of John Perreault" by Inez Dahlberg. *Serif Quarterly*, Vol. 11 No. 3 (Fall 1974), pp. 28–34. Kent State University Library, Kent, Ohio.

PERSE, SAINT-JOHN. *Saint-John Perse: Praise and Presence* by Pierre Emmanuel. With a bibliography. Library of Congress, Washington, D.C., 1971. 82 pp.

PLATH, SYLVIA. *A Chronological Checklist of the Periodical Publications of Sylvia Plath* by Eric Homberger. University of Exeter, Exeter, Eng., 1970. 17 pp.
Sylvia Plath: A Bibliography by Gary Lane and Marie Stevens. Scarecrow Press, Metuchen, N.J., 1978. 144 pp.

PLAYBOY. *Index to Playboy Belles-Lettres, Articles, and Humor Dec. 1953–Dec. 1969* by Mildred Lynn Miles. Scarecrow Press, Metuchen, N.J., 1970. 162 pp.

POETRY. *Index to Fifty Years of Poetry, a Magazine of Verse, Volumes 1–100, 1912–1962* compiled by Elizabeth Wright. AMS Reprint Company, New York, 1963. 392 pp.

POETRY LONDON. *A Complete Catalogue of Books Published by Editions Poetry London at 26 Manchester Square March 1948.* Editions Poetry London, London, 1948. 68 pp.

PORTER, KATHERINE ANNE. *Katherine Anne Porter: A Critical Bibliography* by Edward Schwartz. Introduction by Robert Penn Warren. New York Public Library, New York, 1953. 42 pp.
A Bibliography of the Works of Katherine Anne Porter and a Bibliography of the Criticism of the Works of Katherine Anne Porter by Louise Waldrip and Shirley Ann Bower. Scarecrow Press, Metuchen, N.J., 1969. 219 pp.

POUND, EZRA. *A Bibliography of Ezra Pound* by Donald Gallup.
Rupert Hart-Davis, London, 1963. 454 pp.
"Corrections and Additions to the Pound Bibliography" by
Donald Gallup. *Paideuma*, Vol. I No. 1 (Spring/Summer
1972), pp. 113–25.
"Corrections and Additions to the Pound Bibliography (Part
2)" by Donald Gallup. *Paideuma*, Vol. 2 No. 2 (Fall 1973),
pp. 315–24.

POWYS, JOHN COWPER. *A Bibliography of the Writings of John
Cowper Powys: 1872–1963* by Dante Thomas. Foreword by
G. Wilson Knight. Paul P. Appel, Mamaroneck, N.Y., 1975.
192 pp.

POWYS, T. F. *A Bibliography of T. F. Powys* by Peter Riley.
R. A. Brimmell, Hastings, N.Y., 1967. 69 pp.

PSEUDONYMS. *The Hawthorn Dictionary of Pseudonyms* compiled by Andrew Bauer. Hawthorn Books, New York, 1971.
312 pp.

PYNCHON, THOMAS. (*See* Hawkes, John.)

RANSOM, JOHN CROWE. *John Crowe Ransom: Critical Essays
and a Bibliography* edited by Thomas Daniel Young. Louisiana State University Press, Baton Rouge, 1968. 290 pp.

REXROTH, KENNETH. *Kenneth Rexroth: A Checklist of His Published Writings* compiled by James Hartzell and Richard
Zumwinkly. Foreword by Lawrence Clark Powell. Friends of
the U.C.L.A. Library, University of California, Los Angeles,
1967. 67 pp.

ROBINSON, EDWIN ARLINGTON. *A Bibliography of the Writings
of Edwin Arlington Robinson* by Lucius Beebe and Robert J.
Bulkley, Jr. Dunster House Bookshop, Cambridge, Mass.,
1931. 59 pp.

ROETHKE, THEODORE. *Theodore Roethke: A Bibliography* by James
Richard MacLeod. Kent State University Press, Kent, Ohio,
1973. 241 pp.

ROHMER, SAX. *Book Collecting & Library Monthly* No. 14 (June
1969), pp. 39–41. A checklist.

Master of Villainy: A Biography of Sax Rohmer by Cay Van Ash and Elizabeth Sax Rohmer. Tom Stacey, London, 1972. Contains a bibliography.

SALINGER, J. D.   *J. D. Salinger: A Thirty-Year Bibliography 1938–1968* by Kenneth Starosciak. The Croixside Press, St. Paul, 1971.   83 pp.

SANDBURG, CARL.   *Carl Sandburg by Mark van Doren with a Bibliography of Sandburg Materials in the Collections of the Library of Congress.* Library of Congress, Washington, D.C., 1969.   83 pp.

SAROYAN, WILLIAM.   *A Bibliography of William Saroyan 1934–1964* by David Kherdian. Roger Beacham, San Francisco, 1965.   204 pp.

SARTON, MAY.   *May Sarton: A Bibliography* by Leona P. Blouin. Scarecrow Press, Metuchen, N.J., 1978.   236 pp.

SASSOON, SIEGFRIED.   *A Bibliography of Siegfried Sassoon* by Geoffrey Keynes. Rupert Hart-Davis, London, 1962.   199 pp.

SHAPIRO, KARL.   *Karl Shapiro: A Bibliography* by William White. Note by Karl Shapiro. Wayne State University Press, Detroit, 1960.   113 pp.

SHAW, GEORGE BERNARD.   *A Bibliography of Books and Pamphlets of George Bernard Shaw.* Bookman's Journal and Print Collectors Company, Ltd., London, 1928.   46 pp.

SITWELL FAMILY.   *A Bibliography of Edith, Osbert, and Sacheverell Sitwell* by Richard Fifoot. Second edition, revised. Rupert Hart-Davis, London 1963; reprinted by Archon Books, Hamden, Conn., 1971.   432 pp.

SNYDER, GARY.   *A Bibliography of Gary Snyder* by Katherine MacNeil. The Phoenix Book Shop, New York. In preparation. *A Biographical Sketch and Descriptive Checklist of Gary Snyder* by David Kherdian. Oyez, Berkeley, 1965.   30 pp.

SOLZHENITSYN, ALEXANDER.   *Alexander Solzhenitsyn: An International Bibliography of Writings by and about Him* compiled by Donald M. Fiene. Ardis, Ann Arbor, 1973.   148 pp.

SPENDER, STEPHEN.   *Stephen Spender—Works and Criticism: An*

Annotated Bibliography by H. B. Kulkarni. Garland Publishing, Inc., New York & London, 1976. 264 pp.

STEIN, GERTRUDE. *Gertrude Stein: A Bibliography* by Julian Sawyer. Arrow Editions, New York, 1940. 162 pp.

A Catalogue of the Published and Unpublished Writings of Gertrude Stein compiled by Robert Bartless Haas and Donald Clifford Gallup. Yale University Library, New Haven, 1941. 64 pp.

A Check-List of the Published Writings of Gertrude Stein compiled by George James Firmage. University of Massachusetts, Amherst, 1954. 8 pp.

Gertrude Stein: A Bibliography compiled by Robert A. Wilson. The Phoenix Book Shop, New York, 1974. 227 pp.

STEINBECK, JOHN. *John Steinbeck: A Concise Bibliography (1930–1965)* compiled by Tetsumaro Hayashi. Introduction by Warren G. French. Scarecrow Press, Metuchen, N.J., 1967. 164 pp.

John Steinbeck: A Bibliographical Catalogue of the Adrian H. Goldstone Collection by Adrian H. Goldstone and John M. Payne. Humanities Research Center, University of Texas at Austin, 1974. 240 pp.

STEPHENS, JAMES. *James Stephens: A Literary and Bibliographical Study* by Birgit Bramsbäck. Irish Institute, Uppsala University, Uppsala/Copenhagen/Dublin/Cambridge, Eng., 1959. 209 pp.

STEVENS, WALLACE. *Wallace Stevens: A Preliminary Checklist of His Published Writings: 1898–1954* by Samuel French Morse. Yale University Library, New Haven, 1954. 66 pp.

Wallace Stevens: Checklist and Bibliography of Stevens Criticism by Samuel French Morse, Jackson H. Bryer, and Joseph E. Riddell. Alan Swallow, Denver, 1963. 98 pp.

Wallace Stevens: A Descriptive Bibliography by J. M. Edelstein, University of Pittsburgh Press, Pittsburgh, 1973. 429 pp.

STYRON, WILLIAM. *William Styron: A Descriptive Bibliography* by James L. West III. Preface by William Styron. G. K. Hall & Co., Boston, 1977. 252 pp.

TATE, ALLEN. "Allen Tate: A Checklist" by Willard Thorp. *Critique Studies in Modern Fiction*, Vol. X No. 2 (1968), pp. 17–52.

Allen Tate: A Bibliography compiled by Marshall Fallwell with the assistance of Martha Cook and Francis Immler. David Lewis, New York, 1969. 112 pp.

TAYLOR, PETER. "A Peter Taylor Checklist" by James Penny Smith. *Critique Studies in Modern Fiction*, Vol. IX No. 3 (1976), pp. 31–36.

THOMAS, DYLAN. *Dylan Thomas: A Bibliography* by J. Alexander Rolph. Foreword by Dame Edith Sitwell. J. M. Dent & Sons, Ltd., London, 1956. 108 pp.

THURBER, JAMES. *James Thurber: A Bibliography* by Edwin T. Bowden. Ohio State University Press, Columbus, 1968. 353 pp.

TZARA, TRISTAN. *Tristan Tzara: A Bibliography* by Lee Harwood. Aloes Books, London, 1974. 48 pp.

UPDIKE, JOHN. *John Updike: A Bibliography* by C. Clarke Taylor. Kent State University Press, Kent, Ohio, 1968. 82 pp.

VAN VECHTEN, CARL. *A Bibliography of the Writings of Carl Van Vechten* by Scott Cunningham. Overture in the Form of a Funeral March by Carl Van Vechten. Philadelphia, The Centaur Bookshop, 1924. 52 pp.

VONNEGUT, KURT. *Kurt Vonnegut, Jr.: A Checklist* compiled by Betty Lenhardt Hudgens. Introduction by Vance Bourjaily. Gale Research Company, Detroit, 1972. 67 pp.

WALEY, ARTHUR. *A Bibliography of Arthur Waley* by Francis A. Johns. Rutgers University Press, New Brunswick, N.J., 1968.

WARREN, ROBERT PENN. *Robert Penn Warren: A Bibliography* compiled by Mary Nancy Huff. David Lewis, New York, 1968. 171 pp.

WATKINS, VERNON. *Vernon Watkins 1906–1967: Biographical*

Note, Original Works and Contributions to Periodicals, Critical Articles by Brynmor Jones. Welsh Arts Council Bibliographies of Anglo-Welsh Literature, 1968. 6 pp.

WAUGH, EVELYN. *Evelyn Waugh: A Checklist of Primary and Secondary Materials* by Robert Murray Davis, Paul A. Doyle, Heinz Kosok, and Charles E. Linck, Jr. Whitston Publishing Co., Troy, N.Y., 1972. 211 pp.

WELLS, H. G. *Herbert George Wells: An Annotated Bibliography of His Works* by J. R. Hammond. Garland Publishing, Inc., New York & London, 1977. 257 pp.

WELTY, EUDORA. "A Eudora Welty Checklist" by Noel Polk. *Mississippi Quarterly* Vol. 26 No. 4 (Fall 1973), pp. 663–93.

WEST, NATHANAEL. *Nathanael West: A Comprehensive Bibliography* by William White. Kent State University, Kent, Ohio, 1975. 209 pp.

WHARTON, EDITH. *A Bibliography of the Collected Writings of Edith Wharton* by Lawson McClung Melish. The Brick Row Bookshop, New York, 1927. 97 pp.
Edith Wharton: A Bibliography by Vito J. Brenni. West Virginia University Library, Morgantown, 1966. 99 pp.

WHITE, E. B. *E. B. White: A Bibliography* by A. J. Anderson. Scarecrow Press, Metuchen, N.J., 1968. 199 pp.

WIENERS, JOHN. "John Wieners: A Checklist" by George Butterick. *Athanor Magazine* No. 3 (Summer/Fall 1972), pp. 53–66.

WILBUR, RICHARD. *Richard Wilbur: A Bibliographical Checklist* by John P. Field. Note by Richard Wilbur. Kent State University Press, The Serif Series No. 16, Kent, Ohio, 1971. 85 pp.

WILDE, OSCAR. *Bibliography of Oscar Wilde* by Stuart Mason [Christopher Millard]. T. Werner Laurie, Ltd., London, 1914; reprinted by Bertram Rota, Ltd., London, 1967, with a new introduction by Timothy d'Arch Smith. 605 pp.

WILDER, THORNTON. *A Bibliographical Checklist of the Writings of Thornton Wilder* compiled by J. M. Edelstein. Yale University Library, New Haven, 1959. 62 pp.

WILLIAMS, TENNESSEE. "Tennessee Williams: A Selected Bibliography" by Nadine Dony. *Modern Drama Magazine*, Vol. I, No. 3 (Winter 1958), pp. 181–91.

WILLIAMS, WILLIAM CARLOS. *I Wanted to Write a Poem: The Autobiography of the Works of a Poet* by William Carlos Williams. Reported and edited by Edith Heal. Beacon Press, Boston, 1958. 99 pp.

A Bibliography of William Carlos Williams by Emily Mitchell Wallace. Wesleyan University Press, Middletown, Conn., 1968. 354 pp.

WILSON, EDMUND. *Edmund Wilson: A Bibliography* compiled by Richard David Ramsey. David Lewis, New York, 1971. 345 pp.

WODEHOUSE, P. G. *A Bibliography and Reader's Guide to the First Editions of P. G. Wodehouse* by David A. Jasen. Archon Books, Hamden, Conn., 1970. 290 pp.

WOLFE, THOMAS. *Thomas Wolfe: A Bibliography* by George H. Preston, Jr. Charles S. Boesen, New York, 1943. 127 pp.

Of Time and Thomas Wolfe: A Bibliography with a Character Index of His Works by Elmer D. Johnson. Scarecrow Press, New York, 1959.

Thomas Wolfe: A Checklist by Elmer D. Johnson. Kent State University Press, Kent, Ohio, 1970. 278 pp.

WOOLF, VIRGINIA. *A Bibliography of Virginia Woolf* by B. J. Kirkpatrick. Revised edition. Rupert Hart-Davis, London, 1967. 212 pp.

WRIGHT, JAMES. "Bibliography." *Ironwood Magazine* No. 10 (special James Wright issue), pp. 156–65.

WRIGHT, RICHARD. "Richard Wright (1908–1960): A Bibliography" by Michel Fabre and Edward Margolies. *Bulletin of Bibliography and Magazine Notes*, Vol. 24, No. 6 (Jan.–Apr. 1965), pp. 131–33, 137.

YEATS, WILLIAM BUTLER. *A Bibliography of the Writings of W. B. Yeats* by Allan Wade. Second edition, revised. Rupert Hart-Davis, London, 1958.   449 pp.; third edition, revised, Rupert Hart-Davis, London, 1968.   514 pp.

"Additions to Allan Wade's *Bibliography of W. B. Yeats*" by Russell K. Alspach. *The Irish Book (Magazine)*—(special Yeats issue), Vol. II Nos. 3 & 4 (Autumn 1963), pp. 91–114.

ZUKOFSKY, LOUIS. *A Bibliography of Louis Zukofsky* by Celia Zukofsky. Black Sparrow Press, Los Angeles, 1969.   52 pp.

BIBLIOGRAPHIES
COVERING NUMEROUS AUTHORS

———

BLANCK, JACOB, COMPILER. *Bibliography of American Literature.* 6 vols. Yale University Press, New Haven & London, 1955–73.
Volume One (1955) Henry Adams to Donn Byrne   474 pp.
Volume Two (1957) George W. Cable to Timothy Dwight   532 pp.
Volume Three (1959) Edward Eggleston to Bret Harte   482 pp.
Volume Four (1963) Nathaniel Hawthorne to Joseph Holt Ingraham   495 pp.
Volume Five (1969) Washington Irving to Henry Wadsworth Longfellow   643 pp.
Volume Six (1973) Augustus Baldwin Longstreet to Thomas William Parsons   594 pp.

BRUCCOLI, MATTHEW J., AND CLARK, C. E. FRAZER, JR., editors. *First Printings of American Authors: Contributions Toward Descriptive Checklists.* Gale Research Company, Detroit, 1977–79. Four volumes covering twentieth-century American authors. Vol. One: 432 pp., Vol. Two: 407 pp., Vol. Three: 412 pp., Vol. Four: 406 pp.

BRUSSELL, I. R. *Anglo-American First Editions.* New York 1935–36. R. R. Bowker Co. Vol. One: *East to West 1826–1900* covers editions of British authors first published in the U.S. Vol. Two: *West to East 1786–1930* covers editions of American authors first published in England.

CONNOLLY, CYRIL. *The Modern Movement: One Hundred Key Books from England, France and America 1880–1950.* Andre Deutsch/Hamish Hamilton, London, 1965. 148 pp.

DEODENE, FRANK, AND FRENCH, WILLIAM P. *Black American Fiction Since 1952: A Preliminary Checklist.* The Chatham Bookseller, Chatham, N.J., 1970. 25 pp.
Black American Poetry Since 1944: A Preliminary Checklist. The Chatham Bookseller, Chatham, N.J., 1971. 41 pp.

HAWKINS, SHERMAN. *Seven Princeton Poets.* Princeton University Press, Princeton, N.J., 1963. Covers Louis Coke, Galway Kinnell, George Garrett, William Meredith, Theodore Holmes, W. S. Merwin, and Bink Noll. 115 pp.

JOHNSON, MERLE. *Merle Johnson's American First Editions.* Revised and enlarged by Jacob Blanck. Fourth Edition. Reprinted by Research Classics, Cambridge, Mass., 1962. 553 pp.

KHERDIAN, DAVID. *Six Poets of the San Francisco Renaissance: Portraits and Checklists.* Introduction by William Saroyan. The Giligia Press, Fresno, 1967. Covers Brother Antoninus (William Everson), Lawrence Ferlinghetti, Michael McClure, David Meltzer, Gary Snyder, and Philip Whalen. 183 pp.

KING, KIMBALL. *Twenty Modern British Playwrights: A Bibliography 1956–1976.* Garland Publishing, Inc., New York & London, 1977. Covers John Arden, Alan Ayckbourn, Peter Barnes, Robert Bolt, Edward Bond, Simon Gray, Christopher Hampton, Ann Jellicoe, Peter Nichols, Joe Orton, John Osborne, Harold Pinter, Anthony Shaffer, Peter Shaffer, N. F. Simpson, Tom Stoppard, David Storey, Arnold Wesker, Heathcote Williams, and Charles Wood. 289 pp.

LEPPER, GARY. *A Bibliographical Introduction to Seventy-five Modern American Authors.* Serendipity Books, Berkeley, 1976. Covers Nelson Algren, John Ashbery, Louis Auchincloss, James Baldwin, John Barth, Donald Barthelme, Saul Bellow, Thomas Berger, Daniel Berrigan, Ted Berrigan, Wendell Berry, John Berryman, Paul Blackburn, Robert Bly, Paul Bowles, Richard Brautigan, Charles Bukowski, William S. Burroughs, Hortense Calisher, Truman Capote, John Cheever, Tom Clark, Robert Coover, Cid Corman, Robert Creeley, James Dickey, Diane di Prima, Edward Dorn, Robert Duncan, George P. Elliott, Clayton Eshleman, William Everson (Brother Antoninus), Lawrence Ferlinghetti, Bruce Jay Friedman, John Gardner, William H. Gass, Herbert Gold, Paul Goodman, William Goyen, Shirley Ann Grau, Donald Hall, John Hawkes, Joseph Heller, Jack Hirschman, Robert Kelly, John Oliver Killens, Kenneth Koch, Philip Lamantia, Denise Levertov, Ron Loewinsohn, Norman Mailer, Bernard Malamud, Michael McClure, Larry McMurtry, David Meltzer, Josephine Miles, Warren Miller, Wright Morris, Joyce Carol Oates, Frank O'Hara, Reynolds Price, James Purdy, Philip Roth, Jerome Rothenberg, Gary Snyder, Jack Spicer, William Styron, Harvey Swados, Paul Theroux, John Updike, Diane Wakoski, Edward Wallant, Lew Welch, Philip Whalen, and John Wieners. 428 pp.

MURPHY, ROSALIE, EDITOR. *Contemporary Poets.* Preface by C. Day Lewis. St. James Press/St. Martin's Press, London & New York, 1970. Contains checklists of each poet plus a separate listing of anthologies. 1,243 pp.

Contemporary Novelists. St. James Press/St. Martin's Press, London & New York, 1972. Contains checklists of each novelist included.

Contemporary Dramatists. St. James Press/St. Martin's Press, London & New York, 1973. Contains checklists of each dramatist included.

TATE, ALLEN, EDITOR. *Sixty American Poets 1896–1944.* Revised edition. Selected, with Preface and Critical Notes, by Allen Tate. The Library of Congress Reference Department, Washington, D.C., 1954. Covers Léonie Adams, James Agee, Conrad Aiken, Hilda Doolittle Aldington, Howard Baker, Stephen Vincent Benét, John Peale Bishop, Richard P. Blackmur, Louise Bogan, Malcolm Cowley, Hart Crane, E. E. Cummings, Donald Davison, Richard Eberhart, T. S. Eliot, Paul Engle, Kenneth Fearing, Kimball Flaccus, John Gould Fletcher, Robert Frost, Horace Gregory, Langston Hughes, Randall Jarrell, Robinson Jeffers, James Weldon Johnson, Alfred Kreymborg, William Ellery Leonard, Vachel Lindsay, Amy Lowell, Archibald MacLeish, Norman MacLeod, Edgar Lee Masters, Edna St. Vincent Millay, Marianne Moore, Merrill Moore, Howard Nutt, Ezra Pound, Frederic Prokosch, Howard Phelps Putnam, John Crowe Ransom, Laura Riding, Edwin Arlington Robinson, Muriel Rukeyser, Carl Sandburg, Delmore Schwartz, Karl Jay Shapiro, Gertrude Stein, Wallace Stevens, Jesse Stuart, Genevieve Taggard, Allen Tate, Sara Teasdale, Mark van Doren, Robert Penn Warren, James Whaler, John Brooks Wheelwright, William Carlos Williams, Yvor Winters, Elinor Wylie, and Maria Zaturenska. 155 pp.

WHITEMAN, MAXWELL. *A Century of Fiction by American Negroes, 1853–1952. A Descriptive Bibliography.* Published by the author, Philadelphia, 1955. 64 pp.

WHITLOW, ROGER. *Black American Literature: A Critical History. With a 1,520-Title Bibliography of Works Written by and about Black Americans.* Nelson Hall, Chicago, 1973. 287 pp.

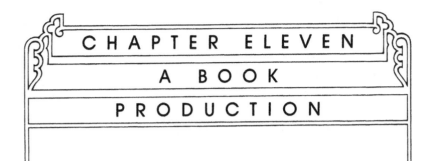

CHAPTER ELEVEN

A BOOK

PRODUCTION

In an earlier chapter, mention was made of galleys, proof copies, advance reading copies, and such other items involved in the production of a book which precede actual publication. Since the nature and function of these objects are often confused or misunderstood, even by some dealers (to say nothing of beginning collectors), this chapter will be devoted to a step-by-step account of the process by which an author's manuscript becomes a book. An understanding of it is more important than it once was; book collectors have become more sophisticated in their tastes and interests in the past couple of decades. Prior to World War II, one collected first editions, period. Virtually no one paid any attention to anything else—either later editions, or earlier states or forms of a book—other than the actual first edition as issued. Later revisions, variant bindings, and the like were never listed in catalogs and were apparently regarded as lacking in significance. Likewise, states of a book before the final, published format were not collected at all. Yet these preliminary states often reflect earlier versions of the text and are in many respects of great interest, scholarly and otherwise. Nowadays such early state material is keenly sought after.

While the basic processes involved in making most books are consistent, there are many variations. For example, works of nonfiction generally involve matter that does not appear in works of fiction—indexes, appendixes, forewords, introductions (although sometimes works of fiction by new authors have introductions by better-known, well-established authors), tables of contents, illustrations, etc. However, as most collected books are fiction (or poetry), the following description involves the production of a typical novel.

Naturally, the first step is for the author to submit a completed manuscript to the publisher. No matter whether or not this is a cleanly typed text, it is generally known as a rough working manuscript. It may be an actual manuscript in the original sense of the word—that is, handwritten—although this is highly unlikely; most publishers insist on typed copy. Most standard contracts, in fact, call for two sets of finished manuscript. At one time this consisted of the ribbon original and a carbon typescript. This still tends to be the case in England, but nowadays in the United States the submission generally consists of the original typescript and a photocopy. Quite often, in fact, contemporary authors submit only the original copy of their manuscript, assuming that the publishing firm will have its own photocopying machine and can run off copies readily. The submitted manuscript may itself be a photocopy, since the author will usually want to keep at least one copy himself, for obvious reasons. The final copy submitted to the publisher, whether original typescript or photocopy, may have some last minute corrections in the author's hand.

Having received the original from the author, the publisher proceeds to make photocopies for internal house use, usually five or six of them. These will be used to plan the book in the production department, to prepare a book design in the art department, and to begin work on a jacket, either inside the house or with an outside artist. Other copies go to various persons in the office for reading or scanning. The book's editor uses one for his editing, and he will probably go through these changes with the author, ultimately transferring them to the original copy (by now known as the "setting copy"—the copy of the manuscript that will go to the typesetters). At this point a copy editor must read through this top copy, or setting copy, correcting any punctuation or spelling errors and making style consistent. Once again, the author must read through the copy to make sure that he approves all the items marked before it goes to the typesetters. He also has an opportunity now to make final changes of his own. If the revisions have been extensive, it may be necessary to retype the entire manuscript. This will seldom happen, although a glance at a single page of revisions made at this point by James Joyce makes one wonder how Maurice Darantière's typesetters managed to decipher anything at all when setting type for *Ulysses*, the more especially in view of the fact that they were setting in a language unknown to them.

More likely it is an odd page or two that would be retyped and inserted in place of the one bearing numerous corrections. All of these changes will appear on the setting copy, but no effort will be made to correct the photocopies of the original text that went to the production departments. They usually remain uncorrected, since textual revisions will rarely affect the work of the jacket design department or even the physical makeup of the book. (Unless, of course, the changes are so extensive as to require that the book itself be redesigned. This is very rare.)

Finally, typesetting takes place. Once the type has been set, the printer pulls about three sets of loose galleys, or long galleys, called such because they are printed on long sheets of proof paper, each sheet bearing approximately two and a half printed pages. (If the book is being set, as is increasingly the case, by a computer, the long galleys may come through at this stage already broken into single pages.) These are then read by the author, by a professional proofreader, and sometimes by the book's editor. To distinguish the source of changes made at this stage, each set of galleys is generally marked at the top of the first sheet—for example, "Author's set." The various corrections are then collated and

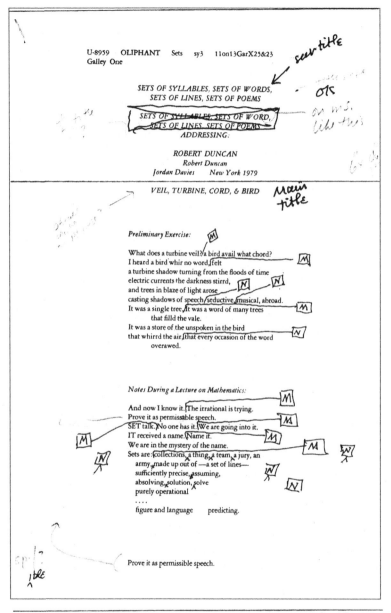

U-8959 OLIPHANT Sets sy3 11on13GarX25&23
Galley One

SETS OF SYLLABLES, SETS OF WORDS,
SETS OF LINES, SETS OF POEMS

~~SETS OF SYLLABLES, SETS OF WORD,~~
~~SETS OF LINES, SETS OF POEMS~~
ADDRESSING:

ROBERT DUNCAN
Robert Duncan
Jordan Davies   New York 1979

VEIL, TURBINE, CORD, & BIRD

Preliminary Exercise:

What does a turbine veil? a bird avail what chord?
I heard a bird whir no word, felt
a turbine shadow turning from the floods of time
electric currents the darkness stirrd,
and trees in blaze of light arose
casting shadows of speech/seductive, musical, abroad.
It was a single tree, It was a word of many trees
   that filld the vale.
It was a store of the unspoken in the bird
that whirrd the air, that every occasion of the word
   overawed.

Notes During a Lecture on Mathematics:

And now I know it. The irrational is trying.
Prove it as permissable speech.
SET talk. No one has it. We are going into it.
IT received a name. Name it.
We are in the mystery of the name.
Sets are: collections, a thing, a team, a jury, an
   army, made up out of —a set of lines—
sufficiently precise, assuming,
absolving, solution, solve
purely operational
. . . .
figure and language   predicting.

Prove it as permissible speech.

*First page of a set of author's galleys, corrected by the poet Robert Duncan.
Courtesy of Jordan Davies.*

transferred to one master set. This may or may not be the author's set. One reason for the importance of identifying the corrections at this point is the matter of financial responsibility for the changes. Since typesetting, like everything else, is a costly matter, the publisher quite naturally wishes to avoid expensive changes insofar as possible. The errors of the typesetter—PEs—are legitimately his expense. However, if the author has made errors, or wishes to make changes in the text originally submitted, these are known as author's alterations—AAs—and the cost of making them, beyond a certain reasonable number, will be charged to the author's account. The final corrected set then goes back to the printer, who will make the corrections.

When the first proofs are received, the publisher will send a set to a company that produces bound galleys. These are usually made from the original uncorrected, unproofed typesetting. They are printed by offset onto somewhat shorter sheets (although generally still taller than the finished book), still on a cheap variety of paper, and usually bound in stiff wrappers, sometimes glued and sometimes fastened by spiral plastic bands. The resulting "books" are intended primarily for publicity purposes. Some are sent as advance copies to important reviewers, some are circulated within the publishing house to the sales force, some are sent out for comment or quotes in advance of publication, some may be submitted to book clubs, such as the Book-of-the-Month Club or the Literary Guild, for consideration as a selection. The number of copies of such bound galleys may vary from half a dozen for a volume of poetry or a long, expensive deluxe book all the way up to as many as seventy-five or a hundred copies of a book that will receive widespread publicity.

Occasionally a firm will have a book that warrants the expense of producing a special "Advance Issue." This is usually printed on something better than proof paper, often the same paper that will be used in the final format of the book, and has a better quality cover than the normal set of bound galleys—possibly even the actual dust jacket, glued around the book. Or the advance issue may have a printed wrapper bearing a message from the publisher or some famous author explaining why the book is felt to be of particular interest or importance. These copies are usually produced from the final text, or as close to the final state of the text as is possible at the time. They generally resemble the finished book in size and general appearance except for the paper binding. Such a book is usually identified on the cover by the words "Advance Reading Copy" or some similar designation. These are usually produced in fairly large quantities, at least five hundred—as was the case with Truman Capote's *In Cold Blood*—or even several thousand copies, particularly if the book is to be publicized at the American Booksellers Association annual convention. Advance copies are usually distributed rather generously at the ABA conventions in the hope of securing large advance orders from retail bookstores. They are of course eagerly sought after by collectors, since they are obviously the earliest form of the book to be released to the public. In some cases they may contain material that does not appear in the final issued version.

When all corrections have been made, the columns of type are separated into page lengths by the compositor. Then (assuming the book is being printed by offset) such things as running heads, chapter headings, page numbers, etc., are stripped in (i.e., actually pasted onto the appropriate page), and all other material is added—such front and back matter as title page, foreword, dedication, table of contents, index, or whatever nontextual material was not actually set in the original galleys. When this work has been okayed by the publisher, the printer photographs the paste-up, strips the resulting negatives to a "flat" roughly the same size as the sheet of paper the book is to be printed on, and makes a set of blueprints (much like an architect's) of the finished flats. These, folded, are known as "blues." Once again, the publisher gives them one final check to make sure that everything is in its correct place, in sequence, and right side up—especially the front and back matter, which has been added. Then a set of printing plates is made from the approved flats, and actual printing begins.

At this stage it is possible for the publisher to request sets of the folded and gathered sheets—actually finished copies of the printed portions of the book, lacking only the binding. This is not often done nowadays, since the binding process takes a very short time, but it means that the reviewers can be supplied with material a few days earlier. These folded and gathered sheets—known as "f and g's"—are generally requested only in the case of art books or illustrated books that could not be judged fairly on the basis of the text alone.

The publisher will ideally receive completed books, bound and dust-jacketed, five to six weeks (sometimes less) before the official publication date of the book. This allows time for the books to be shipped to bookstores so that there will be stock on hand when the actual publication date arrives. It also allows time for review copies to be sent out. Formerly, most publishers employed a rubber stamp inside the front covers of review copies to mark them, but today the common practice is to insert a specially printed slip, giving the price and the official publication date, and requesting that two copies of the review be sent to the publisher. Sometimes a glossy photo and a brief biography of the author may also be inserted. In the past, many publishers double-jacketed review copies so that the newspaper or magazine could, if it chose, use one jacket to illustrate the review. These copies are known as advance review copies and are usually distributed rather liberally by major publishing

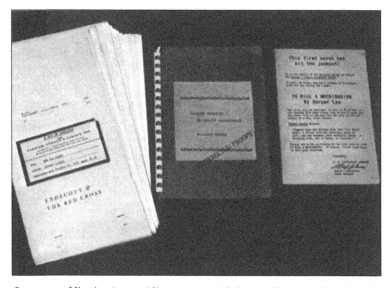

Some prepublication forms of literary material: loose galleys of Robert Lowell's ENDECOTT AND THE RED CROSS; *bound galleys of Galway Kinnell's* FLOWER HERDING ON MOUNT MONADNOCK; *and a special reading edition of Harper Lee's* TO KILL A MOCKINGBIRD. *From the author's collection.*

houses as a form of advertising a new book. Collectors naturally prefer these, since in the normal course of events such copies are issued some weeks prior to the regular copies of the book.

In some cases advance review copies may come to be regarded as extremely desirable first issues, when some vital mistake is discovered after their distribution and corrected before the rest of the books are sent out. There are several instances of this. Even as I write, it has been discovered that such was the case with Bernard Malamud's *Dubin's Lives.* But perhaps the most notable instance, if only for the convoluted sequence of events and the variant copies that it gave rise to, is Marianne Moore's *Collected Poems.* This book was published in 1950 by Macmillan in New York, with a corresponding edition in England by Faber & Faber. At that time it was common for publishers to have the entire printing for a joint edition done in Europe, with either the completed books shipped here, or sometimes the sheets alone, which were then bound and jacketed in the United States. In this particular case, the complete book was printed and bound in England in two editions, one with a Macmillan title page and the Macmillan imprint on the spine, and the other with a Faber title page and the Faber imprint on the spine. Since Miss Moore was an American, it was agreed that the American edition would be released first to protect her copyright, the British edition following some three or four weeks later. Accordingly the Macmillan copies were shipped to the United States. Now, a shipment of three or four thousand books occupies a very large amount of space, and on any bulk shipment comprising identical items in quantity, the standard practice of the U.S. Customs is to release all but one case to the consignee, who is expected to hold all the merchandise, no matter what it is, until the one retained case has been examined by the customs agents and a final clearance given. Not expecting any problem, Macmillan sent out review copies, some sixty-five in all, before word came from Customs that the books were not admissible because they lacked a printed copyright notice on the verso of the title page. If the books were released thus, Miss Moore would lose her copyright. Obviously this could not be allowed to happen, and all the books had to be shipped back to England—all, that is, but the sixty-five review copies, which were at this point irretrievable. Macmillan then hurriedly proceeded with production of a wholly American-printed edition, but this could not be readied in time for issuance before the Faber edition was released in England. Thus the first edition situation is as follows: a total of sixty-five copies, bearing a Macmillan title page and Macmillan imprint on the spine, but no copyright notice; next, a British edition, with Faber on the spine and a Faber title page; then the American-printed American edition (in blue cloth instead of the original orange), with Macmillan on the spine, a Macmillan title page, and bearing a copyright notice. Just to add to the confusion, when the copyright-less batch of Macmillan copies arrived back in England, rather than sacrifice the entire lot Faber sliced out the title page and tipped in a new one, bearing the Faber imprint. This created bastard copies with a Faber title page but a Macmillan imprint on the spine, and these were issued after Faber had sold out its initial supply. So there are four variants of the first edition of Marianne Moore's *Collected Poems*—and the sixty-five advance review copies sent out by Macmillan clearly enjoy priority over all the others.

Most modern books go through all of the production stages described above, although occasionally one of the steps will be bypassed. Material from each stage, however, is of interest to most collectors, especially "in-depth" collectors. The big trick is to get hold of such material. Review copies for most books turn up in the market fairly frequently, for regular reviewers usually supplement their income by selling unwanted books. Advance reading copies also turn up fairly often, for the same reason, and bound galleys sent out as review copies also come into the market occasionally. But the other formats are never released by publishers and, as indicated, often exist in only a very few copies. To recapitulate, here is a list of the possible states of a book, arranged chronologically:

1 Author's manuscript
2 Photocopies of the manuscript, prepared for house use. Either one of these or the author's original will serve as the "setting copy," with corrections thereon.
*3 Long galleys (usually about three sets), including the set with the author's corrections

*4 Bound galleys
*5 Advance reading copies (usually in special wrappers)
 6 "Blues"
 7 Sets of folded and gathered but unbound sheets
*8 Advance review copies of the completed book
*9 Completed book as issued

The starred items are the ones sometimes or often available
in the market. The others are very rarely seen outside the
publishing house. But, of course, whatever exists will be
sought and valued by collectors interested in the work of
that particular author.

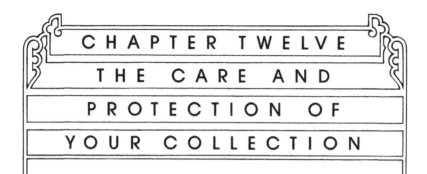

CHAPTER TWELVE
THE CARE AND
PROTECTION OF
YOUR COLLECTION

Every librarian or conservationist will recommend that a collection be housed in a vault or a safe, preferably totally devoid of light and with temperature and climate controls as the best—indeed, the only certain—way of ensuring its preservation. The very minimum that any of them will countenance is an air-conditioned, temperature-controlled room with no windows, and with every book slipcased against light and air and the impurities to be found therein. In other words, human contact with books is to be avoided insofar as possible. This is, of course, sound advice, no denying it. It is also totally impractical, even for libraries and museums, to say nothing of the average collector. While many people nowadays live in air-conditioned homes, few if any collectors are wealthy enough to be able to devote one or more rooms exclusively to the antiseptic preservation of a book collection. Furthermore, kept under such conditions, a collection ceases to be enjoyable and becomes a burden. The slipcases alone, in addition to running into considerable money, take up an enormous amount of space—something that most collectors have even less of than money. Casing denies the collector the simple, unadulterated pleasure of seeing and handling his books whenever he wishes to. To have one's books stored away in a safe-deposit vault, or locked in a light-proof room, or even housed scrupulously in slipcases, seems to me to put one in the same category as those people who possess jewels of such value that the originals are kept locked away in a vault, and paste imitations are worn to avoid the danger of theft or loss.

I am strongly of the opinion that a book collector should not lose sight of the primary purpose for which a book was created. Most books were printed and published to be read and used. This does not mean abused; but the average book is not going to be damaged by being kept in normal surroundings and handled with care. Certain precautions are obvious—shelves should not be above or near radiators, or in a position where the books on them are exposed to direct sunlight during any part of the day. Nor should a collection be kept where there is seepage or dampness. Basement apartments and cellars are subject to this hazard, and any sensible person with a collection to care for will avoid moving into such quarters.

There are other precautions that are not quite so obvious, although still easily taken without being a nuisance. For instance, fluorescent lighting is five times as destructive to paper as ordinary incandescent lighting. Dust and dirt are just as deleterious to books as they are to human lungs. Books are best protected by being kept in cases with doors, such as the old-fashioned glass-fronted bookcases. These, alas, have several disadvantages: they are expensive; they are difficult to purchase today since they are out of style and have gone out of production; and they are bulky. Finally, and perhaps most crucially, they do not house nearly as many books as the same amount of space devoted to open shelves. Most collectors have limited space, and open shelves are therefore more practical. With the widespread use of air-conditioning in private homes and apartments, the problem of dust and dirt has lessened somewhat. But there are other hazards in the use of open shelves. One is bookends, and a word of caution is appropriate here. It is advisable to place a thickness of cardboard, or even a dummy book next to the bookends, particularly if you are using the metal variety. This will prevent the accidental "knifing" of a book inadvertently replaced onto the bookend rather than next to it.

What about protective cases? My own feeling is that, expense aside, row on row of uniformly colored leather-backed boxes rob a collection of its charm and character. There is also one fact that advocates of cases never seem to mention—the wear and tear to books and dust jackets occasioned by their removal from the cases. The dangers of casing probably equal the deterioration that may result from not casing. If you do, however, decide to use cases—and most collections contain one or more gems or pets that deserve a case—there is a wide variety of styles and types to choose from. Any of them can be ordered with either cloth or leather covering, in a multitude of colors. If you wish, you can have a uniform color scheme for the entire collection, or a different color for each author if you collect a number of different writers.

Probably the earliest type of case still in use is the solander case, named for its eighteenth-century inventor, Daniel Solander. Strictly speaking, the solander case is a box, one of whose ends or sides drops down when the lid is lifted. This allows the book to be slid in from the side, and the cover then replaced. It is not as airtight as the other kinds, however.

Another popular type is the slipcase, which is simply a box with one long end open, exposing the spine of the book. Such cases are often found today on signed limited editions and are generally made of cardboard covered with paper. They are the simplest and therefore least expensive kind of case, but obviously still leave the spine of the book subject to light and, therefore, fading. This problem can be defeated by the use of a wrap-around sleeve, or "corset" as it is more properly termed, which is fitted around the book before it is inserted into the case. Slipcases are relatively simple to make, and any collector at all handy with paste and scissors and a little patience can produce them. (If you try this, make certain not to use high-acid-content materials —*see* p. 186.) At least one rather knowledgeable dealer has been so fooled by a homemade slipcase as to catalog the book as being "in the original slipcase, as issued," to the vast amusement of his better-informed colleagues.

A third style is the double-hinged type, the "fall-down back" case, which will lie flat when opened. It is also known as a clam-shell box, since the two sides fit together as snugly as the two halves of a clam shell when closed. It is probably the best kind of case to use, not only because it gives more protection than any other type, but also because it requires the least amount of handling of the book it contains in that it will lie flat and allow the book to be in full view. There is no need to slide the book to remove it, an operation always tinged with the possibilities of damage.

The fourth type is the "pull-off" case, also known as a drop case. This is a vertical box with a lid, much like an ordinary kitchen canister. With the top removed, the book must then be dropped into the case, and the lid replaced. Similarly, to remove a book from such a case involves either pulling or shaking the book out—risky, as noted above.

Pamphlets usually require some sort of protection, being too fragile to stand upright on shelves and, without the strength of bound books, being more prone to wear and tear. Formerly, ordinary brown kraft paper envelopes were believed to be suitable and efficient protection. Now, however, we have become aware of the disintegrating action of chemicals used in the manufacture of most paper, and know that such containers are to be avoided. It is now possible to purchase folders and envelopes made of acid-free paper which will safely preserve anything stored in them. The best known are retailed under the trade name "Permalife." Specially designed pamphlet folders are also available, with fold-over flaps to keep items from slipping out. Since pam-

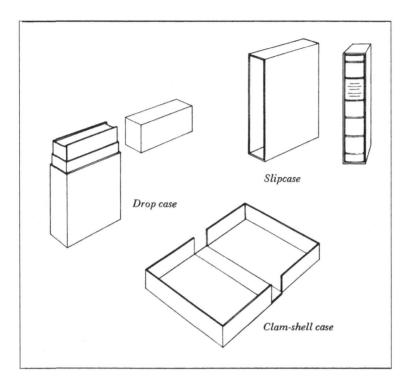

Slipcase

Drop case

Clam-shell case

phlets do not make any appreciable showing on library shelves, many collectors employ boxes or library cases to house groups of pamphlets. A wide variety of sizes and styles of storage boxes and cases, either for flat or upright storage, all made of acid-free materials, is available. But since most collectors like to keep everything by one author together, a pamphlet case may not be the answer for all storage problems. It is also possible to use precut sheets of Mylar, in a thickness of .010", fastened with a "Bac-bone," which slides on easily over the closed edge. These are ideal if you have only one pamphlet or even a group of loose sheets on any one subject to be housed together. These Mylar sheets come in standard sizes and a variety of colors, if so desired. There is still another alternative that is chemically safe, a combination of the Mylar sheets and the format of the Permalife envelopes, known as Markilo Transparent Envelopes, made of cellulose acetate. They come in three standard sizes: 9" x 3"; 9" x 6"; and 12" x 9", with an opening on one long side.

A problem that has become increasingly apparent in recent years is the deterioration of the printed paper itself, because of its acid content. Anyone familiar with the rapid yellowing and crumbling of old newspapers will realize immediately how serious such damage can be, particularly in the case of books or pamphlets printed on cheap wood-pulp paper, the kind used extensively in books published during both world wars. Deacidification of such paper is possible by at least three methods, but they are all intricate processes that can be performed only by specialists with considerable knowledge, experience, and equipment. Since all of them are time consuming, they are correspondingly expensive. It is especially difficult to treat bound books; they must be disbound, treated, and then rebound. Few modern books warrant such expensive treatment. However, this treatment is recommended for rare dust jackets, and particularly for rarities of the Beat writers, many of whose early works were mimeographed on cheap paper guaranteed to self-destruct within a few years. Such items *must* be deacidified as soon as possible. Allen Ginsberg's first book, the pamphlet *Siesta at Xbalba* (*see* p. 12), is an example. Since Ginsberg has become one of the most widely collected of modern poets, this pamphlet fetches four-figure prices whenever it makes one of its rare appearances on the market. Certainly a few dollars' worth of treatment makes sense to preserve such a rarity.

For the collector who likes to display some of his manuscript pages, perhaps a poem in the holograph of one of his favorite poets, there is always the danger of the ink fading due to prolonged exposure to light. In recent years a transparent plastic "glass" has been developed that absorbs ultra-violet light and can be used instead of ordinary glass in a picture frame as a safeguard against fading. It comes in sheets, maximum size 48″ x 96″, and is thick enough (⅛″) and easily enough cut that it can be used to replace regular window glass in the room housing valuable documents. A word of caution, though: If you have plants in the same room, this glass cannot be used; the ultraviolet light that is so dele-terious to books is absolutely essential to a living plant. This plastic—like the other specialized materials recommended in this chapter—can be procured only from specialized library supply dealers, although an occasional item may be found in some of the larger art supply houses. Highly recommended is the firm of Talas, 130 Fifth Avenue, New York, New York 10011, which carries all of the items mentioned, as well as many other aids. A seventy-page catalog is available for a small fee.

The preservation of dust jackets is perhaps the problem that the majority of collectors worry about most. For the collector who does not want to case every book, there is an inexpensive and convenient alternative which will mini-mize the danger of further wear and tear to dust jackets. This is the use of a thin sheet of Mylar as an outside wrapper. Mylar is totally transparent and also chemically inactive. It comes in two styles, one with paper backing and one without. The type with the paper backing is slightly more difficult to fit onto dust jackets, but does provide more protection, since it seals off the top and bottom edges as well as covering the face of the jackets. The paperless variety, easier to use, serves as a second, transparent dust jacket around the original, and is usually an effective safeguard against tearing or snagging, soiling, and other disasters to which jackets are prone. Some collectors, not wishing to go to the expense of Mylar, which must be bought in large rolls, have turned instead to ordinary household waxed paper.

Conservation experts wince when such a suggestion is made, but admit that there is no chemical harm in using such an unsophisticated product. The main drawback is that waxed paper has no strength, and after several handlings must be replaced, whereas the Mylar is virtually indestructible and lasts indefinitely. It does scratch, but only with continued daily handling—and even then can be replaced quickly and inexpensively. Some brands of waxed paper are more opaque than others; in my experience Marcal seems to be the most transparent. With any of them, however, there will be a general dulling of colors, whereas Mylar seems to heighten and freshen the appearance of a collection, a definite aesthetic advantage which helps offset the additional expense involved.

To sum up, general good sense and reasonable care should suffice to protect all but the most fragile items from damage. If there should be damage, don't try home repairs. Most of us are able only to make matters worse. There are experts available who know what to do, and it will save you grief and expense in the long run to employ their services. Finding them may not be easy; however, rare-book librarians at most universities and large institutions will necessarily have employed one or more of these specialists and will probably be glad to give you names and addresses. Similarly, clubs devoted to book collecting will certainly have such names on file or have members who will be able to supply such information. Carolyn Horton Associates, 430 West 22d Street, New York, New York 10011, is one of the best in the field, having headed the American team of expert restorers who helped salvage the irreplaceable books and manuscripts damaged in the Florence flood a few years ago.

Most veteran collectors know that there are also some modern "conveniences" which must be kept away from books—such things as rubber bands, paper clips, cellophane tape (or any other kind of tape for that matter, including

Scotch brand Magic tape), ball-point pens, and felt-tip pens. If you discover a signature or inscription in felt-tip ink in a book, immediately place slips of Mylar (or at the very least our old friend, waxed paper) on either side of the inscribed page to prevent it from bleeding through.

Perhaps the greatest danger to rare books, as to most other endangered species, is man himself, especially in the form of a careless friend or visitor. Never, ever, under any circumstances, allow anyone to handle any of your books while holding a pipe, cigar, cigarette, or drink. The risks of a hot ash burning a hole are obvious, and water damage is probably worse. I learned this the hard way when a famous poet was examining one of his own books in my house with a drink in hand. The inevitable happened, and the drink stained the wrappers and colophon page of a very limited, signed edition (one of only twelve copies). Some days later, when it had thoroughly dried, the poet made amends by making a drawing around the stain and suitably inscribing an explanation. All in all, a reasonably happy ending, but not one that could be expected if someone other than the author had caused the damage. So be firm. No true friend or book lover will be offended.

The following chart, originally issued in 1937 by a mythical "Society for the Prevention of Cruelty to Books," contains sound advice beneath its flippant tone:

HOW TO ABSTAIN FROM BIBLIOLATRY,
BEING A TREATISE ON THE IMPROPER CARE
OF BOOKS

———

Method	*Result*
1 TIGHT PACKING ON SHELVES	*An excellent method for tearing covers when removing.*
2 LOOSE PACKING ON SHELVES	*A quick cover-warping process.*
3 OPENING NEW BOOK VIOLENTLY	*A back-breaking exercise.*

Method	*Result*
4 LAYING FACE DOWN AND WITH OTHER BOOKS PILED ON TOP	*A good system for producing "pop-open" and "bow-legged" books.*
5 USING BULKY OBJECTS FOR PLACE MARKERS	*A short-cut to split backs.*
6 USING TO ELEVATE INFANT CHAIR	*Good means for applying a painful overall strain.*
7 FOLDING CORNER AS MARKER	*Approved manner of paper torture.*
8 USING PAPER CLIP AS MARKER	*Good system for tearing and leaving marks on paper.*
9 USING RUBBER BAND AS MARKER	*The sulphur-rot system.*
10 TURNING PAGES VIOLENTLY	*Endorsed way of creating tears.*
11 PLACING ON ROUGH AND SHARP-EDGED SHELVES	*Favored method for abrading head and tail of books.*
12 PLACING LIGHTED CIGARETTE ON BOOK	*Informal procedure for producing decorations to the binding.*
13 EATING AND CRUMB DROPPING WHILE READING	*The lazy torturer's method, as he entices the assistance of vermin to do his work.*
14 USING AS SERVING TRAY OR COASTER	*Artistic, surrealistic decorations result.*
15 LEAVING OUTSIDE IN HOT SUN	*The sanctioned rule for producing faded colors and permanent warping.*
16 USING BOOKS AS WEIGHTS	*Excellent form for creating interesting cover marks.*
17 USING BOOKS TO KEEP DOORS AJAR	*Ideal for producing flattened corners.*
18 CUTTING ILLUSTRATIONS FROM BOOKS	*This method is particularly enjoyable when employed on borrowed books.*
19 VILIFYING AUTHOR IN MARGINAL NOTES	*The courageous method of anonymous attack on authors.*
20 UNDERLINING SENTENCES	*Decorative and impressive, especially on library books.*

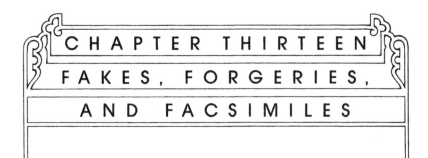

CHAPTER THIRTEEN
FAKES, FORGERIES,
AND FACSIMILES

Fakes, forgeries, and facsimiles do not, fortunately, plague the collector of twentieth-century material as much as they do collectors of earlier material, or even collectors of objects other than books. Still, there is enough of this sort of thing around to warrant some discussion of it.

Forgeries may be defined as spurious productions of books or pamphlets that never actually existed, as opposed to fakes which are conscious reproductions of items made at a later date with the intention of deception. Quite often a facsimile—which has been honestly issued as such—will be manipulated or doctored into a fake. But more about that later. Outright forgeries, the creation of books or pamphlets that never existed, are seldom encountered, thank heaven! But there have been two major attempts to create them, one in the nineteenth century and, surprisingly enough, one in the 1960s. The amazing thing about these two attempts is that the perpetrators employed exactly the same ideas and techniques, and were discovered and tripped up by exactly the same detective tactics.

The earlier forger was the now notorious Thomas J. Wise, certainly one of the least likely candidates for the role. Wise, a businessman of some means, was the leading British bibliophile in the latter half of the nineteenth century. He held every position of honor in the field, and rightly so, as author of comprehensive pioneering bibliographies of such authors as Tennyson, Browning, Ruskin, Swinburne, Wordsworth, and other contemporary writers, all of whom were at that time just beginning to be collected seriously. Wise's bibliographies were based on his own magnificent collections, unrivaled for scope and depth. But some flaw in Wise's character led him astray and ultimately negated all his accomplishments, to the point where he is now principally remembered as one of the most unscrupulous forgers of all time. For reasons we shall probably never know, he began issuing little pamphlets that purported to be early rarities of important Victorian authors, all dated in the 1840s and 1850s. None of them actually appeared before 1888, however, and each one that surfaced was somehow "discovered" by Wise and parceled out by him to eager collectors. This went on for a considerable number of years; in fact, for several decades. Not until the early 1930s, when two serious doubters and students of bibliography had assembled enough evidence to publish a book modestly entitled *An Enquiry Into the Nature of Certain Nineteenth Century Pamphlets* was he at last unmasked. Written by John Carter and Graham Pollard, *An Enquiry* appeared in 1934 and was the biggest bombshell ever to hit the book-collecting world.

Improbabilities concerning the Wise pamphlets had already touched off a certain amount of suspicion. For instance, the most famous of them, Elizabeth Barrett Browning's *Sonnets from the Portuguese*, supposedly had been issued in Reading in 1847, three years prior to the earliest known appearance of these poems. Yet not a single copy bore an inscription, although the edition was purportedly "not for sale" and produced for Mrs. Browning's private distribution among her friends. Further, all the copies were in superb condition, showing no signs of ever having been read. This was also the case with most of the other pamphlets. While such facts may cause suspicion, they are not legally damning, but they inspired Carter and Pollard to employ modern scientific methods to make a case against Wise. A chemical analysis of the paper from one of the Browning pamphlets—and God bless

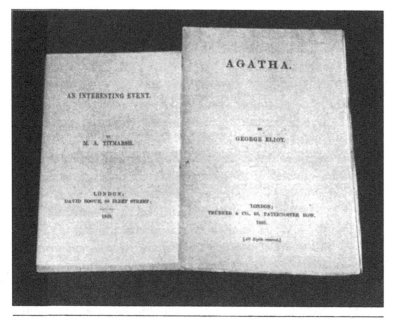

Two pamphlets forged by Thomas J. Wise late in the nineteenth century. Courtesy of the Grolier Club.

the one rare-book librarian who had courage enough to snip a small strip from her copy—proved that it had been manufactured long after 1847, when the book was presumably printed. Then there was the evidence of the typefaces, which also could be demonstrated not to have been in use until long after the imprint dates of the pamphlets. Wise refused all comment, and died shortly afterward in disgrace. Ironically, Wise's fame is such that his forgeries today are collected in their own right; a "genuine Wise forgery" may bring more now than it did in the days when an unsuspecting collector believed he was buying a genuine early rarity.

No serious attempt at anything similar occurred until the late 1960s. Back in the 1930s, in fact almost precisely at the time when the Wise scandal broke, a young poet-novelist named Frederic Prokosch commissioned the printing, quite legitimately and with the knowledge and permission of the various authors concerned, of a series of small pamphlets of poems by such poets as W. H. Auden, T. S. Eliot, and W. B. Yeats. The pamphlets were always limited to an extremely small number of copies (usually twenty or twenty-two—although there is beginning to be a suspicion that there may have been some duplication of numbers), printed on a variety of papers. Prokosch was personally acquainted with the poets, and copies of most of the pamphlets exist with genuine presentation inscriptions dated at the time of issuance. A choice copy is T. S. Eliot's *Two Songs*, inscribed by the author to the then-fledgling W. H. Auden on the eve of the latter's birthday. As the pamphlets were known and catalogued immediately upon publication, there can be no question that they were genuine.

However, in the late 1960s and the early 1970s, additional Prokosch pamphlets by these poets suddenly began appearing at auction, along with titles by other authors not previously known to have been published by him. They appeared chiefly in sales at one of the principal London auction galleries, where most of them were bought by one of the oldest and most honored of British booksellers. At first, collectors were dismayed. Here was a whole series of hitherto unknown and important items—and there were virtually none to be had. What was one to do, when one prided oneself on having a complete author collection—and that collection had suddenly developed an expensive, and perhaps unfillable, gap? I had such collections of Marianne Moore and Gertrude Stein, each of whom now appeared to have permitted a "Prokosch" pamphlet. Gradually, as the first shock wore off, experienced dealers and seasoned collectors began to be suspicious. It seemed odd in the extreme, with the earlier pamphlets well documented since the date of their imprints, that these had never come to light before. Some of the pam-

A genuine T. S. Eliot pamphlet published by Frederic Prokosch in 1934, inscribed by Eliot to Auden and dated. From the author's collection.

phlets had in addition a manuscript note, apparently in Prokosch's own hand, describing the exact circumstances in which each had been printed, at various towns in Europe, between 1934 and 1940. All this added color to the supposition that more pamphlets had been printed than had previously been known. Inevitably collectors, bibliographers, and other experts discussed these new rarities, and inevitably, each voiced his suspicion. For my own part, having been for many years an avid collector of the works of both Stein and Moore, I found it hard to believe that I would never have heard of these had they legitimately existed. Both ladies were meticulous with regard to their own publications, and had Miss Moore, a longtime friend, known of their existence, she would certainly have at least shown me one, if not given me a copy. With respect to Gertrude Stein, the evidence against such a pamphlet was even more weighty. Being convinced of her own genius and immortality from the very beginning, she preserved every scrap of paper she ever received—every letter, card, note, and household bill, right down to the bills for the clipping and grooming of her pet poodle, Basket. She also religiously kept all her manuscripts, written in longhand in school notebooks. These were then transcribed by the faithful Alice Toklas into typewritten copies to send out for possible publication. In all of her massive archive, carefully stored at Yale, fully catalogued, there is no correspondence from Prokosch about any such publication, nor any trace of the poem he issued under her name. Prokosch claimed that he lost the manuscript of "Lily" (the title of the poem he caused to be printed). It does not even sound like genuine Stein, thus posing the possibility of a double forgery—not only of the imprint, but also of the text as well.

All this came into the open when a supposedly complete set of these pamphlets was put up for sale on 1 May 1972. The majority were bought by Bernard Quaritch, Ltd. of London; Arthur Freeman, of that firm, doubtful from the first, asked Nicolas Barker, editor of *The Book Collector* and a bibliographer specializing in the analysis of the physical attributes of books, to examine them. As with the Wise forgeries, Mr. Barker was now able to establish that typeface, paper, or text condemned 75 percent of the pamphlets as manufactured later than the date on the title page. Mr. Barker's account of the entire episode is scheduled for publication soon.

In the United States, in the 1960s, a series of piracies—that is, books issued in violation of copyright—were issued by the New York firm of Haskell House. These were not intended to defraud collectors, since for the most part they did not attempt to reproduce the formats of the original editions. They were intended primarily to fill the demand for scarce, out-of-print texts. The technique was to photocopy a first edition, sometimes in the same size and approximate format, sometimes in larger or smaller size. This firm flourished for a few years, long enough to issue at one point a catalog listing a hundred of these productions. Eventually they were forced to desist when they started issuing titles by Eliot, Stein, and other authors whose estates or literary executors took offense. Some of these books are of interest to in-depth collectors who want every imprint of a title. In the main they are not dangerous, for they cannot possibly fool a collector of even small experience.

Somewhat more serious to collectors is the matter of fakes—that is, the sale of a reproduction as an original. This occurs fairly often in other collecting fields—notably antiques, paintings, and stamps. Generally speaking, for most books the expense of the faking is prohibitive. To set up type, print pages, bind the book, and go through all the necessary mechanics normally involves so much time and labor that the process is self-defeating. Naturally, the simpler the production format, the greater the chance there is that a fake can be produced. Pamphlets are easier to make than hardbound books, and mimeographed items easier still. It is in this last category that some fakes have been produced, especially since the mimeograph revolution of the late fifties. Mimeography was one of the principal methods employed by the Beats to issue their works. To my knowledge, however, only one fake of a mimeographed rarity has been identified definitely—an early book by Larry Eigner entitled *Look at the Park*, where the stencils were retyped, run again, and reissued in identical format. Luckily for collectors, a slight error was made on the reissue: it was stapled at the top left corner only. The original had been stapled all along the left side. The telltale staple holes in the upper corner make identification of this fake very easy. But there well may be other mimeographed fakes in existence that have never been identified.

The conversion of honest facsimiles into fakes is another matter and once again it is not something easily accomplished in the case of bound books. To begin with, very few facsimiles are issued, and those that are usually have various kinds of marking on them so as to render faking difficult, although, of course, not totally impossible. The gambit is rare enough, however, not to need further elaboration here. In most cases, attempted conversions of facsimiles into fakes are so clumsy as to be obvious to almost any collector with a modicum of experience.

The area where there is, alas, a considerable amount of dishonesty and faking is in the field of signed or inscribed copies. This mainly takes the form of forged signatures in books that are genuine. While entire inscriptions can be forged, they are much more difficult to accomplish than signatures and much easier to identify as fraudulent. What usually appears is merely a forged signature copied, with varying degrees of skill, from a genuine specimen. The model is usually a signature in a signed limited edition because there is generally no question of its genuineness. (Not that there is *never* a question in such a case: In one notorious instance, Delacorte Press in 1967 announced a signed limited edition of *A Christmas Story* by Katherine Anne Porter, illustrated by Ben Shahn, to be signed by both. Shahn signed all five hundred of the copies, but Miss Porter became ill and could not sign them. As this was an item aimed specifically at the Christmas market it would have been disastrous to have waited for her to recover. So a modern "auto-pen" was employed, a mechanical device that copies the signature fed into it. Such machines are sometimes used by busy executives who must sign great numbers of letters and became well known to the collecting field when employed by the late

President Kennedy. A couple of sharp-eyed dealers noted the repetitious similarity of the Porter signatures and protested to the publisher. Delacorte permitted unsold copies of the book to be returned for signing—post-Christmas—by the author.)

Some signed book forgeries are good enough to fool even the experts. Luckily, though, most of them are fairly easily recognizable by anyone familiar with a genuine signature. Here again, it pays to have established a working relationship with a reliable and experienced dealer who has seen a considerable number of genuine signatures and is likely to be able to spot fakes and forgeries.

The growing interest in, and demand for, autograph and manuscript material has given rise to another unscrupulous dodge, to which many amiable authors have unwittingly lent their aid. This takes the form of getting an author to sign a typed extract from one of his works, which is then offered in the trade as a typed "manuscript, signed." Of course, it is nothing of the kind, since it was not typed by the author and in no way can be considered anything more than an example of the author's signature. Some authors who have been victimized by this practice now quite rightly refuse to sign any typed extracts, and one hopes that the practice is on the wane.

Human nature being what it is, there will always be fakes and forgeries as long as there are customers for material that can be faked or forged. To understand why some collectors are so gullible as to buy things that even on the surface should sound suspicious, it is necessary to understand the deep urge felt by every collector—including the innocent and the unskilled—to own something unique, something dazzling, that no one else has. One old-time dealer, Samuel Loveman, now dead, played this tendency to the hilt in the last twenty years of his long life, offering all sorts of things that common sense should have told anyone could not possibly be genuine. He was fond of signing famous authors' names into worthless books, offering them in his catalogs as having come from the famous authors' own libraries. It once emerged that no fewer than three of his customers had bought Cabell's *Jurgen* with Dylan Thomas' "signature of ownership." But, despite his ability to make reasonably good copies of genuine signatures, Loveman had a slight palsy, and the handwriting on his spurious products was always a little tremulous, a dead giveaway most of the time. He had acquired, on the death of Hart Crane's mother, her entire archive of her son's letters, books, and papers, a lot that included a large supply of Crane's unused bookplates. Well into the late 1960s Loveman was pasting these into otherwise valueless books, offering them as books from Hart Crane's library. At least once, to my knowledge, he slipped up and put a bookplate into a book not published until after Crane's death.

As senility set in, Loveman got more and more careless about signing books, using ball-point pens for signatures of authors who had died before the ball-point pen was invented. His catalogs were an endless source of amusement to those familiar with his wares. To my mind, he reached the peak of his forging career when he offered, for a mere $50, a book on whaling "annotated in pencil by Herman Melville." I've often wondered who bought this treasure.

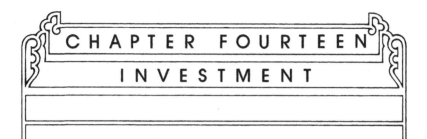

CHAPTER FOURTEEN

INVESTMENT

Most dealers have, at best, ambiguous feelings about customers who are frankly collecting for investment, and while no dealer in his right mind will refuse to sell a book to a customer for this reason alone, dealers usually prefer to place their better books with customers who are collecting primarily for the love of the sport. Realistically, of course, no collector is ever completely unconcerned about the value of his books. One of the many satisfactions in owning a collection is the pleasure of watching a book you have purchased at a nominal price, perhaps even at publication price, start on an upward spiral.

In the past couple of years there has been a considerable amount of discussion in newspapers and national magazines about the investment potential of rare books. Part of the reason for their attractiveness is the fact that several other popular inflation hedges have performed erratically recently, or moved beyond the reach of the average investor. Gold coins, after a boom, stayed more or less level for several years. Impressionist and other modern paintings (which first took the lead in price rises) are now far beyond the means of all but millionaires. Antique furniture, while a good potential investment, presents a massive storage problem. So attention has turned to the field of rare books, where prices are still moderate, supplies available, and storage problems not overly burdensome.

A sure sign of the widespread belief in the attractiveness of rare books as a form of investment is the sudden proliferation of companies purveying what they term "collectors' editions." These are supposedly deluxe limited editions, sold at fancy prices by direct mail and by means of heavy advertising in mass magazines. The advertising is not at all hesitant to tout the investment potential of these books, implying that they are bound to increase in value. All the more reason to bear in mind that several factors must obtain for this to occur. First of all, the book has to be truly scarce, if not rare. (These two terms are vague at best, and are quite often used interchangeably in dealers' catalogs. However, most collectors and many dealers will agree that "scarce" means that a book will be difficult to find immediately or even soon, but will, in all probability, eventually turn up within a reasonable period of time. A truly "rare" book may not be seen for years, perhaps not for decades.) To be scarce or rare, the initial number of copies in existence must be relatively small. "Relatively small" can mean as many as a thousand copies, but certainly no more than that, and probably far fewer. Secondly, it should have the advantage of being either a first edition or, at the very least, an edition that offers something that no other edition can boast—perhaps the signature of the author, or illustrations by a well-known artist, perhaps original etchings or lithographs bound in or an extraordinarily fine binding. The firms offering "collectors' editions" currently meet very few, if any, of these requirements. One firm does advertise that all of its books are first editions—in fact, uses the words "first edition" in the club's name. Much of the time it is true that their edition is a legitimate first, but in several documented cases their editions were in fact issued later than the corresponding trade edition. Ultimately, when bibliographies of the various authors involved are compiled, this lack of priority will be spelled out. As a result, the book is scarcely likely to command any kind of premium.

The prospectuses and advertising copy of these various

clubs are shrewdly calculated to trap the unwary. While nothing that they state is actually untrue, a lot of information that is crucial and relevant is carefully omitted. When the most prominent of these companies started its series, an advertisement listed the authors whose new books the firm would publish and then elaborated in considerable detail the high prices that certain titles by those authors were now bringing. For example, W. H. Auden's *Sonnet* was quoted as being worth anywhere from $400 to $600, and William Faulkner's *Marble Faun* $1,700. Both of these price indications were correct (perhaps even underestimated), but it takes very little research to show how little they have to do with the prospective value of books issued by the club. Auden's *Sonnet* was privately issued in 1934, early in the poet's career, in an edition of only twenty-two copies. Faulkner's *Marble Faun* was virtually worthless for nearly forty years after its publication in 1924, during which time the never very large number of copies in the initial printing became very small indeed. The number of copies actually issued by the club of Auden's *Collected Poems* and the *Selected Letters of William Faulkner* (two of the authors singled out as prime examples of good investment possibilities) exceeded 40,000—more, in fact, than were published in the regular trade editions of the books. Now, it is possible for these books to increase in value—but I wouldn't wait for it to happen! So, the first trap for an investor to avoid is that of joining a book club that promises him, even by implication, books for investment.

There have been, and still are, many other book clubs devoted to the production of fine books in limited editions, most of which are legitimate and do produce handsome books. The Limited Editions Club has been in existence since 1929, producing, usually, a book every month; but not for investment. Many people join this club for a couple of years and then are distressed to learn that they seldom can get their original investment back when they go to sell the books. Handsome as they are, very few of them have increased very much in value over the years.

Among the most notable of Limited Editions Club books that have appreciated is James Joyce's *Ulysses* with six original etchings by Matisse. This edition was originally announced as being signed by both Joyce and Matisse, and Matisse did actually sign the colophon sheets for all 1,500 copies. Joyce, however, signed only slightly more than 250 sheets, ceasing when he realized—on looking at a set of the etchings airmailed to him—that Matisse had not illustrated his work at all but, through a misunderstanding, had illustrated Homer's *Odyssey*. So copies bearing both signatures command a far higher premium than those with only Matisse's signature, although, naturally, any copy of the book, containing as it does six original Matisse etchings, brings a healthy sum. The Limited Editions Club edition of *Lysistrata*, illustrated by Picasso, also always brings a high price, as do the two *Alice* books signed by Alice Hargreaves (the original Alice for whom Lewis Carroll wrote the stories) and two or three other titles in the series, mainly those with illustrations by such notable twentieth-century artists as André Derain and Thomas Hart Benton. But such wanted books account for fewer than a dozen titles out of nearly six hundred. It bears out the principle that book club editions, no matter how fine, *must* have some other important distinction ever to become valuable.

Investing in books as a form of profit making is just as risky as investing in stocks and bonds. Seemingly "safe" authors may fall from grace and favor and never again find popularity among collectors. The classic example, known to every dealer, is that of John Galsworthy, who in the late 1920s and early 1930s was *the* twentieth-century author to collect. His first book, *From the Four Winds*, written under the pseudonym of John Sinjohn, was eagerly sought after

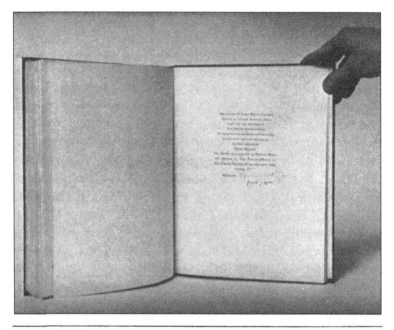

Colophon page of one of the few copies of the Limited Edition Club's edition of James Joyce's ULYSSES, *illustrated by Henri Matisse, that were signed by both Joyce and Matisse. From the author's collection.*

and sold readily for $500 or $600 in 1933, when that amount of money represented a staggering figure. (To gain perspective on this, remember that a married man could raise a family, own his home and perhaps even an automobile, on a salary of $45 a week. The best cut of sirloin steak was 25¢ a pound.) After World War II, Galsworthy fell from popularity and has never recovered with either collectors or readers. Even the success of the television version of *The Forsyte Saga* a few years ago failed to create any demand for his work other than a brief flurry of interest in that one sequence of novels. Nowadays, you can buy *From the Four Winds* for well under $100, and the complete combined *The Forsyte Saga* for not much more, even in the deluxe edition. The other titles cannot be given away. So anyone who invested in Galsworthy has taken a terrific beating.

Nor is that an isolated example. Forty or fifty years ago, the popular authors to collect were H. L. Mencken, James Branch Cabell, A. E. Coppard, Joseph Hergesheimer, Carl Van Vechten, Willa Cather, Robinson Jeffers, Eugene O'Neill, and Edna St. Vincent Millay. Mencken and Cabell slumped badly. Cabell today commands only a very limited audience, and his books sell at modest prices. Mencken has started a comeback, but there is absolutely no interest whatever in Hergesheimer or Coppard, and only a modicum in the works of Van Vechten. Millay, Cather, O'Neill, and Jeffers, of course, are still widely collected. But the same precipitous decline may—and undoubtedly will—strike some of today's top favorites during the next two decades. It would be patently foolish at this point to try to predict which ones they will be. But certainly very few of the much sought after novelists of the present generation will remain in great demand at such inflated prices as are now current.

My belief, based on nearly forty years of experience and observation, is that poets fare better in the long run, for many reasons. For one thing, they arrive much more slowly at peaks of eminence and, in the nature of things, also decline —if they ever do—far more slowly than popular novelists. Another important factor is that the number of copies printed of a book of poetry is extremely small in most cases, especially when compared with the quantity printed of a popular novel. A book of poetry may well have only five hundred or a thousand copies in its first printing (if, indeed, it ever reaches a second). For example, Robert Lowell's first book, *The Land of Unlikeness*, was published in 1944 in an edition of 226 copies, at $2 each. Four years earlier, Hemingway's *For Whom the Bell Tolls* appeared in an edition of 75,000 copies. Hemingway's reputation was well established by that time and copies of his book were readily bought up by col-

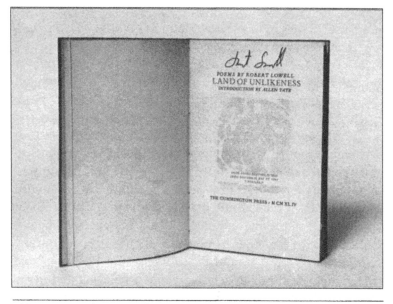

Title page of Robert Lowell's first book, signed by him. From the author's collection.

lectors. Very few people had ever heard of an unknown poet named R. T. S. Lowell, and only a small number of people bought the book. Those who did buy it were mostly fans of the Cummington Press, which printed it, and they purchased it as an example of fine printing. Some three or four decades later, the price of the Hemingway book has done little more than keep pace with inflation, not because of any decline in Hemingway's popularity with collectors but simply because of the enormous number of copies available. On the other hand, Lowell's book is now recognized as one of the key books in any collection of postwar American poetry, and easily fetches four figures when a copy comes on the market. Lowell's second book, *Lord Weary's Castle*, was published by a commercial firm, Harcourt, Brace and Co., and earned him his Pulitzer Prize. While the firm will not disclose the actual number of copies printed, it was almost certainly fewer than five thousand—far, far fewer than that of a Hemingway novel. Today, of course, a copy will cost far more than a copy of Hemingway's *Bell*. This parallel can be drawn all along the line between poetry and fiction. Among living novelists in the late 1970s, John Updike is far and away the most collected fiction writer. His books are produced in enormous quantities, and most also appear in book club editions. Updike novels usually have large initial printings— up to fifty thousand copies—and sometimes go into later printings. His signed, limited editions (issued concurrently with the regular trade edition) are always oversold before publication. On the other hand, the books of the poet Howard Nemerov, a recent National Book Award and Pulitzer Prize winner, are produced in relatively small editions and often remain available for several years in the first printing (most never go into later printings at all). In all probability, decades hence the later novels of Updike will, like Hemingway's *For Whom the Bell Tolls*, be available at reasonable prices despite a continued interest in Updike. The volumes of Nemerov's poetry, all other factors being equal, should rise appreciably over the years simply because there are so few of them.

There are, of course, as with everything, exceptions to this generalization. If a poet such as Carl Sandburg, Marianne Moore, or Allen Ginsberg becomes a public figure (usually, it must be admitted, because of his or her picturesque personality), large editions of his or her work will be printed, though still not nearly as big as those of popular novels. Thus, Marianne Moore's last few volumes will probably never be high-priced items since there are sufficient quantities available to satisfy any and all collectors. The same applies to the later books of Ginsberg, produced in editions of thousands of copies. But Ginsberg's first two books, the aforementioned mimeographed *Siesta in Xbalba* and *Howl*, a watershed volume in the history of American poetry, climb steadily in value. It is fairly safe to say that they will always command a large price, since, whatever one may think of Ginsberg's *oeuvre* overall, his impact on the course of modern poetry has been (in my opinion) greater than that of any other single poet in this century. His books will always have a unique place in literary history—and among collectors.

Many collectors do not have a realistic idea of how much a dealer can or will pay for books. This is often a source of disappointment and sometimes even anger. Especially in the case of modern books, which are often in fairly adequate supply, the would-be seller may be startled to find that he cannot get as much as he paid in the first place, even if he has kept the book for a considerable time, unless for some reason the price for that particular volume has increased significantly. With very few exceptions, no dealer can or will pay more than half of what his ultimate retail selling price will be, and many dealers pay even less than this. Fifty percent is the absolute top price that should be expected. Thus, if the collector has bought novels of an established author such as Norman Mailer or John Updike or Colin Wilson, particularly the middle and later titles of such authors, he should expect to experience difficulty in breaking even. These later titles were all issued in extremely large quantities and are therefore not difficult to find. When such books as these are offered, most dealers will be only mildly interested. Chances are they have at least one copy in stock and perhaps many more, with no prospects of immediate sale. So an offer below the original purchase price can be quite honest and is in no way intended to cheat the owner. In fact, by offering to buy the books at all, the dealer may be doing the seller a favor. There is one way for the seller in such a predicament to realize somewhat more on his investment, and that is by taking other books in trade rather than cash. Most dealers will allow a higher price if it is in trade for other merchandise, the usual offer being approximately another 15 to 20 percent above the cash price.

If the collector has bought books after the particular author has come into widespread collector popularity, he has probably paid premiums for some of them, making his chance of breaking even on resale even less. Once again, the rule of thumb of one-half the dealer's prospective retail price applies. Even with today's rapid increases, it takes a long time for a book to double in price—necessary if the owner is to get back his original investment—or to increase beyond that point—necessary if he is to make a profit. As always, there are exceptions, but as a general rule, little or no profit can be expected on books held for less than a decade. As has been repeatedly said, book collecting should be done for the fun and love of it, not primarily for profit.

Still another factor playing a part in determining prices is one that many people fail to take into consideration. Yet it is probably the most important one of all. Condition has been stressed in other chapters of this book. Modern books, and particularly books published in the last thirty years, are, with very few exceptions, not difficult to find in fine condition and usually with presentable dust jackets. Therefore, many dealers refuse to buy copies without dust jackets, and few dealers, if any, will buy worn copies of books published since World War II. Many beginning collectors hear about phenomenal prices, especially after an important auction, or read high prices in catalogs, but fail to comprehend that these high prices are based very largely on the fact that the book's condition is splendid. They think that their dog-eared copy should bring just as much and cannot understand why the dealer either offers very little or refuses to buy. The importance of condition in a book is much the same as condition in a used automobile. A used Ford in fine running condition is worth far more than a smashed-up Cadillac beyond repair.

CHAPTER FIFTEEN
DONATING OR SELLING
YOUR COLLECTION
TO AN INSTITUTION

The problem of what to do with a large or important collection is one that every collector thinks about from time to time. We have already discussed selling at auction. A second option, and one that is favored by a large segment of the serious book-collecting fraternity, is placement en bloc in an institution. As with other ways of disposing of a collection, this option presents both advantages and disadvantages to the owner, to say nothing of surprises, dangers, and pitfalls along the way.

If you decide not to sell the collection on the open market and thus to break it up, but want to keep it intact by placing it in an institutional library, you have several important choices to make, each with legal ramifications for you and for the institution you select. First of all, most basically, you must decide which institution you want it to go to. This is usually one's alma mater. However, a great many eminent colleges and universities have neither rare-book libraries nor facilities for using or caring for a collection of first editions and related material. And even if your college or university does have a rare-book library, it may not, for a variety of reasons, want your collection. A university's library, including its rare-book section, must be related to the curriculum being offered and to the interests and needs of the student body and the academic staff. An institution devoted primarily to medicine and science, for example, is unlikely to have much interest in a collection—fine as it may be—of avant-garde literature. By the same token an institution lack-

ing a medical school is a poor place for a collection of landmark books on the history of medicine. And a university in
the depths of Idaho might prefer not to have a collection devoted to pictorial material on the history of New York City.
Even if the university of your choice does have a legitimate
interest in the area covered by your collection, it still may
prefer not to accept it because it duplicates books already in
the institution's possession. There are several universities
both in this country and abroad that have been quietly acquiring all the more unusual literary items as they were
issued for the past three or four decades, long before prices
for twentieth-century British and American first editions
began to skyrocket. Few of these institutions would be particularly interested in taking over a collection that in large
measure duplicates their existing holdings, especially if it
bears any sort of restrictions—that it be maintained in toto,
for example, or never be sold.

Thus, before you write a clause into your will leaving
your collection to an institution, you should have some serious discussions with the resident librarian. You might, in
the long run, do the library more good by having the collection sold, with the library to receive the proceeds. Many collectors naturally like to think of their personal collections
living on after them as monuments to their taste and perspi-
cuity. More and more, however, it becomes necessary to
endow a library building or a special room, and to furnish
maintenance; costs have risen so high that few institutions
are otherwise prepared to cope with gifts of rare-book collections. Very few people are wealthy enough for this, even
though they may have spent a considerable amount of money
putting together an important and impressive library. Therefore, more often than most people realize, an institution will
prefer to extract the volumes it needs from a donated collection and quietly dispose of the duplicates. This process is not
as reprehensible as it sounds, even though it may go counter

to a donor's intentions. Unwanted duplicates do no one any good, especially when they can be turned into cash for the acquisition of needed items. More positively—and any true collector will appreciate the value of this—such dispersal sends many scarce and desirable items back into the market for other collectors and institutions to acquire and enjoy. Some institutions, of course, do not part with duplicates; one of the largest and most venerable of American universities has in its collections as many as six copies of a certain extremely rare book, causing considerable unhappiness to collectors who know of them—frozen, held there to no purpose. A serious discussion with the institution's rare-book librarian, on a frank basis, will often prevent a miscarriage of intentions. If you want your collection to be kept intact, despite possible duplication of holdings, this should be made unequivocally clear before the collection is donated or willed.

Once an agreement on the library's treatment of the collection has been reached, there are several ways of negotiating the actual transfer. Some universities are both willing and able to purchase large collections en bloc. If you hope to make such a sale, you will need a written, itemized listing of every piece in the collection, with adequate description, along with a specific total price, based on an item-by-item evaluation. It probably will be necessary to go to a professional appraiser, most likely an experienced dealer, for such a summary. (When placing a price on a unified collection that is complete, or nearly so, in special areas of coverage, it is customary for an appraiser to add a bonus for completeness, for intangibles, or for extraordinary condition.) With such documentation in hand, the institution can be approached. The librarian can use the itemized list to determine whether or not he is interested in acquiring the collection; if he is, he can then use it as the basis for a presentation to his library committee, or trustees, or whatever group controls the appropriation of funds.

The other means of placing your collection with an institution is of course by gift. This can be of benefit to you in terms of tax deduction, but must be planned with care. Many people make occasional minor gifts of books to institutions as a convenient way of disposing of unwanted duplicates, with no thought of any particular benefit to themselves other than, possibly, some much-needed bookshelf space. But a major gift can have important tax consequences. An absolutely basic requirement is to have an itemized appraisal, prepared in triplicate, by a recognized dealer or appraiser. One copy goes to the library with the books; the original goes with your income tax papers; the third copy is for your own files.

Before you dispose of your collection—whether to a dealer, to another collector, or to an institution—make sure you understand the tax situation. The American tax laws were changed as of January 1, 1978, and now require possession of an item for nine months, rather than six as was previously the case, before the increase in its value can be claimed on resale as a capital gain. Capital gains are taxed at a maximum rate of 50 percent. But the most critical fact to be remembered, one that cannot be stressed too much, is that you *must* keep some kind of record of the acquisition date and actual purchase price or cost of each item in the collection, in order to be able to prove to the United States Internal Revenue Service the exact amount of profit (or possibly loss) on each item in the collection. Many collectors, especially when they are beginning, don't keep itemized records. With most modern books this is not a serious failing; it is fairly easy to reconstruct the prices paid for books as they were issued, at least in the case of books produced by the major publishing firms, since the price is generally printed on the dust jacket. Nevertheless, small-press publications in many cases do not have such notations, and here some record should be kept. Obviously, it should also be kept on books for which a premium price has been paid. The best thing, from a tax accountant's point of view, is to have the bill of sale from the dealer. A file of these, kept over the years, will forestall many a headache at the time when you dispose of your books, and may avoid—or at least resolve speedily—an IRS audit. If you don't want anyone else to know in the meantime what you have paid for an item, be it friends viewing your books or perhaps even your wife, work out a number code that can be penciled lightly somewhere in the book in an inconspicuous place—for instance, under the rear flap of the dust jacket. Any ten-letter word or phrase—to represent in order the numbers one through nine, plus zero—will suffice as a key so long as there are no duplications of letters. One collector that I knew of early in my collecting days was delighted when he realized that the name of the only author he collected worked out exactly to ten letters with no repeats—Ezra L. Pound. Thus the $185.00 he paid for his copy of *A Lume Spento*—whose value is now perhaps 3000 percent higher—worked out in code as EULDD.

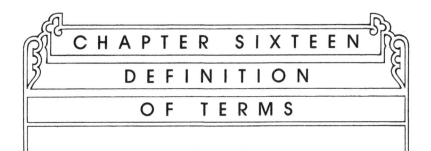

The terms employed in book collecting are fairly standard-
ized. At the same time they have special uses restricted to
this field, and a complete understanding of them is essential,
especially when reading auction catalogs and dealers' catalogs. In such publications these terms will be used repeatedly, on the assumption that anyone reading the catalog is familiar with them. The following is a list of terms
and definitions commonly used among dealers and collectors
of modern rare books.

-ANA   A suffix denoting, originally, a collection of sayings,
anecdotes, or other material regarding a person or subject. Nowadays it refers to any kind of material about
the author or subject to which it is attached. For instance,
Hemingwayana means any book or item *about* Hemingway, but not *by* him.

AS ISSUED   A term indicating that a given book (or some aspect of it) is in the original condition as published, despite appearances to the contrary. The term is most often
encountered today in dealers' catalogs in cases where a
book being described was published without a dust jacket,
the normal assumption being that most modern books are
issued with dust jackets.

ASSOCIATION COPY   A book or pamphlet that has some indication of having belonged to, or at least passed through the
hands of, the author or someone closely related to him.
Properly speaking, an association copy should carry more
than a signed presentation inscription to an unknown per-

son. Any book from the library of an esteemed author, with his annotations, would be an association copy. Likewise, a copy of the author's book presented by him to someone important in his life, such as a wife or mistress; even better, a copy presented to someone who was known to have served as the model for one of the characters in the book. An example of the latter would be a copy of Hemingway's *The Sun Also Rises* with the signature of Harold Loeb, who was the model for the character of Robert Cohn.

BACKSTRIP   The covering over the spine of a book. If this has been replaced, the book is spoken of as having been rebacked.

BLIND-STAMPING   An impressed mark, decoration, or lettering, not colored or gilded, usually appearing on the binding. A modern example of this can be found in the plays of Edward Albee, published by Atheneum, where all of the lettering on the front covers of the books is blindstamped. It can also denote an impressed mark or name used by some persons in preference to a written signature. A familiar example of blind-stamping is the old-fashioned notary public's seal.

BOARDS   The stiff binding material for most modern books; generally cardboard covered with cloth or paper. In the early days of printed books during the fifteenth and sixteenth centuries, actual wooden boards were used—hence the term. Nowadays, the term is almost exclusively used to describe books whose covers—or boards—have been covered with paper. If they have been covered with cloth, the single word "cloth" is generally used.

BOOK BLOCK   The entire book sewn together before it is bound.

BOOK LABEL   A label indicating the ownership of a book. It generally bears only the owner's name and is as a rule smaller and simpler than a bookplate.

BOOKPLATE   A pasted-in sign of ownership, usually larger and more elaborate than a book label, and often incorporating a design or artwork. Bookplates themselves form a fascinating field for collecting. Probably the most sought-after bookplate in the United States is that of George Washington.

BROADSIDE   A single sheet of paper, usually printed on one side only. Originally these were public proclamations or notices, but later became a popular means of distributing songs and ballads. In the twentieth century, the term generally refers to a single poem printed on a fairly large sheet of paper. Since the end of World War II there has been a virtual mania among small press owners for producing broadside poems, with artwork and typography (and poetry) of varying quality.

CANCEL   A tipped-in (i.e., pasted-in) page to replace a page removed after a book has been bound. This is done for a variety of reasons, most commonly to correct a serious misprint discovered too late. A recent example of this occurred with the publication of John Updike's *The Music School*, where three lines of verse occur on page 446. Two of these three lines were transposed, and the error was not discovered until a quantity of copies had been not only printed but shipped. The balance of the edition was then withheld until a new page could be printed with the lines in correct order, the page with the error sliced out, and the correctly printed one pasted in, thus creating a "cancel."

CASE-BOUND   This term indicates that a book is hardbound as opposed to a paperback.

CHAPBOOK   Properly speaking, a chapbook is a cheaply printed book of the kind sold by street vendors in the eighteenth and nineteenth centuries. It is today often used to refer to any small pamphlet.

CHIPPED   A term used to describe dust jackets or the fragile

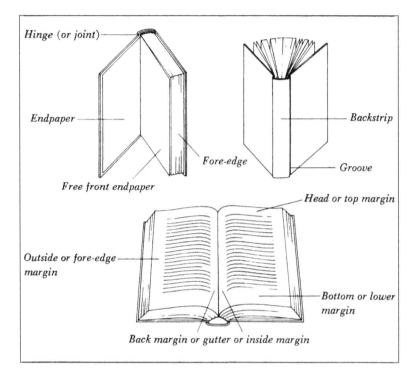

Hinge (or joint)

Endpaper

Free front endpaper

Fore-edge

Backstrip

Groove

Head or top margin

Outside or fore-edge margin

Bottom or lower margin

Back margin or gutter or inside margin

edge of a paperback where small pieces are missing or fraying has occurred.

CLOTH   In many catalogs, the word "cloth" used to describe a copy of a book means simply that the book, cloth-bound, lacks the dust jacket, whether or not it originally had one.

COLLATION   Technically, the examination and notation of the physical makeup of a book. By checking for the presence of every leaf or page originally in the volume when issued, a book may be collated as complete. While few modern books will be found to be lacking any printed pages, books issued with illustrations, especially original etchings or lithographs by well-known artists, often, alas, lack one or more of them. Some art dealers make a practice of removing these items and then reselling the book itself. Sometimes there is no indication in the printed text that the illustration should have been present. The unwary neophyte may be trapped into buying an incomplete copy. Aside from those with important artwork, most modern books do not require collation.

COLOPHON   A statement from the printer or publisher appearing at the end of a book. In the early days of printing, when books did not have title pages, the printer placed his personal seal or device on the last printed page of the book. He generally indicated the location of his press and the date the printing was completed, often to the very month and day. Today, when most publishers place their names and sometimes devices on title pages, colophons are usually encountered only on limited editions. They may give the number of copies in the edition, and sometimes such printing details as the kind of paper and the typeface used, especially if these differ from the trade edition. If the edition is signed by the author, the signature usually—although not always—appears here.

CONJUGATE LEAF   The unsevered second half of a printed page. Books are generally sewn together in signatures (i.e., groups of pages) made up of anywhere from twelve to sixteen sheets of paper, folded so that one single leaf will bear four pages of print. Thus, in a signature of twelve sheets, the leaf bearing pages 1 and 2 will have as its conjugate the leaf bearing pages 23 and 24.

CUT   Many modern books are smooth-trimmed after binding so that all edges are even, or flush. This is described as having been "cut," to differentiate it from books where the edges are left "rough," or slightly uneven. This term is often confused with "unopened." (*See* uncut.)

DECKLE EDGES   Another term for uncut or untrimmed edges. (*See* uncut.)

DEDICATION COPY   The copy of the book inscribed by the au-

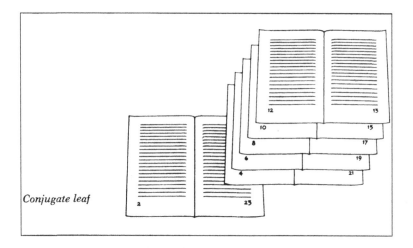

Conjugate leaf

thor to the person to whom the book is dedicated. Obviously, there can be only one such copy, and it is usually regarded as the most desirable of all possible copies of any book. In recent years there has been a widespread misuse of the word "dedication" when the word "inscription" is actually intended, when describing a copy that bears an author's handwritten inscription. This misuse probably stems from the fact that in French such an inscription is called a *dédicace*.

DEVICE A printer's ornament. Also an insignia that is the publisher's identifying mark, generally found on the title page and also sometimes on the binding of a book. For instance Random House employs a drawing of a house; Knopf uses a Borzoi dog, and the Hogarth Press a wolf's head. This is also sometimes called a logotype or "logo."

DISBOUND This term refers to a book or pamphlet, once bound, from which the binding has been removed. Not to be confused with "unbound," which refers to a book that has never been bound. The term is usually encountered in connection with older pamphlets that were often

bound up together in volumes and have since been separated again.

DUST JACKET   A term synonymous with dust wrapper, indicating the usually decorative paper wrapper placed
around a book to protect the binding. Dust jackets came
into general usage towards the end of the nineteenth century, although they did not come to be considered by collectors to be an integral part of the book until well into
the twentieth century. Today it is unwise to purchase a
book without its dust jacket. Considerable premiums are
now asked for books of earlier vintages that still have
their original jackets. Particularly startling, for example,
is the difference in price between copies of F. Scott Fitzgerald's *The Great Gatsby* with and without the jacket.
The former can be ten times the latter.

ENDPAPERS   The sheets of paper pasted onto the inner covers,
joining the book block to the covers. One half of each
sheet is pasted onto the board of the binding, leaving the
other half free, creating the front—or rear—free endpapers. These free endpapers are sometimes mistakenly
referred to as "flyleaves." (*See* book block, flyleaf.)

EPHEMERA   Plural of the Greek word *ephemeron*, meaning
something that disappears quickly. This is now an om-
nium-gatherum word that will include anything not
easily classifiable under any other heading. Ephemera is
perhaps one of the most diverting and intriguing fields
for collecting, and is discussed more fully in Chapter
Two.

ERRATA   Mistakes or errors. Generally encountered in the
term "errata slip," a small sheet of paper laid in loosely
or sometimes glued (or "tipped") into a book by a publisher who has discovered the errors prior to publication
of the book, but too late to correct them. An errata slip
is easily lost, and its presence is generally noted in catalogs as a plus point in the value of a particular copy.

EX-LIBRARY   A term used to indicate that a particular copy
of a book was once in a library, usually a public or institutional library, or even worse, a lending library. It
may be expected to be worn and defaced with call numbers, card pockets, perforated title pages, and other such
distressing features. Lending libraries also usually paste
the flaps of the dust jackets down to the endpapers. Such
copies are to be avoided almost without exception.

EXTRA ILLUSTRATED   A copy of a book into which additional
illustrations have been bound. This was a popular pastime in Victorian days, when years were sometimes spent
in gathering engravings of every person and place mentioned in a book and then having the entire collection rebound. Depending on the type of book, a one-volume
affair could bulk up into three volumes by this process.
Now looked upon askance, except as a curiosity.

FIRST EDITION   Generally used by book collectors and dealers
to mean the first appearance of a work in book or pamphlet form, in its first printing. (*See* pages 111–2.)

FIRST SEPARATE EDITION   The first appearance as a complete
book or pamphlet of a work that has previously appeared
as part of another book. For example, Gertrude Stein's
Four Saints in Three Acts first appeared in a book entitled *Operas and Plays* in 1931. In 1934, after the opera
had become a phenomenal success in its American pre-
miere, it was issued separately by Random House—the
first separate edition.

FIRST TRADE EDITION   The edition produced for general commercial sale, as distinguished from a limited edition. An
example of this can be found in the recent books of John
Updike, most of which have been issued in both signed
limited editions as well as trade editions.

FLYLEAF   A blank leaf, sometimes more than one, following
the front free endpaper, or at the end of a book where
there is not sufficient text to fill out the last few pages. A

term often misapplied to the front or rear endpaper. (*See* endpaper.)

FOXING   Brown spotting of the paper caused by a chemical reaction, generally found in nineteenth-century books, particularly in steel engravings of the period. Seldom encountered in twentieth-century books unless they have been stored for a long time in a humid climate such as Florida or New Orleans. While seldom disastrous, foxing does spoil the appearance of a book, and foxed copies are usually to be avoided. However, because of the nature of the paper used in certain books, unfoxed copies may be impossible to find.

FRONTISPIECE   An illustration at the beginning of a book, usually facing the title page.

GALLEYS   Sometimes called "galley proofs" or "loose galleys" to distinguish them from bound galleys. (*See* page 172.) Long sheets of paper bearing the first trial impression of the type. Usually containing two or three pages per strip, they are used to catch typesetting errors before proceeding with the book. Very few copies are printed (or "pulled"). In recent years they have become much sought after, particularly if they bear the author's manuscript corrections. Newer offset printing methods, especially those involving computer typesetting, may produce galleys that are photocopied and perhaps already page-broken.

GATHERING   A group of sheets folded together for sewing or gluing into the binding. Also called a signature.

HALF LEATHER   A term indicating that the spine and sometimes the corners of a book are bound in leather, while the rest of the binding may be cloth or paper.

HALF TITLE   The leaf carrying nothing but the title of the book, usually preceding the title page. The half title was commonly removed by eighteenth- and nineteenth-century binders. A modern book may have more than one.

HEADBAND   A decorative cloth band, sometimes colored or
   multicolored, appearing inside the backstrip at the top
   (and sometimes also bottom) of the spine of a book.
   Headbands were originally a normal feature of a sewed
   binding but are no longer required; if they appear at all,
   it is mostly as a matter of swank.

HINGE   The joint (either outer or inner) of the binding of
   a book—the part that bends when the book is opened.
   Since this is the part that gets the most wear and tear,
   it is also the part where most defects occur. This is particularly true of leather-bound books kept in a heated room
   and never treated with a leather preservative. If the
   inner hinge is starting to come apart, usually noticeable
   by the endpaper's splitting, the book is said to be "starting." Cataloguers apparently cannot bring themselves
   to complete the phrase by saying "starting to fall apart."

HOLOGRAPH   A term indicating the handwriting of the author. Thus a holograph letter is a letter entirely in the
   author's handwriting. The term *autograph* means the
   same thing, although in recent years it is generally used
   to refer to a handwritten name.

IMPRESSION   A much misused term, but one that, when accurately employed, means the copies printed during any
   given press run.

IMPRINT   A term that can refer either to the place of publication or to the publisher. Imprint collecting is a popular
   field, particularly books and pamphlets printed in a given
   city or state before a specific date. Any book printed in
   what is now the United States prior to 1776 is a pre-
   Revolutionary imprint. Books printed in the Confederate
   States during the Civil War are Confederate imprints,
   and so forth.

INDIA PAPER   An extremely thin yet relatively opaque paper
   used to help reduce the bulk of what would otherwise be
   a book of unwieldy size. Most Bibles, for example, are

printed on India paper. Thus the synonymous term "Bible paper."

INSCRIBED   Usually indicates a book signed by the author, either with an inscription to a specific person or bearing some brief notation along with his signature. An inscribed copy is not necessarily the same as a presentation copy (which is one actually given to the recipient by the author), but it is often difficult to distinguish between the two. Some authors are particularly careful to make this distinction clear. T. S. Eliot, when making an actual presentation to a friend, would write "For ———— from T. S. Eliot"; when asked by a stranger to sign or inscribe a book, he would write "Inscribed for ———— by T. S. Eliot." A book bearing only the author's signature is not an inscribed book, but merely a signed one.

INTEGRAL   A leaf or page is said to be integral when it is one that was sewn and bound into a book during its manufacture. The opposite of a *cancel*. (*See* cancel.)

ISSUE   Generally synonymous today with "state," referring to the priority of copies within the first edition, if indeed any priorities exist. The earliest copies released are known as the first issue. While sometimes it is a matter of varying colors or types of binding (or even in rare cases of the type of paper on which the book has been printed), issues are usually created by errors that may be corrected during the press run. In F. Scott Fitzgerald's *The Great Gatsby*, for example, one of the characters says she is "sick *in* tired." This mistake was caught during the run and corrected to "sick *and* tired," thereby creating a first and second issue within the first edition. Another type of error created two issues in the first edition of Hemingway's *A Farewell to Arms*. The book originally lacked the disclaimer notice about the characters being entirely fictional. Wishing to avoid any possible lawsuits, the publishers stopped the presses before the printing was completed and inserted the notice. Then the press run was completed. The copies without the notice belong to the first issue, those with the notice to the second issue, although both issues are first editions. Anything that distinguishes one issue from another is known as a "point." (*See* points.)

JAPAN VELLUM   A smooth, glossy paper, made in imitation of vellum, generally a light tan color. Quite often used in the production of deluxe editions. Virtually all of the books of the Black Sun Press were printed on Japan vellum.

JUVENILES   Books originally or primarily written to be read by (or to) children, although they are usually highly esteemed by adults as well. *Treasure Island* and *Winnie-the-Pooh* are good examples of juveniles that are collected.

JUVENILIA   Work written when an author was extremely young, often a child.

LAID PAPER   A handmade paper showing parallel lines of the papermaking frame, visible when held up to the light.

LIMITED EDITION   Any book whose publication is deliberately restricted to a comparatively small number of copies, usually numbered, and often signed by the author and/or the illustrator. Such books generally (although not always) are further distinguished by being printed on better paper than that used for the trade edition, and with a more expensive binding. Occasionally they are issued in a slipcase (sometimes referred to as a publisher's box).

LIMP   An adjective describing a flexible binding in suede or imitation leather such as that used on the early titles of the Modern Library. A paperback is not a limp binding.

MADE-UP COPY   A copy of a book whose parts have been assembled from one or more defective copies. Made-up copies of modern books are uncommon but may be found. Making up and other forms of tinkering are also known as "sophistication."

MARBLED Paper decorated with an imitation marble pattern. Marbled papers were especially popular for endpapers in the nineteenth century, and today are most often encountered on deluxe limited editions and occasionally on the page edges.

MINT COPY An absolutely perfect copy, as fresh in all respects as the day it was issued.

MISBOUND Pages or signatures sewn together in an improper order. As long as no pages have been omitted, it is not a matter of crucial importance to most collectors, although a perfectly bound copy is, of course, preferable. A misbound copy is not more valuable, as a misprinted stamp might be.

MONOGRAPH A work, generally short, dealing with a single subject and usually issued in pamphlet form.

MOROCCO A type of leather made from goatskins, especially suitable for book bindings because of its durability and beauty. It has a naturally grainy surface texture. When this is pressed to a smoother finish, it is then referred to as "crushed morocco." Morocco can be dyed a wide variety of colors, red, brown, green, and black being the most common. Black is referred to as "niger morocco" or sometimes merely "niger," from the Latin word for "black."

OUT OF PRINT A book no longer available from the publisher is termed "out of print." Often abbreviated as "o.p."

PASTE-DOWN The portion of the endpaper pasted to the inner cover of a book.

PIRATED EDITION Any edition of a work issued without permission of the author and without payment of royalties to the author or copyright holder. Until the adoption of the International Copyright Law in 1891, it was common for the work of popular authors to be pirated. This practice virtually died out in the twentieth century until recent years when Russia started pirating the works of British and American authors. Since 1949, a flood of piracies has been coming out of Taiwan, printed by photo offset from the original editions and including even the dust jackets. Since they cannot be legally imported into the United States or the United Kingdom, Taiwan piracies have become, in the peculiar but logical manner of such things, sought after by many collectors.

POINTS   Distinguishing characteristics, usually errors, that occur within a first edition and indicate the priority of copies. "Points" differentiate "issues." (*See* issue.) It should be noted, incidentally, that existence of an error is not necessarily proof of an earlier state. In T. S. Eliot's *The Waste Land*, the letter *a* dropped out of the word "mountain" on page 41 approximately halfway through the printing run, so presence of the error is proof of the later state. And certain errors, despite appearances, do nothing to establish priority. For nearly fifty years, many dealers have been cataloguing copies of Faulkner's *Light in August* as "first issue" because they contain an obvious error on page 340, where "Mottstown" is called "Jeffersonville." This is not a point, however, since the error was never corrected, and appears in every copy of *Light in August* ever published, including the Modern Library reprints.

PRESENTATION COPY   A copy of a book actually given by the author (or in rare cases by the publisher) to someone of his acquaintance, usually with an inscription of some sort testifying to this disposition. A mere signature of an author does not make it a presentation copy, since most authors are willing to sign numerous copies of their books at readings or other public appearances. Actual presentation copies are relatively uncommon, because authors seldom receive more than a dozen free copies of their books and cannot afford to give away many. Presentation copies are accordingly the most highly valued category of books for the collector. This is particularly true if the presentation is to another well-known author. Prices for such copies may be several times higher than for unsigned or autographed copies of the same book. (*See* inscribed.)

PRIVATE PRESS   A small press, often operated by one person, usually devoted to the production of small quantities of finely printed books. The work is usually of superior quality, and the collecting of "press books" is an extremely popular field of endeavor.

PRIVATELY PRINTED   This term does not refer to the output of a private press (*see* private press), but to a book or pamphlet whose printing was paid for by an individual or a group, and which is meant for private circulation, not public sale.

PROOF   *See* galleys.

PROVENANCE   The history of ownership or possession of a given book (or painting or other art object). Some extremely rare books have a recorded unbroken pedigree of ownership through the ages. A catalog may, for example, refer to a copy of a book as "the Hoe-Kern-Goodwin" copy, indicating that the book at various times formed part of these distinguished collections. Collectors of twentieth-century books rarely discover the provenance of a particular book (unless it can be pieced together from signatures or bookplates or dealers' information), since there are few examples of modern books so rare as to warrant recording the history of ownership.

PUBLICATION DATE   The date a book is formally placed on sale. Finished copies may be available as much as a month or six weeks beforehand, and will be in bookstores prior to the publication date. "Publishing" a book is the process of placing it on sale, not of printing it.

READING COPY   A copy of a book that is worn or used to such a degree that it is unacceptable to modern collectors, although it may still be textually complete. Such copies are sometimes termed "working copies," and are generally shunned by collectors.

REBACKED   A book that has been repaired by getting a new spine and mended hinges. This is seldom done on modern copies; most twentieth-century books are still in condition not requiring repairs, and few are so scarce as to warrant the expense of such work. Rebacking is usually seen only on leather-bound books of the eighteenth century or earlier.

RECASED   A book that has been glued back into its covers after having been shaken loose. This process entails, at the very least, the replacement of the endpapers and often more extensive surgery.

RECTO   The front side of a leaf in a bound book; in other words, the right-hand page of an opened book. (*Recto* means "right" in Latin.)

REMAINDER   When a book has ceased to sell, a publisher may get rid of his overstock by "remaindering" the title. Sold in quantity at a reduced price, the books will turn up either in special remainder stores or on bargain counters in regular bookstores at a substantial markdown from their original price. It sometimes happens that a publisher has been holding a certain number of copies "in sheets" (i.e., printed but not bound) and, to dispose of them as cheaply as possible, will bind them for remaindering in particularly inexpensive material. Thus while the pages themselves may be from the first printing, the binding is a so-called remainder binding, and a copy so found is less desirable than one in the original binding.

SHAKEN   An adjective describing a book whose pages are be-

ginning to come loose from the binding. This separation
from the casing usually occurs along the inner hinges.

SIGNATURE   In bookmaking, this does *not* mean the author's
name written out in his hand. It refers rather to the
group of pages produced by folding a single printed
sheet, ready for sewing or gluing into a book. A careful
look at the top of a book will show immediately whether
signatures have been inserted into the binding or whether
the edges of single leaves have been glued together to
make what is rather incredibly called a "perfect" binding. A signature is sometimes called a gathering.

STATE   Closely allied to the definition of "issue." "State"
generally refers to a change other than a correction of a
misprint. It can occur anywhere, either in the printed
portion of the book, the binding, or even the dust jacket.
For instance, the photo of Hemingway on the rear panel
of the dust jacket of *For Whom the Bell Tolls* bore no
photographer's credit. This was noted, and the photographer's name added at some point during the printing
of the jackets. Thus while the book itself exists in only
one state, the jacket exists in two. An example of a book
that exists in four states—none of them due to any error
—is Gertrude Stein's *Geography and Plays* (where, incidentally, her famous "rose is a rose is a rose" first
appears). It was published in 1922 in an edition of one
thousand copies. At that time Stein did not sell very well,
and the publisher bound up the sheets in groups of 250
at a time, over a period of ten years. As might be expected, after intervals of several years, he was not able
to obtain exactly the same binding materials, thus creating four states of the binding—and none of them remainder bindings. (*See* remainder.)

STUB   A narrow strip of paper usually remaining where a
leaf has been cut away. Cancels are pasted onto stubs.
Sometimes a stub is a normal part of the book's construc-

tion, as for example when a frontispiece is an etching or engraving on paper other than that used for the printing of the text, and a stub is needed as a base to glue it on. A stub without some reasonable explanation is usually a danger signal that something has been removed from a book.

SUNNED   Faded from exposure to light or direct sunlight. This usually occurs on spines (and can occur even through dust jackets), but may happen to any exposed portion of a book. Green and purple are notoriously unstable colors, and books bound in those colors inevitably become sunned quickly.

TOP EDGE GILT   Usually abbreviated t.e.g., it means that the top edges of the pages have been covered with gold leaf or a gilt material. This was originally done to make the book easier to dust. Today it is mainly employed on deluxe editions as a form of "elegance."

TRIMMED   An adjective indicating that the pages have been cut down to a size smaller than when originally issued. This usually occurs when a book is rebound.

UNCUT   One of the most misused terms in book collecting. It means simply that the pages of the completed book have not been shaved down to a uniform surface. (*See* cut.) It does *not* mean "unopened." An unopened copy of a book is one whose pages need the service of a paper knife before they can be opened and read.

VERSO   The second, or rear, side of a leaf in a book. When the book is opened, the page on the left is the verso (Latin for "turned"). The opposite of recto.

WRAPPERS   The outer covers of a paperbound book or pamphlet. Not to be confused with "dust wrapper."

ABBREVIATIONS

A.L.S.   autograph letter, signed

BDS   boards

D.J. or D.W.   dust jacket or dust wrapper

MS   manuscript

N.D.   no date (of publication)

N.P.   no place (of publication)

O.P.   out of print

T.L.S.   typed letter, signed. It is also an abbreviation for *The Times Literary Supplement*. The context will indicate which.

BOOK SIZES

A full sheet of paper used by printers can be folded in such a manner as to make two or more pages in a book, depending on the size of book desired. When the sheet is folded once, it is termed a "folio"; when folded twice, it becomes a "quarto" (since it then produces four leaves); when folded three times it becomes an "octavo" (eight leaves) and so on. Since the size of the original sheet may vary, it is possible to have a large quarto, or a small folio, or even a "Crown octavo," the latter indicating a somewhat smaller size than the ordinary octavo. These terms are usually indicated numerically:

4to — quarto
8vo — octavo
12mo — duodecimo
16mo — sextodecimo

and so forth. A handy way of correlating sizes is to remember that the larger the number, the smaller the book. Another handy device is to remember that most modern novels are 8vo size.

Note that the book sizes described above are largely based on the traditional sheet-size used by printers until this century. Today, most books are printed on presses capable of handling far larger sheets, so that the standard gathering is 16 or even (less commonly) 32 leaves. Yet the books are no smaller, and a novel "in 32s" will probably still be described as an octavo (that is, about $8\frac{1}{2}'' \times 5\frac{1}{2}''$ to $9\frac{1}{2}'' \times 6''$), even though it is technically a "32mo."

Size has no bearing on the value of a book, but it is customary in dealers' catalogs to note the size so that the prospective customer will have some idea of the size of the book he is ordering. There is one classic tale, known to almost every American dealer, of the collector who had searched for years for a copy of T. S. Eliot's *Ara Vos Prec*, and then, when a dealer triumphantly sent it to him, returned it. When the dealer asked why, his reply was that he had not known that it was so large and it simply wouldn't fit on his bookshelves! Few collectors are so obtuse, but it does sometimes help in the search if you know the physical size and appearance of the item you are searching for.

APPENDIXES

INDEX

APPENDIX ONE

LIST OF BOOK AUCTION

FIRMS HANDLING BOOKS

OF INTEREST TO COLLECTORS

CALIFORNIA BOOK AUCTION CO.   *224 McAllister Street, San Francisco, Calif. 94102*

CHRISTIE, MANSON & WOODS INTERNATIONAL, INC. ("CHRISTIE'S")
   8 King Street, St. James's, London SW1, England

CHRISTIE, MANSON & WOODS INTERNATIONAL, INC. ("CHRISTIE'S")
   502 Park Avenue, New York, NY 10022

SAMUEL T. FREEMAN & CO.   *1080 Chestnut Street, Philadelphia, Pa. 19103*

CHARLES HAMILTON AUTOGRAPHS, INC.   *25 East 77th Street, New York 10021*

HANZEL GALLERIES, INC.   *1120 South Michigan Avenue, Chicago, Ill. 60605*

HARRIS AUCTION GALLERIES, INC.   *873–75 North Howard Street, Baltimore, Md. 21201*

HUNTINGTON-MANN BOOK AUCTION GALLERY   *467 Alvarado Street, Suite 35, Monterey, Calif. 93940*

MONTREAL BOOK AUCTIONS   *750 Sherbrooke Street West, Montreal, PQ, Canada*

PHILLIPS SON & NEALE, BLENSTOCK HOUSE   *7 Blenheim Street, New Bond Street, London, W1, England*

PLANDOME BOOK AUCTIONS   *113 Glen Head Road, Glen Head, NY 11545*

SOTHEBY PARKE BERNET & CO.   *34 & 35 New Bond Street, London W1A 2AA, England*

SOTHEBY PARKE BERNET, INC.   *1334 York Avenue, New York, N.Y.
10013*

SOTHEBY PARKE BERNET-LOS ANGELES   *7660 Beverly Boulevard, Los
Angeles, Calif. 90036*

SWANN GALLERIES, INC.   *104 E. 25th Street, New York, NY 10010*

ABOUT BOOKS   280 Queen Street West, Toronto, Ontario, Canada
M5V 2A1

AM HERE BOOKS   2740 Williams Way, Santa Barbara, Calif. 93105

AMPERSAND BOOKS   P.O. Box 674, Cooper Station, New York, NY
10003

ANACAPA BOOKS   3090 Claremont Avenue, Oakland, Calif. 94705

ANT OPERA BOOKS   P.O. Box 1055, Lawrence, Kans. 66044

ARGOSY BOOK STORES, INC.   116 East 59th Street, New York, NY
10022

ASPHODEL BOOKSHOP   17192 Ravenna Road, Route 44, Burton, Ohio
44021

NELSON BALL   686 Richmond Street West, Toronto, Ontario, Canada
M6J 1C3

BARQU BOOKS   216 West 89th Street, New York, NY 10024

BELL, BOOK & RADMALL, LTD.   80 Long Acre, London WC2, England

DEBORAH BENSON BOOKSELLER   P.O. Box 947, West Cornwall, Conn.
06796

BLACK SUN BOOKS   667 Madison Avenue, New York, NY 10021

BROMER BOOKS   127 Barnard Avenue, Watertown, Mass. 02172

JOHN R. BUTTERWORTH   742 West 11th Street, Claremont, Calif.
91711

H. ALAN CLODD   22 Huntington Road, E. Finchley, London N2 9DU,
England

CHLOE'S BOOKS   *PO Box 255673, Sacramento, Calif. 95865*

COLOPHON BOOKSHOP   *Box E, Epping, N.H. 03042*

COMPENDIUM BOOKSHOP   *240 Camden High Street, London NW1 8QS, England*

LLOYD CURRY RARE BOOKS   *Church Street, Elizabethtown, NY 12932*

WILLIAM DAILEY ANTIQUARIAN BOOKS   *P.O. Box 69812, Los Angeles, Calif. 90069*

DALIAN BOOKS   *14 Remington Street, Islington, London N1 8DH, England*

JORDAN DAVIES   *356 Bowery, New York, NY 10012*

PHILIP C. DUSCHNES   *699 Madison Avenue, New York, NY 10021*

I.D. EDRICH   *17 Selsdon Road, London E11 2QF, England*

ELYSIAN FIELDS   *81–13 Broadway, Elmhurst, NY 11373*

JOHN F. FLEMING   *322 East 57th Street, New York, NY 10021*

FULLER D'ARCH SMITH, LTD.   *30 Baker Street, London W1, England*

MICHAEL GINSBERG BOOKS, INC.   *P.O. Box 402, Sharon, Mass. 02067*

GOODSPEED'S BOOKSHOP   *18 Beacon Street, Boston, Mass. 02108*

GOTHAM BOOK MART   *41 West 47th Street, New York, NY 10036*

HAMILL & BARKER   *400 N. Michigan Avenue, Chicago, Ill. 60611*

HERITAGE BOOKSHOP   *847 N. Lacienega Boulevard, Hollywood, Calif. 90069*

WILLIAM HOFFER   *570 Granville Street, Suite 101, Vancouver, B.C., Canada V6C 1W65*

JOHN HOWELL BOOKS   *434 Post Street, San Francisco, Calif. 94102*

IN OUR TIME   *P.O. Box 386, Cambridge, Mass. 02139*

THE JENKINS CO.   *P.O. Box 2085, Austin, Tex. 78767*

JOSEPH THE PROVIDER   *903 State Street, Santa Barbara, Calif. 93101*

KENNETH KARMIOLE   *2255 Westwood Boulevard, Los Angeles, Calif. 90064*

JAMES LORSON BOOKS   *Villa del Sol, Suite B-6, 305 N. Harbor Boulevard, Fullerton, Calif. 92632*

PAUL GARON/BEASLEY BOOKS   *1533 W. Oakdale, Chicago, Ill. 60657*

GEORGE S. MACMANUS CO. *1317 Irving St., Philadelphia, Pa. 19107*

IAN MCKELVIE BOOKSELLER *45 Hertford Road, London N2 9BX, England*

GEORGE R. MINKOFF *Rowe Road, R.F.D. #3, Box 147, Great Barrington, Mass. 01230*

JAMES MOREL *241 Central Park West, NY 10024*

BRADFORD MORROW *33 W. 9th St., New York, NY 10011*

KENNETH NEBENZAHL, INC. *333 N. Michigan Avenue, Chicago, Ill. 60601*

MAURICE NEVILLE *835 Laguna Street, Santa Barbara, Calif. 93101*

THE PHOENIX BOOK SHOP *22 Jones Street, New York, NY 10014*

BERNARD QUARITCH, LTD. *5–8 Lower John Street, London W1, England*

BERTRAM ROTA, LTD. *30 & 31 Long Acre, London WC2E 9LT, England*

SAND DOLLAR BOOKS *1205 Solano Avenue, Albany, Calif. 94706*

JUSTIN G. SCHILLER, LTD. *36 East 61st Street, New York, NY 10022*

BARRY SCOTT *15 Gramercy Park S., New York, NY 10003*

SERENDIPITY BOOKS *1790 Shattuck Avenue, Berkeley, Calif. 94709*

G. F. SIMS RARE BOOKS *Hurst, Reading, Berkshire, England*

ERIC & JOAN STEVENS *82 Fortune Green Road, Hampstead, London NW6 1DS, England*

THE STRAND BOOKSTORE *828 Broadway, New York, NY 10003*

SYLVESTER & ORPHANOS BOOKSELLERS *2484 Cheremoya Avenue, Los Angeles, Calif. 90068*

THE TURRET BOOK SHOP *43 Floral Street, London WC2E 9DW, England*

UNIVERSITY PLACE BOOKSHOP *821 Broadway, New York, NY 10003*

THE VILLAGE BOOKSTORE *239 Queen Street, West Toronto, Ontario, Canada M5V 1Z4*

BERNICE WEISS *36 Tuckahoe Avenue, Eastchester, NY 10707*

EDNA WHITESON *66 Belmont Avenue, Cockfosters, Hertfordshire, England*

JEFF WEINBERG *The Beat Bookshop, PO Box 438, Sudbury, MA 01776*

SECOND LIFE BOOKS *PO Box 242, Lanesboro, MA 01237*

JOHNSON & O'DONNELL LTD *1015 State Tower Bldg., Syracuse, NY 13202*

J. HOWARD WOOLMER BOOKS   *Revere, Pa. 18953*

WORDS, ETC.   *89 Theberton Street, London N1, England*

XIMENES RARE BOOKS   *120 East 85th Street, New York, NY 10028*

HERB YELLIN   *19073 Los Alimos Street, Northridge, Calif. 91324*

WILLIAM YOUNG ASSOCIATES   *P.O. Box 282, Wellesley Hills, Mass.*
    02181

ZEITLIN & VERBRUGGE   *815 N. La Cienega Boulevard, Los Angeles,*
    Calif. 90069

With the exception of Fleming of New York, Hamill and Barker of
Chicago, and Alan Clodd in England, all of the above dealers issue
catalogs periodically, some more frequently than others.

APPENDIX THREE

CLUBS FOR

BOOK COLLECTORS

UNITED STATES

THE ACORN CLUB *1 Elizabeth Street, Hartford, Conn. 06105.* Limited to twenty-five members, all of whom must be Connecticut residents. Devoted solely to books relating to Connecticut. Issues occasional publications. Membership by recommendation only, and when there is a vacancy.

THE AMERICAN ANTIQUARIAN SOCIETY *185 Salisbury Street, Worcester, Mass. 01609.* One of the oldest active clubs of any type in America, having been founded in 1812. Large membership, limited to 325. Some publication activity. Membership by recommendation when a vacancy occurs. Primarily devoted to Americana.

ASSOCIATES OF THE JAMES FORD BELL LIBRARY *472 Wilson Library, University of Minnesota, Minn. 55455.* Membership of exactly 300, open to anyone paying the annual fee of $7.50. Several annual publications. Devoted primarily to the art of book production.

THE BAKER STREET IRREGULARS *33 Riverside Drive, New York, NY 10023.* One of the most famous clubs in the entire world, founded in 1934, devoted solely to the lore of Sherlock Holmes. Open to all who are conversant with the doings of their hero.

THE BALTIMORE BIBLIOPHILES *Evergreen House, 4545 N. Charles Street, Baltimore, Md. 21210.* Membership limited to 85, new members admitted by recommendation when a vacancy occurs. Three publications per year (for members only). For bibliophiles of all categories.

THE BIBLIOGRAPHICAL SOCIETY OF AMERICA *P.O. Box 397, Grand Central Station, New York, NY 10017.* Membership unlimited, open to anyone. Publishes a quarterly journal as well as occasional papers on the subject of bibliography.

THE BIBLIOGRAPHICAL SOCIETY OF THE UNIVERSITY OF VIRGINIA   *Alderman Library, University of Virginia, Charlottesville, Va. 22901.* Membership of 1,000, open to anyone interested in books, manuscripts, printing, and bibliography. Publishes an annual journal as well as occasional papers.

THE BOOK CLUB OF CALIFORNIA   *545 Sutter Street, Room 202, San Francisco, Calif. 94102.* Membership limited to 950, open to the public whenever a vacancy occurs. Publishes a quarterly journal as well as three other books or pamphlets per year. Covers all phases of book collecting.

THE BOOK CLUB OF DETROIT   *In care of Robert C. Thomas, Gale Research Co., Book Tower, Detroit, Mich. 48226.* Open to anyone interested in book collecting, printing, graphic arts, bibliography, book auctions and sales, libraries, and other book-related subjects. Publishes a journal irregularly.

THE BROTHERS THREE OF MORIARTY   *1907 Fort Union Drive, Santa Fe, NM 87501.* Membership limited to 50, by invitation only. No publications. Another Sherlock Holmes club.

THE CAXTON CLUB   *60 W. Walton Street, Chicago, Ill. 60610.* Membership limited to 265, open to the public by recommendation whenever a vacancy occurs. Publishes occasional monographs and pamphlets pertaining to literary studies and the art of the book.

THE CLUB OF ODD VOLUMES   *77 Mount Vernon Street, Boston, Mass. 02108.* Membership limited to men only. No publications.

THE COLLECTOR'S INSTITUTE   *P.O. Box 7219, Austin, Tex. 78712.* Membership open to anyone interested in book collecting and literary matters. Publishes occasional broadsides and keepsakes.

THE DELAWARE BIBLIOPHILES   *680 S. Chapel Street, Newark, Del. 19713.* Membership open to anyone with a love for books or book collecting. Publishes minutes of its meetings as well as catalogs of exhibitions at the University of Delaware.

THE GROLIER CLUB   *47 East 60th Street, New York, NY 10022.* Membership limited to 300 resident and 325 nonresident members. Publishes a semiannual gazette and other occasional catalogs and bibliographies. Membership upon recommendation for anyone with a sincere devotion to books or allied subjects.

HROSWITHA   *In care of Mrs. Sherman P. Haight, Sr., Chestnut Hill, Litchfield, Conn. 06759.* Membership limited to women book collectors, by invitation. Publishes occasional books.

THE LONG ISLAND BOOK COLLECTORS   *In care of Library Director's Office, Adelphi University, Garden City, NY 11530.* Membership by recommendation for any bona-fide book collector. Publishes an irregular journal and occasional catalogs.

THE MANUSCRIPT SOCIETY   *1206 N. Stoneman Avenue #15, Alhambra, Calif. 91801.* Membership open to any collector of autograph material. Publishes a quarterly journal as well as occasional volumes.

THE OLD SOLDIERS OF BAKER STREET OF THE TWO SAULTS   *909 Prospect Street, Sault Ste. Marie, Mich. 49783.* Membership open by invitation only to military men (or ex-military men) interested in Sherlock Holmes. Publishes a journal.

THE PHILOBIBLION CLUB   *In care of Hunt Institute for Botanical Documentation, Carnegie Mellon University, Pittsburgh, Pa. 15213.* Membership unlimited by nomination of two members. Occasional publications.

THE ROUNCE AND COFFIN CLUB   *1600 Campus Road, Los Angeles, Calif. 90041.* Membership upon recommendation for anyone interested in promoting book design and production in the West. Publishes an annual catalog of an exhibition of western-produced books.

THE ROWFANT CLUB   *3028 Prospect Avenue, Cleveland, Ohio 44115.* Membership upon recommendation for anyone interested in any phase of book collecting or study. Publishes an annual yearbook and one or two yearly volumes.

THE ROXBURGHE CLUB OF SAN FRANCISCO   *545 Sutter Street, San Fran-*

cisco, Calif. 94102. Membership limited to 100 men only, by invitation. No publishing program.

THE SACRAMENTO BOOK COLLECTORS CLUB   *7440 Alexander Court, Fair Oaks, Calif. 95628.* Membership upon recommendation for anyone interested in the printed word, especially as it pertains to the West. Publishes occasional pamphlets.

THE SOCIETY OF BIBLIOPHILES   *140 Manning Boulevard, Albany, NY 12203.* Membership for anyone interested in book collecting and the art of the book. No publications.

THE TYPOPHILES OF NEW YORK, INC.   *140 Lincoln Road, Brooklyn, NY 11225.* Membership limited to 500, by invitation, open only to professionals in the field of publishing. Publishes several pamphlets or chapbooks annually.

THE WICHITA BIBLIOPHILES   *207 N. Pinecrest, Wichita, Kans. 67208.* Membership limited to 12, by invitation only. No publications.

THE ZAMORANO CLUB   *P.O. Box 465, Pasadena, Calif. 91102.* Limited to 80 members, upon recommendation and approval of the board of governors. Publishes a journal, *Hoja Volante,* three times a year as well as other occasional items.

BRITAIN

THE BIBLIOGRAPHICAL SOCIETY   *In care of the British Library, Great Russell Street, WC1, England.* Open to the public. Publishes a journal.

THE PRIVATE LIBRARIES' ASSOCIATION   *Ravelston, South View Road, Pinner, Middlesex, England.* Publishes a journal.

THE ROXBURGH CLUB   *In care of His Grace the Duke of Northumberland, Alnwick Castle, Alnwick, Northumberland, England.* Membership upon recommendation. The most exclusive British club (no bookseller may be a member).

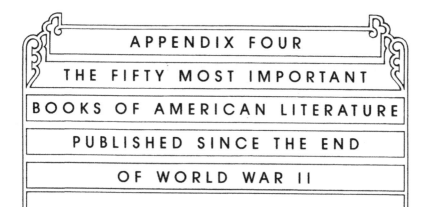

APPENDIX FOUR
THE FIFTY MOST IMPORTANT
BOOKS OF AMERICAN LITERATURE
PUBLISHED SINCE THE END
OF WORLD WAR II

The following is my own list of the fifty most important and influential books published in the field of American literature since the end of World War II. Most of the giants of the first half of the twentieth century were either dead by then or had already produced the main corpus of their works. There were, however, three poets of enormous importance in the years before the war, who continued to publish books that have been so deeply influential that they must perforce lead the list. The three men I refer to are Ezra Pound, William Carlos Williams, and Louis Zukofsky. I place them at the head of the list, which is otherwise arranged in alphabetical order.

EZRA POUND *The Pisan Cantos* New Directions (New York, 1948). These form part of his major work, *The Cantos,* and are perhaps the strongest and most controversial section of the entire work.

WILLIAM CARLOS WILLIAMS *Paterson.* This long poem was published separately in five parts, in successive volumes, by New Directions in 1946, 1948, 1949, 1951, and 1958, and subsequently reprinted in 1963 in one volume that also contained unfinished fragments of a sixth section. The impact of Williams on new poets is becoming more widespread as the influence of Eliot declines. Williams' first fame rested mainly on his miniature vignettes, but his main opus, *Paterson,* while an amalgam, is much more accessible to the general reader than are Pound's *Cantos* or Zukofsky's *A.*

LOUIS ZUKOFSKY   *A*. Issued, like Pound's and Williams' long works, serially, over a period of years between 1959 and 1975 (*A 1–12* Origin Press 1959; *A 13–21* Jonathan Cape, Ltd., 1969; *A 24* Grossman Publishers, 1962; *A 22–23* Grossman Publishers, 1975), the complete work was released in one volume by the University of California Press in 1979. Zukofsky, acknowledged as a peer by both Pound and Williams, is almost totally unknown to the general American and British public. However, his influence on the younger poets, particularly those of the Black Mountain School (Creeley, Duncan, Niedecker, et al.) is widely recognized and acknowledged. He is slowly but surely gaining a wider reading audience.

EDWARD ALBEE   *The Zoo Story*, which first appeared in the March/April 1960 issue of *Evergreen Review*, and had its first performance in Berlin, catapulted Albee into immediate fame and launched him on his meteoric career. He is now firmly established in the ranks of major American playwrights along with Eugene O'Neill, Tennessee Williams, and Arthur Miller.

JOHN ASHBERY   *Some Trees*, which was Ashbery's second book, and appeared in the Yale Younger Poets' Series in 1956, remains Ashbery's most accessible and appealing work. His recent receipt of the Pulitzer Prize, the National Book Award, and the National Book Critics Circle Award confirms the promise of this early work.

JOHN BARTH   *The Sot-Weed Factor*. Published in 1960 by Doubleday and Company, this was Barth's third novel, and the one on which his fame mainly rests. He is not a ground breaker, but rather a revitalizer of the technique of digression upon digression within a single narrative framework, virtually abandoned in literature since the death of Laurence Sterne. For collectors, this particular book has the added bonus of a dust jacket that is one of the earliest published works of Edward Gorey, now feverishly collected in his own right.

JOHN BERRYMAN *Homage to Mistress Bradstreet* (illustrated by Ben Shahn; New York, 1956). One of the best poets to come out of the Kenyon College group, Berryman gained the Pulitzer Prize late in his career for his *Dream Songs*. However, his best work seems to me to belong to his earlier period. This is his fifth book.

ELIZABETH BISHOP *Questions of Travel* (New York, 1965). Miss Bishop was a meticulous worker, never rushing into print until each poem had been finely polished to a gemlike luster. As a result, she issued a book no more often than every few years, but made them so marvelous that it is virtually impossible to single out one as being better than another. However, this title contains much work that is representative of her very best.

JANE BOWLES *Two Serious Ladies* (New York, 1942). In her tragically short life Mrs. Bowles produced only three books—a play, a group of short stories, and this novel, which while not widely known has attained a cult status. Its artistry is self-evident; it is a book one returns to periodically with ever increasing admiration.

PAUL BOWLES *The Delicate Prey and Other Stories* (New York, 1950). Bowles has been producing splendid work for nearly three decades and may well be our most underrated author. He has long been a resident of Tangier, and most of his work has a Moroccan background. He is at his best in the short-story form. What is perhaps his best story, "Pages from Cold Point," appears in this volume.

WILLIAM BURROUGHS *The Naked Lunch* (Paris, 1959). Burroughs' impact on modern fiction technique is undoubtedly the most widespread of any postwar writer's. His "cut-up" method, while far from accepted, has revolutionized narrative writing more than anything since the publication of Joyce's *Ulysses*. This seminal work, his second book, was issued in Paris in the now famous Traveller's Companion series of the Olympia Press.

TRUMAN CAPOTE   *The Grass Harp* (New York, 1951). Capote, at the beginning of his career, was almost universally regarded as little more than a picturesque and slightly decadent aesthete. However, since the publication of *In Cold Blood*, the critics have acknowledged his gifts both as a consummate storyteller and as a fine stylist, probably the best we now have. *The Grass Harp*, both as a novel and in its later play version, illustrates Capote's gifts superbly.

TRUMAN CAPOTE   *A Christmas Memory*, which first appeared as a piece to fill out *Breakfast at Tiffany's* in 1958, was not widely known until its television adaptation gave it a life of its own, making it a serious competitor of Dickens' Christmas classic. It is to my mind the finest piece of evocative writing produced in America since World War II.

GREGORY CORSO   *Gasoline* (San Francisco, 1958). By now, the so-called Beat poets are not only here to stay, they have almost become establishment. Their works are being taught in university courses, and many of them have become part-time professors. Corso, who in his private life in many ways resembles Rimbaud, has not produced a great volume of work, but has gained the respect of his peers to an extraordinary degree. Allen Ginsberg once proclaimed that Corso was "the one true poet of us all." *Gasoline*, his third publication, shows him at his strongest.

ROBERT CREELEY   *A Form of Women* (New York, 1959). Creeley is one of the major poets of the now famous Black Mountain School, founded by Charles Olson. His work has been uniformly characterized by a spareness and terseness that no doubt reflect his New England upbringing and clearly follow his own personal speech rhythms. His recurrent theme is that of the love of women, and this book, from his mid-period, is thus far most representative.

DIANE DI PRIMA   *Memoirs of a Beatnik* (New York, 1969). Beyond question the leading female member of the Beat group, di Prima is both a poet and a playwright of extreme sensitivity and perception, and one whose reputation is still growing. Despite the high quality of her poetry at its best, I have selected this volume of memoirs because of its overwhelming honesty, and also because it is the only book I have encountered that presents a totally accurate and at the same time moving account of the Beat period.

ROBERT DUNCAN *Selected Poems* (San Francisco, 1959). Along with Robert Creeley and Denise Levertov, Duncan is one of the triumvirate of Black Mountain poets who are the principal disciples of Charles Olson. Duncan is the most erudite of the group, and his work possesses a richness and density unequaled anywhere else in contemporary poetry. The body of his work is impressive, rendering a choice difficult. This early collection, however, shows him at his best.

WILLIAM EVERSON Known as Brother Antoninus during a long period as a Dominican friar, he has now returned to secular life and is producing work again under his original name. He actually started publishing before World War II, but the bulk of his poetry has been written in the period after it. The major influence on him has been Robinson Jeffers, and his *The Poet Is Dead* (San Francisco, 1964), a moving tribute to Jeffers, is his strongest and most impassioned book. Like Jeffers, his main preoccupation has been the conflict between man's physical nature and his spiritual aspirations.

LAWRENCE FERLINGHETTI *A Coney Island of the Mind* (New York, 1958). Ferlinghetti is a first-rate poet whose work has been overshadowed by his importance as the original champion and first publisher of many young poets who are now among the best known in America. Operating from his City Lights Book Shop in San Francisco, he was a major factor in the San Francisco Renaissance, with his "Pocket Poets Series" bringing to public attention such figures as Duncan, Corso, Levertov, and most famous of all, Allen Ginsberg, whose epochal *Howl* first appeared in this series. *A Coney Island of the Mind,* Ferlinghetti's second book, has been one of the best-selling books of poetry ever issued in the United States. In the twenty years since its publication it has never gone out of print.

ALLEN GINSBERG   *Howl* (San Francisco, 1956). Without any doubt, Ginsberg is *the* figure in postwar poetry, both here and abroad. The publication of *Howl* marks a watershed in American poetry as definitely as did *Leaves of Grass* in 1855. Virtually every American poet now writing has been influenced by Ginsberg's modern adaptation of the long, loose line of Whitman, whose spiritual and literary heir he is.

RANDALL JARRELL   *Little Friend, Little Friend* (New York, 1945). Another of the Kenyon group, Jarrell's comparatively early death robbed us of one of our best talents. He was both a superb poet and a critic of exquisite acumen, as well as a witty novelist. "The Death of the Ball-Turret Gunner," one of Jarrell's most famous poems and perhaps the best antiwar poem ever published, appears in this early volume.

RANDALL JARRELL   Jarrell is another author who must be represented by two books. His only novel, *Pictures from an Institution* (New York, 1954), is based on his teaching experiences at Bennington College. For sheer wit and inventiveness, it has had no equal since Beerbohm's *Zuleika Dobson.*

JAMES JONES   *From Here to Eternity* (New York, 1951). While his later work tends to be repetitive and verbose, this first novel deserves its fame as the best American novel to come out of World War II.

LEROI JONES   *Preface to a Twenty-Volume Suicide Note* (New York, 1961). Although somewhat sidetracked recently from poetry by his black nationalist activities, Jones (who now prefers to be known as Amiri Baraka) is a poet and playwright of exceptional qualities. This first book of poetry introduced him as the finest black poet since Langston Hughes.

JACK KEROUAC *On the Road* (New York, 1957). As with Ginsberg among the poets, Kerouac became *the* novelist of the immediate postwar world. This was his second novel, and it brought him instant and lasting fame. It became the vade mecum for the youth of all countries of the Western world, and has had probably a greater impact on its readers than any other work of fiction in this century.

GALWAY KINNELL *Body Rags* (Boston, 1968). Kinnell is a younger poet whose reputation is steadily increasing, whose technical accomplishments are staggering, and whose work continues to gain in strength and intensity. This volume contains two of his very best poems—"The Bear" and "The Porcupine."

JOHN KNOWLES *A Separate Peace* (London, 1959). Published in 1960 in the United States, Knowles' first novel bore the endorsement of both E. M. Forster and Truman Capote, the latter an author seldom given to praising the work of a potential competitor. The book deals with the aches and pains of adolescence and the loss of innocence, familiar themes, but in this case handled in a manner unmatched in recent years. To my mind, *A Separate Peace* is far superior to that other epic of adolescence, *Catcher in the Rye.*

JERZY KOSINSKI *The Painted Bird* (Boston, 1965). Polish-born Kosinski, now a naturalized American, writes in English, parallelling the practice of his compatriot Joseph Conrad. His first novel is a brilliant tour de force of terror and horror.

HARPER LEE *To Kill a Mockingbird* (Philadelphia, 1960). The author's only book to date is one of the most poignant and moving evocations of childhood ever published. It has no peer in the latter half of this century. Interestingly, her childhood companion Truman Capote appears as a character in this book, as she did in his first book, *Other Voices, Other Rooms*.

DENISE LEVERTOV   *Here and Now* (San Francisco, 1957). Some years back Kenneth Rexroth termed Denise Levertov "the finest female poet in America under the age of forty," obviously meaning to except her elders, Marianne Moore and Louise Bogan, now both deceased. This is her second book, showing her clearly to be a major poet from the very beginning.

ROBERT LOWELL   *Life Studies* (New York, 1959). Lowell, the acknowledged heir of T. S. Eliot, was the best known of the "academic" poets (as opposed to Beat poets). Much of his work betrays his personal inner conflict and turmoil. His fourth book represents an important stylistic departure from his earlier work, and probably strikes the best balance between his private agonies and his lyric gifts.

MICHAEL MCCLURE   *Dark Brown* (San Francisco, 1961). McClure may be the most interesting of all the San Francisco poets because he dares more than any other. Of course, he is not always successful, but he is never dull, and improbable ventures often yield fresh delights. *Dark Brown*, an early collection, shows all of his best traits.

CARSON MCCULLERS   *The Member of the Wedding* (Boston, 1946). Although the body of writing she left us at the time of her early death is relatively small, McCullers is assured a permanent position in American literature. This novel, later successfully transferred to the stage, is one of her best works.

NORMAN MAILER   *The Naked and the Dead* (New York, 1948). In his first novel, before he became an instant expert on almost anything topical, Mailer displayed a new style with a telegraphically direct impact.

JAMES MERRILL   *Nights and Days* (New York, 1966). Merrill is that rarest of all literary phenomena, the poet who starts out quietly and steadily improves and grows with each succeeding volume instead of thinning out as the years go by. A recent Pulitzer Prize elevated him to the forefront of American poets, a place he has honored by his unfailing accuracy of eye combined with an exceptional grace and felicity of style.

W. S. MERWIN *The Miner's Pale Children* (New York, 1970). Merwin belongs to no school or group, making his own way in every sense of the word. He will not accept teaching jobs, believing that poetry should support the poet. Luckily, this has sometimes required him to turn to translating, and he has brought us superb versions of many works, particularly from the Spanish, that we would not otherwise have had. The book cited here is prose and appeared the same year as his Pulitzer Prize–winning *The Carriers of Ladders*. It is a book of parables and is for me his finest work. It will remain in your mind for the rest of your life.

ARTHUR MILLER *Death of a Salesman* (New York, 1949). For a man who is generally conceded to be one of the century's leading playwrights, Miller's output is relatively small. It is nonetheless excellent, and by general consensus this heartrending portrayal of the tragic defeat of a man is a modern classic.

VLADIMIR NABOKOV *Lolita* (Paris, 1955). An American by naturalization, Nabokov wrote in English during the latter half of his life. His fondness for puns and word games sometimes carried on in two or even three languages simultaneously are a never-ending challenge to readers. *Lolita*, with its sensational theme of adolescent sexuality, catapulted him into fame; but it is also an extremely clever, subtle, and profound commentary on American culture.

HOWARD NEMEROV *Guide to the Ruins* (New York, 1950). Nemerov is a man of multiple talents—a superb poet, a good novelist, an excellent short-story teller, and a knowledgeable critic. Of his several volumes of poetry, all of them excellent, I personally prefer the book cited, if only because it was the first I read and it therefore made the strongest impact upon me.

FRANK O'HARA *Meditations in an Emergency* (New York, 1957). O'Hara's untimely death in a car accident robbed us of one of the best of the group known as the New York School of poets. He was one of the very few modern poets since Auden who could write good light verse that was not merely lightweight. Some of his best work appears in this book.

CHARLES OLSON *The Maximus Poems.* Appearing in installments in 1953, 1960, 1961, and 1969, *The Maximus Poems* are Olson's ongoing long poem. He is the patriarch of postwar poetry, and his position in many respects parallels that of Pound between the two wars. He was the founder of the Black Mountain School, and as a critic propounded the projective verse theory of poetry. The figure of "Maximus" is Olson's persona in this long work. It directly influenced many of the major poets now writing.

SYLVIA PLATH *The Colossus, and Other Poems* (London, 1960). The fact that Sylvia Plath has become the object of cult worship since her suicide in no way negates the fact that her poetry shows extraordinary power. Her first book of poems contains work of such emotional intensity that it is almost impossible to read more than one or two poems at a sitting.

SYLVIA PLATH *The Bell Jar* (London, 1963). Originally published under the pseudonym of Victoria Lucas, this harrowing novel was tragically prophetic. It chronicles a young woman's attempts, eventually successful, to commit suicide. The control Plath displays in this book is nothing short of marvelous.

JAMES PURDY *Malcolm* (New York, 1959). Purdy, never destined to be a popular writer like Updike, Roth, or O'Hara, may very likely endure much longer than the commercially successful novelists, despite the fact that the content of many of his books seems almost grotesque. The small-town characters who are his specialty are genuine, and his stories have the unmistakable ring of truth, disquieting and troubling as it may be. *Malcolm* is his third book, his first novel, and remains unsurpassed as yet in his work.

J. D. SALINGER *Nine Stories* (Boston, 1953). Despite the enormous popularity of *Catcher in the Rye*, I feel that his short stories are Salinger's strongest claim to fame. In them, his depiction of a segment of middle-class American life has an accuracy that will rank him with Sherwood Anderson. *Nine Stories*, his second book, is incidentally also the scarcest of them all.

GARY SNYDER *Regarding Wave* (Iowa City, 1969). Snyder is one of the most controlled poets now practicing. A longtime Zen Buddhist, he spent many years in the monasteries of Kyoto. This left an indelible impression on his work, which combines in a unique manner the finest traditions of Japanese delicacy of phrasing with the vigor and directness of the American idiom. *Regarding Wave*—published first in a limited signed edition, and later available in a commercial edition—shows him at the height of his powers.

DIANE WAKOSKI *The Motorcycle Betrayal Poems* (New York, 1971). While not an active feminist, Wakoski in her work displays the best results of women's liberation. She manages to convey women's feelings accurately without being either maudlin or didactic, and her poems are vigorous and direct.

JOHN WIENERS *Ace of Pentacles* (New York, 1964). One of the Black Mountain poets, and direct disciple of both Olson and Duncan, Wieners enjoys the recognition of his peers to an extraordinary degree. His recent work has been marred by recurrent personal problems, but of this early book, his second, Denise Levertov remarked that it could be used to show visitors from another planet what the word "poetry" meant.

RICHARD WILBUR *Things of This World* (New York, 1956). Wilbur is a man of dazzling wit and brilliance, who in addition to being one of our very best poets is a skilled translator (especially of Molière), a successful Broadway songwriter (*Candide*), and a competent critic and editor. His multiple levels of meanings are absolutely astounding, and he has a verve and humor rarely seen in this or any age. This volume was his third, and won him the Pulitzer Prize.

TENNESSEE WILLIAMS   *A Streetcar Named Desire* (New York, 1947). Certainly one of the greatest dramatists of the twentieth century, Williams considers this play his own favorite. It ranks by all standards as one of the finest plays ever written by an American.

ABEBOOKS.COM RARE BOOK ROOM *www.abebooks.com/books/RareBooks*
Includes directories for rare books, antique book fairs, and book appraisers.

ANTIQUARIAN BOOKSELLERS' ASSOCIATION OF AMERICA *www.abaa.org*

ANTIQUES ROADSHOW: PRESERVING ANTIQUE BOOKS *www.pbs.org/wgbh /roadshow/tips/preservingbooks.html* Tips on preserving antique books.

BAUMAN RARE BOOKS *www.baumanrarebooks.com/default.aspx*
Rare book dealer with information on selling and collecting. Also has a list of first edition books and their values.

BOOK COLLECTING TIPS *www.book-collecting-tips.com*

BOOK COLLECTORS' GLOSSARY *www.tappinbookmine.com/glosdefn.htm*

BOOK VALUES *www.djmcadam.com/book-values.html*

BUILDING A RARE BOOK COLLECTION *www.maggs.com/collections /collecting.asp*

THE CLIFTON WALLER BARRETT LIBRARY OF AMERICAN LITERATURE
www2.lib.virginia.edu/small/collections/barrett/index.html Includes notable works from 1775 to 1950.

COLLECTING ANTIQUE BOOKS *hubpages.com/hub/Become-Book-Hound-Collecting-Antique-Books*

COLLECTORS WEEKLY: BOOKS *www.collectorsweekly.com/books/overview*
Collector information for vintage and antique books.

DIGITAL LIBRARIAN *www.digital-librarian.com/bookcollecting.html*
Includes a vast list of websites on book history and collecting.

THE ESSENTIALS OF BOOK COLLECTING *www.trussel.com/books/lucas01.htm*

FINE BOOKS AND COLLECTIONS *www.finebooksmagazine.com/calendar*
  Includes a list of rare book auctions.

FIRSTS, THE BOOK COLLECTOR'S MAGAZINE *www.firsts.com/index.html*
  Includes an eleven-part essay on collecting rare books.

HOW TO SPOT AND IDENTIFY A FACSIMILE BOOK DUST JACKET
  www.artbusiness.com/facsdj.html

HOW TO START AN ANTIQUE BOOK COLLECTION *www.ehow.com*
  /how_2051830_start-antique-book-collection.html

HOW TO IDENTIFY A FIRST EDITION *www.emptymirrorbooks.com/collecting*
  /firstedition.html

THE INFOGRAPHY ABOUT BOOK COLLECTING *www.infography.com*
  /content/426936269470.html

INTERNATIONAL LEAGUE OF ANTIQUARIAN BOOKSELLERS *www.ilab.org*

INVESTING IN ANTIQUARIAN BOOKS *www.historyandnews.co.uk/article*
  .php?story=20060719122921337

THE LIBRARY OF CONGRESS PRESERVATION *www.loc.gov/preserv*

THE LIBRARY OF CONGRESS RARE BOOK & SPECIAL COLLECTIONS READING
  ROOM *www.loc.gov/rr/rarebook* Includes a guide to book
  appraisals.

KEN LOPEZ BOOKSELLER *lopezbooks.com/articles/trends* Includes an
  essay on modern book collecting.

POWELL'S BOOKS: RARE BOOK BASICS *www.powells.com/rarebooks*
  /bookbasics.html Includes interviews, essays, and events for rare
  books.

THE RARE BOOK MARKET TODAY *www.reeseco.com/papers/market.htm*

RARE BOOKS AND MANUSCRIPTS SECTION: YOUR OLD BOOKS *www.rbms*
  .info/yob.shtml Answers to questions about rare and older book
  values.

RARE FINDS—A GUIDE TO RARE BOOK COLLECTING *rarebookfinds.com*

INDEX

ACKNOWLEDGMENTS

Grateful acknowledgment is made to the following for permission to reprint previously published material:

Farrar, Straus & Giroux, Inc., and Faber and Faber Limited: "The Death of the Ball Turret Gunner" by Randall Jarrell, as handwritten by Jarrell on the front page of the book LITTLE FRIEND, LITTLE FRIEND *and reprinted in* THE COMPLETE POEMS. *Copyright 1945 by Mrs. Randall Jarrell. Copyright renewed 1972 by Mrs. Randall Jarrell. Used by permission of Farrar, Straus & Giroux, Inc., and Faber and Faber Limited.*

The Grolier Club of New York: Two pamphlets forged by Thomas J. Wise late in the nineteenth century. From the collection of the Grolier Club of New York. Used by permission.

Harcourt Brace Jovanovich, Inc., and Faber and Faber Limited: "Two Quatrains for First Frost" by Richard Wilbur. Copyright © 1959 by Richard Wilbur. Reprinted from his volume ADVICE TO A PROPHET AND OTHER POEMS *by permission of Harcourt Brace Jovanovich and Faber and Faber Limited.*

The Limited Editions Club: Page from The Limited Editions Club edition of ULYSSES *by James Joyce. Copy number 804, signed by James Joyce and Henri Matisse. Courtesy of The Limited Editions Club.*

New Directions: Inscription by Ezra Pound. All rights reserved. Published by permission of New Directions, Agents for the Trustees of the Ezra Pound Literary Property Trust.

Sotheby Parke Bernet, Inc.: Sample page from catalogue courtesy Sotheby Parke Bernet, Inc.

Jill Faulkner Summers: Inscription by William Faulkner on page from INTRUDER IN THE DUST, *Random House, copyright © 1948 by William Faulkner, copyright renewed 1975 by Jill Faulkner Summers. Previously unpublished poem by William Faulkner on page 55 copyright © 1980 by Jill Faulkner Summers.*

Photographs on pages 9, 13, 26, 29, 33, 35, 41, 45, 47, 98, 173, 177, 193, 195, 205, and 207 were taken by Coe Younger and Ben Asen.

A NOTE
ABOUT THE AUTHOR

Robert A. Wilson was proprietor of the
Pheonix Bookshop in Greenwich Village
in New York City. He is a passionate
writer; author of bibliographies of
Gertrude Stein, Gregory Corso, and
Denise Levertov; and specializes
in rare books and manuscripts.

A NOTE ON THE TYPE

The text of this book
was set in Waverley, a typeface
produced by the Intertype Corporation.
Named for Captain Edward Waverley,
the hero of Sir Walter Scott's first novel,
it was inspired by the spirit of Scott's
literary creation rather than actually
derived from the typography
of that period.

Composed by
American–Stratford Graphic Services, Inc.,
Brattleboro, Vermont
Designed by Betty Anderson

Made in the USA
Las Vegas, NV
02 July 2022

51024701R00164